Corrective Reading

Student Book

SRA

Skill Applications

Decoding C

A Direct Instruction Program

Siegfried Engelmann

Gary Johnson

Linda Carnine

Linda Meyer

Mc
Graw
Hill
Education

Photo credits: **197** ©hywit dimyadi/Alamy; **212** ©Bill Gozansky; **274** (t to b)Nobumichi Tamura/Stocktrek Images, (2)©dieKleinert/Alamy, (3)©The Natural History Museum/Alamy, (4)LEONELLO CALVETTI, (5)ROGER HARRIS/SPL; **313** ©Library of Congress Prints and Photographs Division; **370** (b)NASA; **395** (tl)NASA; **410** (l)Kees Smans/Getty Images, (r)©NHPA/David Chapman; **448** (bl) Wyatt Rivard/123RF, (bc)©Andrey Nekrasov, (br)W. ROBERT MOORE/National Geographic Creative; **cover** ©Chairat/RooM the Agency/Corbis.

SRAonline.com

The McGraw·Hill Companies

Contents

1 ai

A	B
sailed	bailing
painting	remain
pail	sailor
strain	nails
chain	wait

2 ou

A	B
out	shout
account	slouch
pounded	bound
grouch	sour
snout	

3

count
counter
counting
counted

4

A	B	C
ir	Bert	turn
ur	clerk	jerked
er	Shirley	third
	buster	dirty
	thirst	shirt
	first	surf

5

1. stout
2. churn
3. perch
4. ail
5. strain

6

felt   laughed   left   sticking

boats   woman   anchor   dollars

didn't   don't   without   sooner

catching   dragged   thinking

tired   can't   asked   people

7 Bert Meets Shirley

Bert had a job in a sailing shop. He was a clerk, and he didn't like ⟨16⟩
his job. ❶ Every day without fail, he went to the shop and waited for ⟨30⟩
people to buy things. Then people came to the shop. They picked up ⟨43⟩
paint and nails and containers for bailing. But every day Bert said to ⟨56⟩
himself, "I'm tired of this job." ⟨62⟩

Then one day a big sailor came into the sail shop. This sailor was a ⟨77⟩
woman who spoke loudly. "Hello, buster," she said to Bert. "My name ⟨89⟩
is Shirley. I am the best sailor you will ever see. And I need a long ⟨105⟩
anchor chain." ❷ ⟨107⟩

"Do you have to shout?" Bert asked. ⟨114⟩

"Shout?" she shouted. "Don't be such a grouch." She pounded the ⟨125⟩
table. "Get that chain. The sooner I sail, the sooner I will catch ⟨138⟩
perch." ❸ ⟨139⟩

"The chain is upstairs," Bert said. "Wait here, and I will get it for ⟨153⟩
you." ⟨154⟩

"No," Shirley shouted. "You don't look very stout. I'll go with you ⟨166⟩
and carry the chain down." ⟨171⟩

So Shirley and Bert went upstairs. She grabbed the chain and gave it a ⟨185⟩
jerk. Then she turned to Bert and said, "How much for this anchor ⟨198⟩
chain?" ⟨199⟩

"<u>Ten</u> dollars," Bert said. ⟨203⟩

Shirley said, "That sounds fair. I'll take that chain on account." ❹ ⟨214⟩

"You haven't opened an account here," Bert said. "How can you ⟨225⟩
take it on account?" ⟨229⟩

The sailor said, "I'll take it on account of I don't have any cash." ⟨243⟩
She laughed and laughed. Then she turned with a jerk. "That's a ⟨255⟩

joke," she said. "You'll get paid without fail. Don't stand there with 267
that sour look." 270

Shirley dragged the chain down the stairs. When she was at the 282
bottom of the stairs, she said, "You're out of shape. Get out of this sail 297
shop. Go fish for perch." 302

"I can't do that," Bert said. "I must remain here and do my job." 316

"Don't you thirst for the sound of the surf? ❺ Don't you want to see 330
the waves churn around your feet? Didn't you ever get out under the 343
clouds and the birds?" 347

"Oh, yes," Bert said. "But—" 352

"Don't but me," she said. "Get rid of your slouch and fish for perch. 366
It will fix what ails you." ❻ 372

Bert found himself thinking of the birds and the waves. Then he 384
said, "When can we go?" 389

"Now," she said. She pounded the counter. Then she slapped Bert 400
on the back. "Pick up the anchor chain and follow me." 411

When Bert tried to lift the chain, he said to himself, "This is a 425
strain. I don't know if I will be much of a sailor." ❼ 437

1 ai

A	B
m<u>ai</u>n	faint
cont<u>ai</u>ner	waist
b<u>ai</u>ling	afraid

2

A	B	C
ir	d<u>ir</u>ty	stir
er	t<u>ur</u>ning	another
ur	p<u>er</u>ched	churn
	st<u>er</u>n	further
		surf

3 ou

A	B
s<u>ou</u>nd	around
p<u>ou</u>nding	shouted

4
1. sound
2. hull
3. stern
4. flounder
5. faint
6. waist

5

wouldn't you'll you've should cannot

didn't don't that's can't tried tied

begin hear toward mast anchor

those these side dragged asked

asks grapes could slapped yourself

sure bobbing grabbed below knee

deck hull heard fishing away farther

6   On the Open Sea

Bert had left the sail shop to go fishing for perch with Shirley. They 14
went to the dock. Bert counted six sound boats at the dock. ❶ The 27
third boat didn't look sound. It needed paint. Nails were sticking out 39
of the side of the boat. The deck was dirty. "This is my house," Shirley 54
said loudly. "I can't wait to get it under sail." 64

"This boat is a turkey," Bert said. ❷ 71

Shirley said, "Be fair, Bert. This is a swell home." 81

Bert dragged the chain on board. "Some boat," he said. 91

"It's time to sail," Shirley said. "Run up the main sail." 102

"Where is the main sail?" Bert asked. 109

Shirley slapped a big mast. "Here it is," she said. 119

"I can't run up that thing," Bert said. "I can't even climb up that 133
thing." 134

"You don't run yourself up that mast," Shirley said. "You run the 146
sail up that mast. I'll show you how." ❸ 154

So she did. And then, as Bert stood there, not sure what he was 168
doing or why he was doing it, the boat began to turn and go out 183
to sea. 185

Soon the boat was in the open sea, bobbing up and down in the 199
surf. Bert began to feel sick. But Shirley was singing. She was perched 212
in a chair under the main sail. ❹ And the boat churned a path in the 227
surf. At last Shirley shouted, "Bert, grab a container, go below, and 239
start bailing. Our hold must be filled with water." 248

Bert went below. The water was up to his waist. ❺ He felt faint as 262
the boat pounded this way and that way. He bailed and bailed and 275
bailed. At last the water was only knee-deep. Then Bert went back to 288
the deck. ❻ 290

"What ails you?" Shirley shouted. "You look like you just ate sour   302
grapes."   303

"I'm sick," Bert said.   307

"Take a turn around the deck," Shirley said. "The sea air will take   320
care of what ails you."   325

Bert went to the stern of the boat. Just then the boat began to   339
flounder as a big wave slapped the side of the hull. Bert fell into the   354
water. ❼ He came up just in time to see another big wave churn   367
toward him. Before he could shout, the wave hit him like a train of   381
water. He came up and tried to shout, but he had water in his mouth.   396
"Blurp," he said. The old boat and Shirley were farther away.   407

"Help," he yelled, but his shout was faint over the sound of the   420
pounding sea. ❽ Suddenly Bert was very afraid. But just then he   431
heard somebody say, "Hello." ❾   435

1 **ai**

A	B
afr**ai**d	br**ai**n
f**ai**th	p**ai**ned
str**ai**ned	f**ai**nt

2

A	B	C
er	m**er**maid	swirled
ur	surf**er**	surfboard
ir	st**ir**red	thirsty
		clerk

3 **ou**

A	B
out	sounds
surr**ou**nds	shouted
ar**ou**nd	without

4
1. flounder
2. flail
3. fret
4. snout
5. swirl
6. surfer

5

won't   don't   didn't   wasn't   staring

weren't   wouldn't   starting   swim

swam   middle   paddled   yourself   worry

shark   anybody   rather   floating

talking   head   reached   submarine

attack   while   hungry   brushed

6

The Merman

Bert was flailing in the surf, but he was failing to get close to the old boat. ❶ Then suddenly somebody said, "Hello." 16 / 22

Bert turned around and saw a head bobbing in the water. "You must be a mermaid," Bert said. ❷ 34 / 40

"Don't be a jerk," the head said. "Do I look like a maid?" 53

"No, no," Bert said. "You look like a man. So you must be a merman." ❸ 67 / 68

"Don't be a jerk," the head said again. "I am a surfer. I took the wrong turn, and here I am, out in the middle of the sea." ❹ 83 / 96

The surfer paddled over to Bert. Bert said, "I am afraid we won't be able to get back to the beach." 110 / 117

"Don't get yourself stirred up," the surfer said. "Things will take a turn for the better if you just keep the faith." 129 / 139

"How do you do that?" Bert asked just as a big wave swirled over his head. 153 / 155

"Grab hold of my surfboard and play it cool. Don't strain your brain. Somebody will come by if you just wait." ❺ 167 / 176

"How long will we have to wait?" Bert said as he reached for the surfboard. 190 / 191

"Don't be a pain, man," the surfer said. "<u>Don't</u> worry about how long it will be. Don't start thinking about how we are shark bait sitting out here. Don't think about how thirsty you are. Think of how much fun this is. Like what would you be doing if you weren't out here?" ❻ 203 / 216 / 229 / 243 / 244

"I would be working as a clerk in a sail shop," Bert said. 257

"See what I mean?" the surfer said. "Anybody would rather be out here floating around like a flounder." 269 / 275

Bert said, "I don't know about that. I think I would rather—" Bert stopped talking. He was staring at a fin that was cutting a path in the water. Bert said, "Isn't that a shark fin?" ❼

"That's not a submarine," the surfer said. "Look at how that shark can swim. Wouldn't it be neat to swim that well?"

"But—but—won't that shark attack us?" Bert said.

"I'll tell you in a while," the surfer said. "But don't fret about it. If that shark is hungry, we will be its supper."

"But I don't want to be a shark's supper," Bert moaned.

"Well," the surfer said, "if you don't dig it here, why don't you just take the next bus home?" ❽

Just then the shark swam under the surfboard. The shark's snout brushed against Bert's foot. "I think I'm going to faint," Bert said.

"That's cool," the surfer said. "You'll feel better after a little nap." ❾

Bert felt sick. He wished he were back in the sail shop.

Lesson 4

1 **ar**

A	B
h<u>ar</u>d	tardy
st<u>ar</u>t	park
<u>ar</u>mor	sparkler

2 expl<u>ai</u>ned c<u>ou</u>ntless f<u>ai</u>nt cl<u>er</u>k hours

w<u>ai</u>led gr<u>ou</u>nd p<u>ai</u>nful p<u>ou</u>ting <u>ai</u>d

surr<u>ou</u>nd s<u>er</u>ve b<u>ou</u>nding s<u>ur</u>fer sn<u>ai</u>l

p<u>er</u>ched compl<u>ai</u>n ar<u>ou</u>nd fl<u>ou</u>nder

3
1. perch
2. wail
3. survive

4 slipped climbed bucket strain

anchor tripped yawned simply

hanging hunger away mount

spotted craft ahoy morning

line move ready

5 Back on Board

Bert was sick. He was hanging on to a surfboard in the middle of   14
the sea. A shark was swimming around and around the surfboard.   25
The surfer didn't seem to mind, but Bert felt faint. ❶   35

He asked the surfer, "How many hours can we survive out here?"   47

The surfer said, "If that shark gets a hunger pain, you won't have to   61
worry about surviving." ❷   64

Bert asked, "What if I make loud sounds? Will it go away then?"   77

"Sharks dig loud things," the surfer said. "If you do that, sharks   89
will surround us." ❸   92

At that moment Bert spotted a sailboat bounding over the surf.   103

"Look, look," Bert shouted. "A craft has come to our aid." ❹   114

The surfer didn't look up. He simply yawned. "Oh, well," he said,   126
"looks as if our fun is over."   133

Bert didn't feel that he was having fun. He looked at the   145
sailboat, and he could see somebody perched on the main mast. It   157
was Shirley. ❺   159

"Ahoy," she wailed. "I see a pair of sick fish on a surfboard."   172

The boat seemed to move like a snail, but soon it was next to the   187
surfboard. Bert left the surfboard and floundered over to the boat.   198
Then <u>he</u> climbed up over the rail. ❻   205

"Oh, that was painful," he said. "We were out there with sharks,   217
and we didn't—"   220

"Shut up and stop wailing," Shirley said. "Grab a pail and start   232
bailing." ❼   233

The surfer didn't complain. He slipped his surfboard over the rail   244
and climbed up. Then he said, "When do we eat?"   254

Shirley said, "After you work. Grab a bucket and start bailing."   265

"Wait," the surfer said. "Let me explain. I don't work. I surf and I eat, but I don't work." ❽ 279 284

Shirley said, "And I don't serve eats to them that don't work." 296

"I dig," the surfer said. "I don't feel much hunger, so I'll just sit in a deck chair and take a nap." And that's just what he did. 312 324

Bert bailed and bailed. Then he bounded up to the deck and said, "This life at sea is too much strain. Take me back to the sail shop." 337 352

"We came out here to fish," Shirley said. "And that's what we're going to do. Drop the anchor chain, and get ready to count the flounder." ❾ 364 377 378

"I like the ground under my feet," Bert said. "It's plain that I'm no sailor. Take me back." 392 396

"Stop your pouting," Shirley said. ❿ "There are countless fish out there just waiting for a fish line." 406 413

Bert wailed, "I can't stand the smell of fish. I can't stand the sound of the surf. Take me back to my job as a clerk." 427 439

The boat bobbed over the waves. Shirley handed Bert a long fishing pole. She slapped Bert on the back. "You'll come around," she said, "after you feel the joy of fishing." ⓫ 451 463 470

1   **ar**

A	B
hardly	marks
jarred	started
tarnish	parts

2   surrounded   spurted   hounding   sounded

first   ground   thirst   mailed   sternly

another   mouth   jerked   tiller   around

wailed   sputtered   ouch   survive

3
1. serious
2. termites
3. suddenly
4. tiller

4   line   slump   sawdust   crack   tossed

dropping   rolled   pulled   tugged

splash   fooling   handle   swam   swing

splat   races   morning   reach   clowning

really   you've   hasn't   we're

haven't   weren't   I'll   shouldn't

didn't   I've   wouldn't   doesn't

couldn't   don't   I'm   you'll

5 | Thousands of Flounder

Shirley tossed a pail of little fish over the side of the boat. "This bait 15
will get them," she said. Soon big fish surrounded the sailboat. ❶ 26

Shirley dropped her line into the sea. She jerked up and pulled a big 40
flounder over the rail. She dropped the fish on the surfer. The surfer 53
rolled over and said to the fish, "I was here first, fish." ❷ 65

Shirley pulled another fish from the sea and then another. Then she 77
shouted, "Come on, Bert, you grouch, it's time to fish." 87

Bert dropped his line into the sea. He felt a tug. He jerked up the 102
fishing pole. But Bert didn't pull a flounder from the sea. The flounder 115
pulled him into the sea. Splash. "Cut it out," Shirley yelled. "This is 128
no time to fool around." 133

Water spurted from Bert's mouth. "I'm not fooling," he sputtered. ❸ 143
"That fish is too big to handle." 150

Bert swam back to the rail of the boat. He tossed his pole over the 165
rail. The surfer grabbed it and said, "Is this work or fun?" 177

Shirley said, "This is more fun than playing in the rain." ❹ 188

"Then I'll do it," the surfer said. He jerked up on the pole and 202
pulled a stout flounder from the sea. The flounder swung around and 214
hit Bert just as Bert was trying to climb over the rail. Splat. Bert fell 229
on a fish that was on the deck. ❺ He slid across the deck on that fish 245
and went sailing over the other side of the boat. Splash. 256

"Cut it out," Shirley said sternly. "This is no time to play around." 269

Again water spurted from Bert's mouth. "I'm not playing," he said. 280

"I'm playing," the surfer said. "This is about as much fun as 292
surfing." 293

The surfer and Shirley ate flounder that night. Bert didn't eat. He 305
sat near the main mast and talked to himself. 314

He was still talking to himself the next morning when Shirley 325

shouted, "Now it's time to go back to port." ❻ 334

Shirley grabbed the tiller and turned it to one side, but the boat 347

didn't turn. The tiller broke in her hand. Then she yelled, "Men, we've 360

got termites on this ship. They ground the tiller into sawdust. I don't 373

know how long it will take them to eat the rest of this fine ship." ❼ 388

"Oh, not that," Bert wailed. "I'm a clerk. Why didn't I just stay and 402

be a clerk? Why did I—" ❽ 408

"It's full sail," Shirley said. "We must reach port before the termites 420

have ground this boat into bits." 426

"This is the life," the surfer said. "I dig races, and I dig termites." 440

Bert got up to see what the termites did to the tiller. As he walked 455

near the rail, he felt the deck begin to crack under his feet. Slump. A 470

hole formed in the deck, and Bert fell into the hole filled with a 484

thousand flounder. ❾ 486

"Stop clowning around," Shirley said. "This is serious." 494

"But," Bert hollered as he floundered around with the flounders, 504

"the termites really know how to eat wood." 512

"I just hope they don't eat the main mast," Shirley said. ❿ 523

Lesson 6

1
ar

A	B
f<u>ar</u>	sh<u>ar</u>pen
<u>ar</u>en't	sh<u>ar</u>pened
ch<u>ar</u>ming	st<u>ar</u>ting
c<u>ar</u>penter	

2
h<u>ou</u>r   s<u>ai</u>lor   ch<u>ai</u>r   s<u>ou</u>th

th<u>ir</u>d   p<u>ou</u>ting   till<u>er</u>   gr<u>ou</u>nded

excl<u>ai</u>med   cl<u>er</u>ked   ar<u>ou</u>nd

3
1. collapse
2. craft
3. skid

4
shouldn't   hadn't   wasn't   suddenly   hasn't

you've   isn't   weren't   what's   couldn't   that's

into   onto   unto   tottered   serious   really

pointed   shore   rented   clowning   toward

eaten   crafted   chewing   landed   filler   front

board   casting   place   raced   grabbed   during

aground   something   through   passed

5
responded   generate   imagination

1. responded   2. generate   3. imagination

   a. She responded to my letter the same day she received it.
   b. The dam they are building will generate electricity for the valley.
   c. You have to use your imagination to be a good artist.

6 A Race with Termites

It was a race between the termites and the sailboat. The termites   12
had eaten the tiller, and now they were working on the deck. Shirley   25
was saying, "Let out more sail."   31

Bert was saying, "Why did I ever leave the sail shop?" ❶   42

And the surfer was saying, "This is really fun. I dig it."   54

Hour after hour dragged by. Then suddenly, the rail on the left side   67
of the boat fell down.   72

"Look at those termites eat wood," the surfer said.   81

"Oh, no," Bert said.   85

"Let out more sail," Shirley said.   91

An hour later more rail fell down. Bert was sitting in a deck chair   105
talking to himself. "We're not going to make it," he was saying.   117
Suddenly his chair collapsed, and Bert was sitting on the deck. ❷   128

"Stop clowning around," Shirley shouted.   133

Another hour passed. During that hour the rest of the rail around   145
the boat collapsed. Shirley said, "Men, I think we're too far south to   158
make it back to the dock. We're going to have to turn toward shore   172
before water starts to spout through the bottom of this boat." ❸   183

The surfer said, "Why don't you go to my dock? It's over there." He   197
pointed toward the shore.   201

"Do you rent a dock there?" Shirley asked.   209

"No," the surfer said. "I own that part of the beach. My uncle left it   224
to me. But I can't stand it because the surf is poor."   236

"Stop talking and start turning," Bert said. "I want to feel dry   248
ground under my feet." ❹   252

So the boat turned toward the shore. Just then the top third of the   266
mast tottered and fell over. The surfer said, "Those termites are   277
something."   278

The boat came closer and closer to the shore, and the boat got lower   292
and lower in the water. "I think we spouted a leak in the hull," Shirley   307
said. ❺   308

"I'll nail some boards over the hole," Bert said. He grabbed a   320
hammer and some boards. He went down the stairs and flailed   331
around in the water with the flounder. But when he tried to use the   345
hammer, the handle broke. The termites had eaten holes in it. Bert   357
was about ready to start pulling out his hair.   366

"We're going to make it," Shirley shouted from the deck. "I'll just   378
run this craft aground next to the dock." ❻   386

The old boat was spouting new leaks. It was sinking lower and   398
lower into the water. Bert was chewing his fingernails. He ran up the   411
stairs. And just when he got to the deck, the boat made a loud sound   426
as it came aground next to the dock. The boat stopped so suddenly   439
that Bert skidded on the deck and went sailing over the front of the   453
boat. He landed nose first on the beach. His mouth was filled with   466
sand. "We made it," he yelled. ❼   472

"Stop clowning around," Shirley said. "Bert, you just don't seem to   483
know when things are serious."   488

1

ship

sheep

sharp

shark

shake

2 ge

A	B
strange	charge
gem	change
dodge	manage
gent	

3

lousy   started   flounder   stairs

fisher   sharks   sounding   parking

around   spark   repair   turned

4

1. business
2. respond
3. exclaim

5

broken   enough   responded   hey

wouldn't   didn't   doesn't   shouldn't

don't   couldn't   business   picked

holding   fishing   pulled   share   poster

loan   along   across   away   always   replied

right   following   people   period

6

tremendous   exclamation   unbelievable

1. tremendous   2. exclamation   3. unbelievable

a. The lightning was followed by a tremendous explosion of thunder.

b. The exclamation point at the end of a sentence shows what that sentence says is really important!

c. I was shocked to discover that his unbelievable story was true.

7   What Will Bert Do?

Bert was on the beach yelling, "We made it." The boat was   12
grounded next to the dock. ❶ The surfer picked up his surfboard,   23
turned to Shirley, and said, "That trip was a real treat." Just then the   37
front of his surfboard collapsed and fell to the deck. He was left   50
holding a third of his surfboard. "Hey," he said. "That's not fair. How   63
can I go surfing with a broken board?"   71

Shirley slapped him on the back. "You're born to fish," she shouted.   83
"Stick with me and we'll go after the big flounders." ❷   93

Bert got up and spit sand from his mouth. Then he yelled, "I'm not   107
going with you. I'm going back to the sail shop. I'm a clerk, not a   122
sailor."   123

Shirley said, "How can you go back to that place after you've had   136
the sound of surf in your ears?"   143

"I dig," the surfer said.   148

"No, no," Bert yelled. "I like to feel the ground under my feet. I'm   162
sick of the surf, and I can't stand boats with termites." ❸   173

The surfer tossed his broken surfboard on the beach. Then he   184
grabbed a fishing pole and made a long cast along the beach. ❹ In an   198
instant <u>he</u> pulled out a big fish. "This fishing is a lot of fun," he said.   214
He swung the fish onto the deck. Then he cast again. He jerked up on   229
the pole and pulled out another fish.   236

Shirley grabbed the fish and looked at it. "That's a shad," she   248
exclaimed. "Are there always shad around here?"   255

"Yep," the surfer said as he made another cast. "This water is lousy   268
with shad."   270

Bert said, "This water is lousy—period. I never want to see any   283
more water. I'm going back to the sail shop." ❺   292

Shirley said to the surfer, "How much of this beach is yours?" 304

The surfer said, "About a third of a mile up the beach and about a 319
third of a mile down the beach." ❻ 326

"Wow," Shirley exclaimed. 329

By now Bert was walking across the beach, away from the boat. 341
"I'm leaving," he said. 345

"Stop pouting," Shirley said. "First you're clowning around 353
when things are serious, and now you're pouting when things are 364
beautiful." ❼ 365

"What's beautiful?" Bert shouted. 369

"Well, come on back here and I'll tell you," Shirley responded. "I've 381
got a plan that will make everybody happy. It will make you happy; it 395
will make the surfer happy; and it will make old Shirley happy." 407

Bert stopped and looked back at the boat. He was thinking. ❽ 418

1 ge

A	B
char**g**e	ran**g**e
stran**g**er	lar**g**e
bar**g**e	mana**g**er
gem	lod**g**e

2 ce

A	B
for**c**e	pri**c**e
cent	**c**enter
fa**c**e	spi**c**e
cell	spa**c**e
pla**c**e	

3

farmer   turning   painted   third

jar   charge   plaster   aren't

lousy   first   hailed   tarp

4
1. convert
2. purchase
3. probably
4. reply

5

behind   ducked   alive   station   chief

posters   either   business   our   shuffling

money   replied   game   booming   rubbed

hardly   fire   fired   your   neither

gone   waist   slowly   equipment

6

information   enlargement   remainder

1. information   2. enlargement   3. remainder

a. The information they gave us was not complete.
b. An enlargement of the photo I took hung over the fireplace.
c. We ate the remainder of the chicken salad for lunch.

7   A Business on the Beach

Shirley told the others that she had a plan. Bert was standing on the   14
beach shuffling his feet. The surfer was casting his line into the water.   27
Shirley was waiting for Bert to make up his mind about leaving. ❶   39

Finally Bert shuffled over to Shirley. "Let's hear your plan," he said.   51

"Here it is," Shirley replied. "The surfer owns this beach. I own this   64
boat. And you, Bert, are a clerk."   71

"Right," Bert said.   74

"Cool," the surfer said as he reeled in another shad.   84

Shirley said, "And this beach is lousy with fish. So what if we   97
opened a business right here on the beach? We could fix up the old   111
boat and convert it into a sail shop. Bert, you could work in the sail   126
shop. We could charge people to fish here. I could be in charge of the   141
fishing. And we would pay the surfer for using his beach." ❷   152

"Cool," the surfer said. "I really dig money."   160

Bert rubbed his chin. "You may have something there," he said   171
slowly. "We could sell sails and bait and anchors and all the other   184
things you would buy in a sail shop."   192

"Right," Shirley said. "People would get a <u>charge</u> out of coming to   204
our shop. It would be a real boat right here in the water." ❸   217

The surfer said, "And I could take the money you give me and buy a   232
new surfboard. And I could fish for free."   240

"Right," Shirley said. "And I could fish too and sell some fish."   252

Everybody began talking at the same time. They talked and talked.   263

On the following morning they began to work. They repaired the   274
old boat. It wasn't in any kind of shape to go back to sea, but it was   291
good enough for resting in water that was waist-deep.   300

Bert got a loan from the bank and purchased goods for the sail 313
shop. ❹ Then he made posters. He plastered the posters all around. 324
Some said, "Seashore Sail Shop—Marine supplies, diving equipment, 333
fishing goods." Other posters said, "Fish at Seashore Sail Beach. Pay 344
for the fish you catch. No fish, no pay." ❺ 353

That's how the business got started. Hardly a month had gone by 365
before the business was booming. And it's going strong today. Bert 376
and Shirley are pretty rich. You can see them down at Seashore Sail 389
Beach almost any time. But if you go down there, you probably won't 402
see the surfer. You'll probably find him up the beach about five miles, 415
where the waves are good. He comes back to Seashore Sail Beach now 428
and then, either to fish or to pick up his share of the money the 443
business makes. ❻ 445

So Shirley was right. The business had made everybody happy. 455

1 ce

A	B
pla<u>c</u>e	pie<u>c</u>e
dan<u>c</u>ed	<u>c</u>ents
for<u>c</u>e	sli<u>c</u>e
ri<u>c</u>e	fen<u>c</u>e

2 K<u>u</u>rt j<u>a</u>r strange f<u>ai</u>nt general
c<u>ou</u>nter s<u>u</u>rge pl<u>u</u>nger s<u>ou</u>nd
th<u>ir</u>st do<u>dg</u>e exp<u>er</u>ts
excla<u>i</u>med ann<u>ou</u>nced dep<u>ar</u>ted

3
1. several
2. inspect
3. future
4. unusual
5. announce

4 I've we're wasn't those what chief station
these touched engines causing arrived examined
stunned different major show glowing mustard
squirt suddenly disappear done picture minutes
planet instead gone toward slowly fighters
appeared quite glanced circle moving quiet

5   remembering   peacefully   accidental

1. remembering   2. peacefully   3. accidental

   a. I kept remembering what she said.
   b. They settled their disagreement peacefully.
   c. It was an accidental meeting.

6

The Mustard Jar

This is an unusual story in several ways. It is a story that takes 14
place in the future, and it is a story about a mustard jar. ❶ 27

The mustard jar looked a lot like any other mustard jar. It was 40
made of glass, and it had a plunger on the top. ❷ When you pressed 54
the plunger, yellow mustard squirted out. This mustard jar was on the 66
counter of a snack bar. Every day things were the same for the 79
mustard jar. Every morning Kurt, the man who owned the snack bar, 91
filled the mustard jar. People then came into the snack bar. Some 103
would order a hamburger. They would grab the mustard jar, press the 115
plunger, and squirt mustard onto their hamburgers. Day after day, 125
things didn't change. ❸ 128

But one day was quite unusual. It started out like any other day, 141
with Kurt filling the mustard jar. As usual, people came into the 153
snack bar and squirted mustard on their hamburgers. In the late 164
afternoon the people left the snack bar and Kurt began to clean up. 177
Everything was quiet until suddenly there was a loud sound followed 188
by a strange green light. The snack bar was filled with <u>this</u> green light. 202
Kurt ducked behind the counter and exclaimed, "Oh, no. They've 212
found me." ❹ 214

Suddenly a strange-looking woman appeared in the middle of the 224
green light. In a husky voice she said, "You must come back to the 238
planet Surge with me." ❺ 242

"No, no," Kurt yelled. "I am happy here. I won't go back to that 256
place." 257

"Then I will have to use force," the strange woman said calmly. She 270
pointed her finger at Kurt and—bong—a path of light danced from 283
her hand into the snack bar as the room rang with a wild sound. Kurt 298

had ducked behind the counter, and the dancing light had not hit him. 311
Instead, it hit the counter, and the counter began to burn. ❻ 322

"You cannot hide," the woman announced. Again she pointed at 332
Kurt, who was dodging this way and that way behind the counter. 344
Bong. The path of light hit the wall behind the counter and made a 358
circle of flame on the wall. Bong. The path hit a picture on the wall, 373
causing the picture to burn. Bong. The path hit the mustard jar, but 386
the mustard jar didn't burn. It began to glow. ❼ Bong. The path of 399
light hit Kurt and stunned him. He seemed to freeze. 409

The strange-looking woman jumped over the counter, took Kurt's 418
hand, and led him around the counter. Both of them seemed to 430
disappear in a bright circle of green light. They were gone, and the 443
snack bar was again empty. ❽ 448

Within three minutes after the strange woman and Kurt had 458
departed, fire engines arrived at the snack bar. Somebody had seen 469
smoke coming from the shop. Within two minutes after the fire 480
fighters arrived, they had put out the fires. "We're all done here," the 493
chief said. "Take the truck back to the station. I'll stay here and see if 508
I can find out how these little fires got started." ❾ 518

The other fire fighters left, and the chief began to inspect the place. 531
She examined the walls and the windows. She examined the floor. ❿ 542
As she was inspecting the floor, she glanced to one side and saw the 556
mustard jar. She stopped. "What is this?" she asked herself. "That jar 568
is glowing." Very slowly she moved her hand toward the jar. Then she 581
touched it softly. "It's not hot," she said. "But I think I can feel it 596
moving. It almost seems to be alive." ⓫ 603

1 gi ci

A	B
city	giant
magic	imagine
circle	electricity
engine	

2 mountain plunger dodge

however furnace chance

larger agreed races surge

sparked voice grounded

general sharpener agents

charge discovered several

3 tion

A	B
station	lotion
nation	investigation
relation	

4
1. beaker
2. device
3. expert
4. investigation
5. laboratory

5 crackled staring increased observed

temperature behind wiggle future

disappear different splashing probably

metal carefully people secret

fantastic suggested showers might

huge through million move believe

6 occupation unlimited according

1. occupation 2. unlimited 3. according

   a. For her occupation, she had to travel a lot.
   b. It seemed to the others that he had unlimited cash.
   c. According to the map, we are a long way from the campsite.

7 Nothing Changes the Mustard Jar

The fire chief had discovered the glowing mustard jar in the snack   12
bar. ❶ She held it carefully by the plunger and took it to her car.   26
When she got to the fire station, she called the police chief and told   40
the chief about the mustard jar. The police chief called a major in the   54
army. The major called a general, who called somebody in   64
Washington. ❷ While all this calling was going on, the mustard jar   75
was in a glass case in the fire station. All the fire fighters looked at it   91
and shook their heads. "It's almost alive," several of them observed. ❸   102

Two days after the jar had been discovered in the snack bar, several   115
people from Washington entered the fire station. They were experts   126
on different types of matter. Each looked at the mustard jar, and each   138
observed, "I've never seen anything like this before."   146

After all the experts had inspected the jar, the one in charge of the   160
experts said, "We don't know anything about this jar. ❹ We have   171
never seen matter in this form. We must find out what makes it work."   185
The experts returned the mustard jar to the glass case. Then they   197
placed the <u>glass</u> case in a metal box, which they took to a place high   212
in the mountains. A large fence circled this place, and there were   224
many signs on the fence. Each sign said, "Top Secret. Don't talk about 237
your work." ❺   239

The experts went inside to a laboratory, where they removed the   250
mustard jar from the glass case in the metal box. Then they began   263
their investigation. First, they put the mustard jar in a beaker of water. 276
Nothing changed. The jar kept on glowing. Next, the experts put the   288
jar in a freezer. Nothing changed. At last, they put the jar in a   302
furnace, which heated the jar far above the boiling temperature of   313
water. Nothing changed. Still the experts increased the heat to a   324

temperature that would melt glass. Finally, they turned up the heat as   336
high as it would go. The mustard jar glowed just as it had glowed   350
before. The glass didn't melt. ❻   355

"This is fantastic," one of the experts exclaimed. "That jar should   366
have melted."   368

"I have an idea," another expert suggested. "Let's try electricity."   378

"Yes," a third expert agreed. "Electricity might work."   386

So the experts put the mustard jar in a giant device. Then they   399
turned on the electricity. At first, they sent a charge of five thousand   412
volts through the mustard jar. Nothing changed. They increased the   422
charge again and again. "Let's give it all the electricity we can," an   435
expert suggested. "This is our last chance." So the experts sent a   447
charge of three million volts through that jar. Showers of sparks filled   459
the room. The sound of electricity crackled and sparked. First, the jar   471
appeared to wiggle and shake and then to smoke. ❼   480

"Shut it off," one of the experts yelled. "It's burning up."   491

Suddenly the room became dark. The experts crowded around the   502
smoking jar. Everybody just stood there, staring at the jar and not   513
speaking. Then one expert yelled, "Am I seeing things, or is that jar   526
getting larger?"   528

"You're right," another expert agreed as she looked closer. "Look at   539
it grow." ❽   541

"And I'm alive," a voice said.   547

The experts looked at each other. "Who said that?" one woman asked.   559
They looked back at the jar, which was now as big as a pop bottle.   574

The mustard jar said, "I said that. I am alive." ❾   584

"I'm getting out of this place," one of the experts said. "I don't   597
believe in talking mustard jars." With fast steps, he ran from the   609
room. However, the other experts didn't move. They just stood there   620
with their mouths open, staring at the huge mustard jar.   630

1 gi   ci

A	B
giant	engines
changing	forcing
cinch	dodging
racing	cities
	excite

2 tion

A	B
relation	vacation
solution	imagination
invention	investigation

3
1. crease
2. observe
3. sprout

4
piece   sprouted   experts   change

darted   chance   voice   spout

spaces   huge   nerve   giant

agents   force   plunger   announced

5
flatter   quite   adventure   exactly   something

quiet   future   actually   squirt   instead   touch

wiggled   glowing   enough   replied   moved   skidded

flowed   minutes   stubby   tickled   second   cautioned

laugh   eyes   lying   nobody   covered

6   attention   unsteady   cautioned

1. attention   2. unsteady   3. cautioned

  a. He could not keep his attention on the lesson.
  b. Her legs were unsteady after she got out of the pool.
  c. The doctor cautioned us about eating too much fatty food.

7

Glops of Mustard

Nobody knows exactly how long the experts stood with their   10
mouths open looking at the talking mustard jar. But at last one of   23
them worked up the nerve to talk to the jar. (If you don't think it takes   39
nerve to talk to a mustard jar, try it.) The expert said, "How do you—   54
I mean why are you—I mean what do you—?" **❶**   64

The mustard jar said, "I don't know. I just know that I am alive and   79
I can talk."   82

"Can you move?" one expert asked.   88

"I will try." The mustard jar seemed to shake and wiggle. Then it   101
fell over. It shook some more and stood up. "I can move a little bit,"   116
the jar said.   119

"Maybe you can move more if you keep trying," one woman said.   131

So the jar tried and tried. After trying for a few minutes, the jar   145
said, "I think I can change shape if I really try hard. I will look at   161
something. Then I will change so that I look like that thing." **❷**   173

The mustard jar looked at a wall. The experts observed little glass   185
eyes just under the base of its plunger. As the jar looked at the wall,   200
the jar got flatter and flatter. The jar didn't look like a wall, however.   214
It looked like a flat <u>mustard</u> jar. When the jar was quite flat, it fell   229
over. One of the experts began to laugh. "That was funny," he said. **❸**   242

The jar's eyes darted at the expert. The jar then said, "I will make   256
myself look just like you." As the jar stared at the expert, the jar began   271
to change. It got bigger and bigger and bigger. Then little legs began   284
to sprout from the bottom. And little arms sprouted from the sides of   297
the jar. The mustard jar didn't look like the expert, however. It looked   310
like a huge mustard jar with little stubby legs and arms. All the   323
experts began to laugh. **❹**   327

"Stop laughing," the jar announced, "or I'll let you have it." But the experts were so tickled that they couldn't stop laughing. Suddenly the plunger on top of the jar went down, and a giant squirt of yellow mustard flowed out of the spout. ❺

"Take that," the jar said. The experts were covered with glops of mustard.

"My new shirt," one woman said. But as she was talking—squirt—a second shot of yellow mustard hit her in the open mouth. "Ugh," she said. "I can't stand mus—" A third shot hit her in the mouth.

"I'm getting out of here," one expert said, and he began to dash toward the door. When he was about halfway there, however, a huge squirt of mustard landed on the floor in front of him. When he hit the slippery goop, his left foot shot out from under him. His seat landed in the mustard, and he skidded all the way out the door. He left an ugly yellow path on the floor. ❻

"Now stop laughing," the mustard jar cautioned. "I look just the way you do."

"Yes, you do," one expert said as she wiped mustard from her face. She was lying, but she felt that she had enough mustard on her face to last her for some time.

Another expert said, "You look fine, just fine."

The mustard jar smiled. You could see a little crease form in the glass when it smiled. Then the jar said, "Now that I look just like a person, I want to do the things that people do." ❼

Lesson 12

1   **tion**   imagination   inspection   invention   direction

2   remained   chance   sparkler   imagine

nerves   couches   germ   hardly

largest   plunger   general   surround

fence   crouch   covered   device

3
1. unfortunate
2. waddle
3. hesitate
4. unbelievable

4   slid   slide   spit   quick   suspect

winner   behave   blanket   actually

waddled   squirted   laboratory   neither

elephant   supply   crowded   pretended

believe   built   head   coughing   shoulder

escape   before   either   agreed   repair

insisted   eyes   yellow   sniffing   unlimited

through   disguise   clever   course

5   indication   nitrogen   immediately

1. indication   2. nitrogen   3. immediately

a. The dog gave no indication that it was sick.
b. The divers made sure that there was no nitrogen in the air tanks.
c. When the bell rang, the students immediately left the classroom.

6

The Spy Won't Split
If the Jar Won't Spit

When the mustard jar told the experts that it wanted to do the   13
things that people do, the experts agreed. "Yes, that's a fine idea,"   25
they insisted. They didn't think the idea was very fine, but they didn't   38
want to get squirted with mustard again. ❶   45

So the mustard jar and the experts left the laboratory. The jar,   57
which had made itself about six feet tall, waddled along on its short   70
little legs. Some of the experts started to smile and giggle, but when   83
the jar's eyes darted in their direction, they pretended that they were   95
coughing.   96

When they were close to the huge fence that circled the top secret   109
laboratory, they saw two people running across the grass. One was   120
yelling, "Stop that man. He is a spy."   128

The experts looked at each other. They didn't know how to cope   140
with a spy. ❷ They worked with different kinds of matter, not with   152
fists and guns. But the mustard bottle didn't hesitate. With a quick   164
little waddle the jar moved across the grass. It stopped in front of the   178
spy. The mustard jar remained still for a moment. Then the plunger   190
shot down with unbelievable speed and out came a huge gob of yellow   203
mustard. The unfortunate spy didn't stand a chance when the mustard   214
hit him. It covered him <u>from</u> head to toe like a yellow blanket and   228
gooped up the grass surrounding him. First his left leg went flying.   240
Then his seat hit the grass, and he slid right past the mustard jar,   254
leaving an ugly yellow streak in the grass. ❸   262

"The jar stopped that spy," one of the experts yelled.   272

Another expert asked, "What chance did he have in the face of the   285
mustard jar?"   287

The experts ran to the spy. One of them said to the spy, "If you   302
don't behave yourself, I'll tell the jar, and it will splat you good."   315

The spy said, "I won't split if that jar won't splat me with that stuff." ❹   330

Another expert said, "That's a joke—the spy won't split if the jar   343
won't spit."   345

The woman who had been chasing the spy ran up to the mustard jar   359
and said, "I don't know what kind of clever device this is, but I'm   373
grateful. What imagination—making a disguise as clever as a mustard   384
bottle. Who would suspect a mustard bottle?" ❺   391

The woman patted the mustard jar on the shoulder (the part where   403
the bottle gets wide).   407

Then she patted the mustard bottle on the other shoulder. "Yes,"   418
she said, "we are all grateful."   424

The mustard jar said, "Everybody loves me so much, it makes me   436
sad." Then just below the mustard jar's eyes, a tear began to form. Of   450
course it was mustard. The tear ran down the mustard jar's cheek.   462
Then the mustard jar wiped the tear away with its stubby little hand. ❻   475

One expert said, "There's just one thing that bothers me. If you   487
keep blasting people with mustard, won't you run out of mustard   498
pretty soon?"   500

"Oh, no," the mustard jar said, wiping another mustard tear from   511
its eye and sniffing through its little nose. "I have an unlimited supply   524
of mustard. Watch this."   528

The mustard jar squirted out a pile of mustard that was bigger than   541
a cow and almost as big as an elephant. One expert said, "I think I'm   556
going to be sick."   560

Another expert said, "That's terrible. I've never seen such an   570
unbelievable sight in my life."   575

The mustard jar said, "Isn't that wonderful? I'm still full of   586
mustard." ❼   587

1

changes   chances   reflection   pardon

grounds   starving   hailed   lousy

investigations   gentle   department

operated   naturally   directed   scarf

protection   apartment   device

2

1. flinch
2. innocent

3

bloop   label   flowing   flinched   grown

wag   cafeteria   built   sloshed   angrily

sorry   waddle   hesitate   business   suspect

demanded   either   stroked   covered   proof

wasting   laughing   breath   shower   neither

believe   poked   unusual   barely   suggested

peering   mound   lying   certainly

knees   ahead   tough   once   spies

4

directed   navigation   apartment

1. directed   2. navigation   3. apartment

   a.   The captain directed the ship's navigation through the channel.

   b.   The sailors based their navigation on the location of the stars.

   c.   She directed me to my friend's apartment.

5 The Mustard Jar Becomes a Spy

The mustard jar and the experts were staring at the huge pile of   13
mustard the jar had just squirted onto the ground. The spy chaser   25
said, "Say, I believe I can use this mustard jar on one of my   39
investigations."   40

The mustard jar said, "Oh, wow, maybe I'll be a spy." **❶**   51

The spy chaser stroked her chin with one hand and poked at the jar   65
with the other. This device is a little strange, she observed to herself,   78
but it seems well built.   83

The jar said, "And I can hide very well. Watch this. I'll make myself   97
look like a dog." The mustard jar got down on its stubby little knees.   111
Then it grew a tail, which began to wag. The spy chaser began to   125
laugh. "What in green hills and valleys is that?" she asked. She was   138
laughing so hard that she almost fell down. "A mustard jar with a   151
tail—I can't believe it." She grabbed her belly and bent over in a big   166
hee-haw laugh. When she stood up to take a breath, she must have   179
seen something very unusual. Imagine looking up in time to see a wall   192
of yellow mustard flying at you so fast that you barely have time to   206
hold your breath and close your eyes. Then that wall of goop hits   219
you—bloop. **❷**   221

The spy chaser was on her back. She wasn't laughing any more. Her   234
eyes peered out of the pile of yellow mustard. "What kind of device is   248
this?" she demanded.   251

"Don't get too loud," one of the experts suggested. "There is a lot   264
more mustard where that came from."   270

"All right," the spy chaser said angrily. She stood up and sloshed   282
over to the mustard jar. "All right, I'll use you. But we'll have no more   297
of this mustard wasting. Remember there are people in parts of the   309

world who would give a lot for the mustard that you waste. Save that 323
mustard for the—" There was a loud bloop and once more the spy 336
chaser was flat on her back with her eyes peering from a mound of 350
mustard. ❸ 351

About an hour later, the mustard jar and the spy chaser were in the 365
spy chaser's apartment. The spy chaser had taken a shower and was 377
now putting on clean clothes. "Here's the plan," she announced. "I 388
want you to stand in the window of a department store a few blocks 402
from here. That store is operated by spies. We plan to raid the store 416
soon, but we need an insider, and you're it." The spy chaser looked at 430
the mustard jar. "Well, maybe you're not a real person, but you look a 444
lot like one." Naturally she was lying. ❹ 451

The mustard jar said, "You certainly won't be sorry. I can do a lot 465
of things that the usual spy can't do." The mustard jar pounded itself 478
on the chest. "Nothing can hurt me. Go ahead. Hit me with a 491
hammer." 492

"Not here in the apartment," the spy chaser said, tying her scarf. 504

"Oh, go ahead," the mustard jar said. "You have to make sure that 517
I'm tough, don't you? It's for your protection. Go ahead. Get a 529
hammer." 530

"No, I really—" the spy chaser looked at her clean white shirt, and 543
she remembered how it felt to get hit with a huge mound of yellow 557
mustard. She said, "Well, all right," because she didn't want that to 569
happen again. ❺ 571

She got a hammer. "Where do you want me to hit you?" she 584
asked. 585

The mustard jar exclaimed, "It doesn't matter. Just hit me 595
anywhere." 596

The spy chaser hit the fattest part of the mustard jar's fat body. 609
Then . . . bloop. 611

The spy chaser was covered with mustard again. The mustard jar   622
said, "I'm sorry. I didn't mean to squirt you that time. When the   635
hammer hit me, I flinched, and I must have pulled in my plunger."   648
Then the mustard jar added, "But at least you know I'm tough." **❻**   660

"I'm really glad I found out," the spy chaser said. She didn't look   673
too happy standing up to her knees in mustard.   682

1

my
sly
sty
style
styling
spying
spies

2 ea

A	B
streak	clean
mean	real
hear	screamed
	clear

3

serve   center   swirl   turned
protection   aimed   enlarge   office
giant   charged   startled   strange
innocent   racing   gentle

4
1. helicopter
2. label
3. tremendous

5

pardon   ceiling   celebrate   strain   quart
direction   can't   directly   couldn't
standing   throughout   observe   law   move
climbing   dangling   member   pressure
secret   listened   earth   department
entirely   window   briefcase   swooped
cafeteria   front   strolled   happening
angrily   spies   world   eight   once   posing

6   impossible   astounding   suspended

1. impossible   2. astounding   3. suspended

a.   She found his story to be impossible.
b.   The size of the wave was astounding.
c.   The ball remained suspended in the air.

7 # Ugly Yellow Goop

The next day found the mustard jar standing in a window in a 13
department store with a new label on its front. The label said, 25
"Cafeteria—second floor." The mustard jar didn't like the label very 36
much, but the jar was glad to be a member of the Secret Agents. The 51
jar said to itself, "I'll bet I'm the only mustard jar in the entire world 66
who chases spies." ❶ 69

Throughout the day people walked past the mustard jar, but not 80
one of them seemed to be a spy. The jar looked and listened, but it 95
didn't observe anything that seemed strange. Once it saw a man start 107
to whisper something to another man, and the jar listened very 118
carefully. But all the first man said was, "Pardon me. Do you know 131
where the men's department is?" 136

Late that day a woman strolled by with her son. He was about seven 150
years old. When he spotted the mustard jar, he said, "Mother, please 162
buy me that jar." 166

"No," his mother said, "that jar is much too big for our house." ❷ 179

"I want it," the boy said. "I want that mustard jar." 190

"Now stop talking so loudly," his mother said. "You must behave 201
yourself." 202

The boy began to cry. "I want a big mustard jar," he screamed, 215
running from his mother. <u>He</u> ran up to the mustard jar. "I want it," 229
the boy yelled. "Let me have it. Let me have it." 240

So the mustard jar let him have it with about a quart of mustard 254
that was aimed directly at the center of the boy's mouth. The boy must 268
have been startled indeed, because he stopped crying and stared at the 280
mustard jar. Then he ran back to his mother, who yelled, "How on 293
earth did you get covered with that ugly yellow goop?" ❸ 303

The mustard jar stood very still, posing as an innocent giant   314
mustard bottle and trying not to smile. But just then there was a huge   328
crash and part of the roof caved in. People screamed and began to run   342
from the store. The mustard jar could see a helicopter through the   354
hole in the roof. At that moment three people ran from an office on   368
the first floor of the department store. A rope dropped from the   380
helicopter, and the three people began climbing the rope. One of them   392
had a briefcase.   395

Before the mustard jar knew what was happening, eight Secret   405
Agents ran into the department store and charged toward the people   416
who were dangling from the rope. "Stop in the name of the law," they   430
yelled. ❹   431

But suddenly, the helicopter swooped up in the sky, taking the three   443
spies with it.   446

"They're gone now," one of the Secret Agents said angrily.   456

"Yes," another agent said. "We had better call for a plane to   468
follow them."   470

"I will follow them," the mustard jar said, running toward the   481
Secret Agents. "If I shoot out mustard fast enough, I move in the   494
other direction. I fly. Here I go." ❺   501

With a tremendous blast of mustard, the mustard jar went flying   512
through the department store. It hit one wall and then another. It hit   525
the floor three times and the ceiling once. Then it sailed through the   538
hole in the roof. The entire department store was a sea of mustard by   552
now. A Secret Agent who had mustard all over her said, "There have   565
to be better ways of catching spies than this." ❻   574

1

ea

A	B
hear	screaming
disappear	meanwhile
squeal	beam
piecemeal	clean
	steal

2

circle   sponge   office   blurt

century   imagination   ground

straight   sharper   city   disturb

darted   celebration   generate

location   changing

3

1. situation
2. stunt
3. continue
4. outfit

4

direction   swirling   startled

protection   squirted   huge   tremendous

exclaimed   starting   trouble   through

helicopter   stunt   throw   couple

business   another   before   skidding

replied   landing   proof   below

glops   dive   breath   observed

unbelievably   great   company

5

arrangements   exceptional   inspired

1. arrangements   2. exceptional   3. inspired

adventure

4. adventure

a. They made exceptional arrangements of flowers.
b. They were inspired by their adventure.
c. We agreed that our adventure was exceptional.
d. She was inspired to write a new musical arrangement.

6 The Chase

A great chase was taking place over the city as the mustard jar   13
chased a helicopter. It was a very messy chase. The mustard jar had to   27
squirt mustard out very fast in one direction to make itself move in   40
the other direction. The mustard jar had trouble going in a straight   52
line. So it zigged and zagged and spun around like a pinwheel on the   66
Fourth of July. Sometimes it would dive down, almost to the ground,   78
but then it would turn around, squirt mustard at the ground, and   90
shoot back up in the air. ❶   96

The helicopter that was carrying a pilot and three spies zigged and   108
zagged to keep away from the mustard jar. Below, people were   119
standing on the street, watching the great chase across the sky. From   131
time to time, glops of mustard would fall on them. It was a messy   145
situation. One man who got hit on the head with a large glop of yellow   160
mustard said, "What kind of a stunt is this?"   169

Another man exclaimed, "It looks like mustard."   176

A woman observed, "It smells like mustard."   183

A little girl put some of the yellow stuff on her hot dog and said, "It   199
is mustard."   201

Then someone yelled, "It is mustard gas. Run for your life because   213
mustard gas will kill you."   218

While <u>people</u> were running around or staring into the sky, the chase   230
continued. The helicopter would dart in one direction as the mustard   241
jar chased it. Then the helicopter would stop, and the mustard jar   253
would go flying past it. When the mustard jar passed the helicopter,   265
the helicopter would dart off in another direction. ❷   273

As the chase continued, some of the streets below got pretty   284
slippery. You have to remember that for the mustard jar to move, it   297

had to shoot out mustard very fast, and it had to keep on shooting out 312
mustard. As all the mustard was landing on the city, cars were 324
skidding around on the yellow streets. In one part of the city some 337
boys and girls were sliding down a big mustard-covered hill. They sat 349
in inner tubes, and away they went. "This is great," they agreed. "This 362
mustard is a lot better than snow." 369

A couple of blocks away workers were shoveling the mustard into 380
trucks. These people worked for a mustard company. They were going 391
to load up the mustard, take it to their mustard plant, clean it, and sell 406
it. These people weren't thinking too well. Mustard sales would be 417
unbelievably poor in this city for a long time because people would 429
have had enough mustard to last them for years. ❸ 438

Meanwhile the chase went on over the city. The helicopter stopped, 449
and the mustard jar darted by. The jar made a sharp turn. It was 463
getting better at steering itself. The helicopter kept changing location. 473
The helicopter darted to the left. The mustard jar darted to the left. 486
Suddenly the helicopter stopped, but the mustard jar kept on coming. 497
It was heading right for the helicopter, and it was moving very, very 510
fast. ❹ 511

1 ea

A	B
cleaning	scream
steal	meanwhile
hear	disappear

2 startled sprain outfit dangerous

device instruction enlarger beneath

remain imagine situation

information strain complaining

intersection burned range gathered

3 1. collide
2. instant
3. deceptive

4 celebration thousands giant enough

buildings behind spies chance

changes imagine tremendous shall

instant treasure waddling pressure

badge nearly pocket

5 continent   approaching   ordinary   unexpected

1. continent 2. approaching 3. ordinary 4. unexpected

   a. The ship is approaching the North American continent.

   b. What happened was both not ordinary and unexpected.

   c. They found a lot of unexpected things on the continent.

   d. The ordinary hound dog was approaching the barn.

6 # A Super Job

Over a thousand people were standing on the yellow streets below,   11
watching as the mustard jar headed toward the helicopter. It seemed   22
as if the mustard jar would collide with the helicopter. But at the last   36
instant the helicopter dived down, and the jar did not collide with it.   49
Instead, the jar went right over the top of the helicopter. When the jar   63
passed over the helicopter, a great trail of mustard dropped onto the   75
large blades of the helicopter. A helicopter cannot fly if its blades are   88
covered with ice, so you can imagine what happened when they   99
became covered with a load of mustard. Sputter, sputter went the   110
helicopter, and then down it went—zigging and zagging and turning   121
around. ❶   122

The helicopter landed in the middle of a street where some girls and   135
boys were sliding on inner tubes. The helicopter, which had landed   146
near the top of the hill, zipped down the hill. It slid further than any   161
of the inner tubes had gone. It slid three blocks to an intersection   174
where a police officer was trying to control traffic. The traffic was a   187
mess because the cars were slipping and sliding around on the   198
mustard. ❷   199

The police officer had just allowed a long line of cars to creep   212
through the intersection. He was ready to <u>signal</u> the cars going in the   225
other direction when the helicopter came sliding down the street. The   236
police officer got out of the way just in time. He took a big dive into   252
the mustard and slid to the curb. Zip. The helicopter went through the   265
intersection. Then—bang! It hit the back of a bread truck. The police   278
officer got up and ran over to the helicopter. He pointed to his yellow   292
badge and said to the spies inside, "You're under arrest." ❸   302

One spy said to another spy, "I didn't know that the police dressed in yellow outfits."

The other spy said, "Oh, shut up."

When the spies were getting out of the helicopter, the mustard jar landed. By now a great crowd had gathered around the helicopter. The mustard jar waddled up to the police officer and said, "I am a member of the Secret Agents. I will take charge of these spies." ❹

The police officer looked at the mustard jar. He was going to say, "What is going on around here?" But he didn't. Instead, he looked at the helicopter in the middle of a city street. He looked at streets and sidewalks and buildings covered with mustard. He looked at a talking mustard jar, as big as a person, waddling around on stubby little legs. When he saw all this, he said to himself, "This is so crazy, it can't really be happening." ❺

He slid his badge into his pocket, smiled at the mustard jar, and said, "I'm always glad to help the Secret Agents."

Later that day so many people called the Secret Agents that they burned out the telephone lines. All these people were complaining. The chief of the Secret Agents called the spy chaser who had hired the mustard jar and complained to her. "That mustard device will cost us thousands and thousands of dollars," the chief said angrily. "Get rid of it. And don't hire any more devices like it."

That evening the spy chaser told the mustard jar, "Well, you did a fine job, but—" The spy chaser didn't want to make the mustard jar mad. "But—" the spy chaser said, "we want you to go undercover from now on. We're going to send you to a quiet place far from this city. We want you to stay there until you hear from us."

The mustard jar smiled and said, "I did a super job, didn't I? I think I'll call myself Super Mustard."

315
318
325
337
348
362
374
387
400
414
425
438
453
456
469
478
490
500
513
524
535
547
560
573
585
600
612
626
632

The spy chaser smiled and said, "Yes, you did a super job. Now you   646
must do some undercover work for us."   653

So the mustard jar went to the quiet place. And what happened   665
there is another story. ❻   669

1

peaceful celebration intersection

sponge rounded dangerous practiced

2

1. buoy
2. gear
3. occasional
4. gymnastics

3

Lopez service ceiling deceptive Florida

glided Caribbean unbelievably Olympic

scuba warn taught pressure strain

Dubowski accident treasure woman

classes instructor stripe waddling

women remembering toward coral shadow

great injured during grinder drew

worth coffee knots studied thought

4

unnatural   excellent   surrounded

1. unnatural 2. excellent 3. surrounded

continuous   protection

4. continuous 5. protection

a. His coat felt unnatural but gave excellent protection against the cold.

b. A continuous ring of fire surrounded the lake.

c. Her voice sounds loud and unnatural.

d. The bird's only protection against attack was its continuous calling.

5   # Jane and Doris

The water looked unbelievably blue to Jane. The sand beneath the   11
water looked blue-white. From time to time a dark shadow of a fish   24
glided over the sand. Everything looked very peaceful. The boat   34
slowly bobbed and dipped over the waves. As Jane looked down to the   47
bottom, she had to remind herself, "Don't be fooled. It is very   59
deceptive down there." ❶   62

Jane Dubowski was a teacher. She taught gymnastics and   71
swimming. At one time she had wanted to become an Olympic   82
swimmer, but then she injured her leg in an auto accident. She now   95
has a brace on her leg. She liked her teaching job, but for the past year   111
she had been looking forward to her vacation. She wasn't sure when   123
she first got the idea to dive for sunken treasure, and she wasn't sure   137
when the idea became more than an idle dream. But some time during   150
the fall she had asked herself, "Why not? Why not go to the keys off   165
the coast of Florida and dive for treasure?" The Florida Keys are little   178
islands strung out from the tip of Florida into the Caribbean Sea. ❷   190

She had told a friend of hers, Doris Lopez, about her idea. Doris,   203
who was also a teacher, liked the idea. Doris and Jane studied maps   216
that showed where <u>people</u> think ships carrying gold had sunk. One   227
ship that had gone down off the Florida Keys was supposed to have   240
carried over fifty million dollars' worth of gold. ❸   248

But Doris and Jane hadn't really thought that they would find the   260
ship. They just thought that the diving would be fun. That winter they   273
had taken scuba diving classes. They had saved their money, and   284
when school was out, they bought airline tickets. They packed their   295
scuba gear and flew to Florida, where they rented a car and drove to   309
one of the keys, named Key West.   316

When the women arrived at Key West, they rented a boat. It was an ³³⁰ old boat, about twenty feet long. It had an engine that sounded like a ³⁴⁴ coffee grinder. The engine pushed the boat along at about four ³⁵⁵ knots—not very fast. On their first two days the teachers took their ³⁶⁸ boat out about a mile and made practice dives under the eye of an ³⁸² instructor. They set out buoys with diving flags. These flags are red ³⁹⁴ with one white stripe cutting across them, and they warn other boats ⁴⁰⁶ that divers are in the water. ❹ ⁴¹²

At first Jane and Doris went down only about thirty feet. The ⁴²⁴ pressure of the water hurt Jane's ears. After she had been underwater ⁴³⁶ for about twenty minutes, however, her ears stopped hurting. But her ⁴⁴⁷ mask fogged up quite a bit and water kept leaking in around the edges ⁴⁶¹ of the mask. She wore a blue wet suit. Doris had a yellow wet suit. ⁴⁷⁶ When Jane looked at Doris underwater, the suit looked yellow-green, ⁴⁸⁶ and shadows made by the waves drew little lines over Doris and over ⁴⁹⁹ the bottom. ❺ ⁵⁰¹

"This is great," Jane said to herself. She followed a school of yellow ⁵¹⁴ fish along the bottom. She stopped and picked up a sponge from the ⁵²⁷ bottom. She kept telling herself that she was having a good time, but ⁵⁴⁰ she kept remembering all the things she had heard and read about ⁵⁵² diving near the reefs, which is where the treasure ships had gone ⁵⁶⁴ down. She kept thinking about the next day when she would dive near ⁵⁷⁷ the reefs. And she felt a little afraid. At the same time she kept ⁵⁹¹ thinking, "How blue this water is!" ❻ ⁵⁹⁷

Lesson 18

1

northeast information giant

markers explained dangerous

carved occupation oxygen

ridge peaceful surface

2

1. glimpse
2. air pressure
3. prop
4. stranded

3

large nervous fences patterns sponge

slightly guard weather whistled

sandwich adventure coffee creature

currents coral grinder occasional

tomorrow ocean spare great worry

replied loaded fruit shifted front

compass toward shadows beautiful

million unlimited escape built cafeteria

briefcase couple bothered expect stretched

4

mountainous   furniture   faithfully
1. mountainous   2. furniture   3. faithfully

conditioner   management
4. conditioner   5. management

a. They bought furniture and an air conditioner.
b. The hikers faithfully followed the park rules for the mountainous area.
c. The management of the furniture company received a lot of money.
d. She used that new skin conditioner very faithfully.

5 To the Coral Reef

Doris and Jane got up before six the next morning. Doris called the 13
Coast Guard station to get weather information. The person told her 24
that the day should be calm and that small craft should have no 37
trouble. "But we expect a northeast wind to move in by tomorrow. If 50
the air pressure drops today, the wind may come in sooner." A 62
northeast wind was dangerous. 66

Doris asked, "How long will that wind blow?" 74

The person told her, "Maybe three or four days." 83

Doris hung up and shook her head. "We only have a week," she 96
said. "And we may not be able to go out after today for three or four 112
days." ❶ 113

"Nuts," Jane said. Jane walked to the window of their motel room 125
and looked out. The sun was coming up over the ocean, and the ocean 139
looked like a sheet of glass that was ruffled by an occasional wind. ❷ 152
"Well, we'll worry about tomorrow later," she said. "Let's get going." 163

So Doris and Jane took their gear to the pier where their boat was 177
docked. They filled the boat's main gas tank. Then they filled the 189
spare tank. The woman who filled the tanks said, "Where are you 201
going today?" 203

Jane said, "Out to the coral reef." ❸ 210

The woman whistled and shook her head. "That's dangerous," <u>she</u> 220
said. Jane wished the woman hadn't said that. She knew that it was 233
dangerous. She had read about the reef and about the water currents. 245
She had read about how many people had been injured diving near 257
that reef. 259

The woman explained, "Those currents are bad. They'll suck you 269
down if you don't watch out." 275

Jane smiled and tried to act as if she wasn't bothered. "We'll be   288
careful," she replied. Inside, she was saying to herself, "Maybe we   299
shouldn't go." ❹   301

Before seven o'clock, the boat was loaded. Four air tanks were tied   313
down in the front of the boat. Diving flags and markers were in the   327
boat. On the middle seat was a large cooler filled with fruit,   339
sandwiches, and soft drinks.   343

Jane started the coffee-grinder engine in the old boat. She shifted it   355
into forward, and the boat began to move away from the dock. "Did   368
you bring the suntan lotion?" Doris called from the front seat.   379

"Yes," Jane answered. "It's next to the cooler." But Jane wasn't   390
thinking about suntan lotion. She was looking far out over the ocean,   402
trying to get a glimpse of the coral reef. She checked the compass and   416
turned the boat slightly toward the south. ❺   423

Probably fifteen minutes passed before Jane yelled, "There it is."   433
She pointed, and Doris turned around. A large red buoy marked the   445
reef. The reef stretched out for several miles, sticking out of the water   458
in places, very white and very sharp.   465

Jane steered the boat to a place where the reef was just below the   479
surface of the water. "Watch out," Doris said. "Don't let the prop hit   492
that reef or we'll be stranded out here."   500

Jane looked at the coral reef below. It was beautiful. It looked like a   514
giant white ridge with a million patterns carved in it. It was a network   528
of sharp knobs and knots and ridges and shadows. Jane could see   540
little caves with fish swimming in and out of them. She said to herself,   554
"It's hard to believe that anything so beautiful could be dangerous." ❻   565

1 ee

A	B
eel	screech
feel	steep
reef	peeling

2 charges location markers surface

cautioned sharpness sponges

patterns creature mouthpiece

3
1. location
2. indicate
3. unsteady

4 attention surge breathing burst

purchase special unsteady nitrogen

current grumbling swayed glimpse

watches million worth die razor

anchor twenty smiled backward

bubbles layer sunken adventurous

sunlight purchased according studied

5
adjustment   preventing   exaggerated

1. adjustment   2. preventing   3. exaggerated

production   military

4. production   5. military

a. The president ordered a large adjustment in the size of the military.

b. The report exaggerated the company's production of trucks.

c. The bad weather was preventing military helicopters from landing.

d. Each month they made an adjustment in the production rate of furniture.

Lesson

19

6 Jane and Doris Take a Dive

According to a map that Doris and Jane had studied, a ship with 13
more than fifty million dollars' worth of gold had gone down at a 26
location near the middle of the reef. That ship had gone down more 39
than two hundred years ago, and nobody had ever found it. It was 52
hard to say just where the ship went down because the reef changes 65
shape from year to year. The reef is made up of millions of tiny 79
creatures—some living and some dead. The coral shells of these little 91
creatures can be sharp as razors. 97

"This looks like a good location," Doris said as the boat moved 109
between two lines of coral that stuck up above the water. Doris tossed 122
the anchor over the side. Doris lowered the diving flags into the water. 135
Then Jane slipped her arms into the loops on her air tanks. ❶ 147

"We'll stay down for one hour," Jane said. "Set your watch." Both 159
Jane and Doris had large diving watches with special markers to 170
indicate how long they had been underwater. 177

Doris cautioned, "Now don't get too adventurous. Stay on the east 188
side of the reef. And don't go down more than fifty feet." 200

Jane said, "Right. And don't get too close to the reef. That coral 213
will cut like a razor." ❷ 218

Doris <u>put</u> her arm around Jane and patted her on the shoulder. 230
"Good luck," she said. She smiled, but her eyes looked a little 242
unsteady. 243

Jane sat on the side of the boat with her feet on the boat's floor. 258
Then she fell backward into the water, holding her mask so that water 271
wouldn't leak in. She looked around underwater and could see Doris 282
in a cloud of bubbles. Jane waved. Doris waved. Then the women 294
started to swim along the reef. In some places large plants grew from 307

58 *Lesson 19*

the reef and swayed slowly in the current of the water, like grass 320

bending in a wind. "Watch those plants," Jane said to herself. "They 332

indicate how the current is flowing." ❸ 338

Suddenly Jane heard a funny grumbling sound. She looked around 348

and saw that Doris was pointing to something. Jane swam over and 360

looked. Three sponges were stuck to the reef about twenty feet below 372

Doris. Sponges are worth a lot of money. The sponges on the reef were 386

probably worth five dollars each. Jane pointed down, and then she 397

swam down. She pulled two of the sponges from the rock. Doris 409

pulled off the other sponge. Then Jane and Doris returned to the 421

surface. Jane's mask was fogged. She pushed it up and said, "Doris, 433

we may get rich just finding sponges. Who needs a sunken ship?" ❹ 445

Doris smiled. Jane and Doris swam to the boat and tossed the 457

sponges over the side. Jane explained, "I think I'll go back down there 470

and see if I can find any more sponges." 479

Jane fixed her mouthpiece in her mouth, put her mask in place, and 492

went underwater about thirty feet. She passed through a school of 503

little silver fish that flashed in the sunlight. She peeked into the caves 516

along the reef. She went down another fifteen feet. She was looking 528

very hard for sponges, but she was not paying attention to the plants 541

and how they were waving in the current. ❺ 549

1   ee

A   B

eek   between
creek   succeed
screech fifteen

2   breathing hurt pounding barge decide

started about creature grinder except

3
1. surface
2. ledge
3. nitrogen

4   scream mound burst aloud squint
grumbling farther drifting tilted
continued disk frightened indicate
tried current moving surge suddenly
oxygen mouthpiece hidden heart
nobody hundred relax pressing razor
bottle bubbles sunken caught
goose panic cause thought

5   occasion   selective   improvement

1. occasion   2. selective   3. improvement

incapable   particular

4. incapable   5. particular

a. The team seemed to be incapable of much improvement.
b. It was snowing on that particular occasion.
c. She was very selective about the people she invited to dinner.
d. We saw great improvement from one occasion to the next.

6   Caught in the Current

Jane was about 45 feet below the surface, swimming next to the reef 13
and looking for sponges. Suddenly she felt something tug at her. It was 26
the current. Her legs were pulled by the current that sped through a 39
break in the reef. Jane could hear herself breathing very hard. She 51
kicked and tried to swim up, but she could not move up. She was 65
slowly drifting down. She kicked again and pulled with her arms as 77
hard as she could, but now she was moving down even faster. She 90
reached out and grabbed a ledge of coral. She felt something cut 102
through her rubber glove. She let go and slid down. ❶ 112

The current pulled Jane down about ten feet. Then it began to move 125
her east through the break in the reef. Jane wanted to scream for help, 139
but she remained silent except for the bubbles that came from her 151
mouth and the pounding of her heart. "I've got to get out of here," she 166
said to herself. 169

"Relax," she told herself. "Don't panic. Don't panic." The current 179
pulled her through the break in the reef. Then it started to pull her 193
down again, but not as hard. Jane tried to swim up again. She pulled 207
with her arms. She kicked until her legs hurt, but it was no use. 221

"I'll have to go with the current," she decided. "I just hope that it 235
lets me go pretty soon." The current continued to pull her down, deep 248
into darker water. ❷ Jane could not see the bottom below her. She 260
could see only darkness. When she looked up, the sun didn't look like 273
a white disk anymore. It looked yellow-green. "Relax," she reminded 283
herself as she drifted with the current. 290

She looked down again. "I must be sixty feet deep," she said to 303
herself. "I must—what's that?" Jane looked down. The water was 314
pressing Jane's mask against her face so hard that she had to squint to 328

see the dark form that was on the bottom. Was it a mound of coral? 343
Or was it too dark to be coral? What was that long thin line next to it? 360
Jane was almost afraid to say to herself, "It's a ship." But it was. The 375
mast was next to the ship. The hull was tilted with part of it hidden 390
under sand. 392

"It's a ship," Jane said to herself. "I see a ship." She was all 406
mixed-up. She was frightened. Her heart was beating like the 416
coffee-grinder engine of their boat. She could feel goose bumps 426
forming on her arms. "I am looking at a ship that nobody has seen in 441
over two hundred years. Wow!" At the same time, part of Jane's mind 454
was saying, "I just hope I live to tell somebody about it." ❸ 466

The current was pushing her past the ship, but now it seemed to be 480
pushing her up. Again, Jane tried to swim up. This time she began to 494
go up. "Stop," she thought. "If you go up too fast, you'll get the 508
bends." 509

When somebody gets the bends, bubbles form in the blood. When 520
you open a soft drink bottle, bubbles form because the pressure on the 533
liquid drops when you open the bottle. The same thing happens when 545
divers come up to the surface too fast. As they come up, the pressure 559
on the blood drops. If the pressure drops too fast, bubbles of nitrogen 572
will form in the blood. These nitrogen bubbles can burst blood vessels 584
and cause great pain. 588

Jane wanted to get to the surface so that she could mark the spot 602
where she saw the sunken ship. She was still drifting farther and 614
farther from the ship. But she had to wait before going up to the 628
surface. She waited and drifted. ❹ 633

1   **ch**   **sh**   **wh**

A	B

chin	whether
chip	which
ship	church
whip	

2   surfacing   succeed   remained   burnt

speech   returned   teachers

3
1. decide
2. gasp
3. sprawl
4. immediately

4

darkness   thirty   pounding   warn

meant   warm   exclaimed   water

trembling   wobbly   intended   gauge

might   indicate   gasped   speck

second   closer   pointed   somewhere   right

climbed   scared   caught   grinder   pressing

wrong   trying   realized   however   disk

listen   though   wrist   thought

5   expensive   responsible   approval

1. expensive   2. responsible   3. approval

       unfortunate   entirely

4. unfortunate   5. entirely

   a.   The shoes were entirely too expensive.
   b.   They hoped they would get approval from their friends.
   c.   He was entirely responsible for the unfortunate situation.
   d.   It's unfortunate that the bike is so expensive.

6   Deep in Dark Water

Jane remained underwater for another five minutes before   8
surfacing. During that time she tried not to drift too far from the   21
sunken ship. But when she came up, she saw that she was far from the 36
reef, which meant that she was far from the ship. Jane's boat looked as 50
if it were half a mile away. A yellow speck was in the boat. "That's   65
Doris," Jane said aloud. Jane was glad to see Doris, even though   77
Doris was far away. Jane waved and yelled, "Hello." ❶   86

A few seconds passed. Then Doris waved back. Jane put her mask   98
down and started to swim back to the boat. When she was about fifty 112
feet from the boat, she yelled, "I saw a ship. I saw it."   125

Doris said, "What?"   128

Jane swam closer. Then she yelled, "I saw a sunken ship."   139

Doris dove into the water without her mask or air tanks. She swam   152
over to Jane. Out of breath, Doris gasped, "Where is it?" Jane turned 165
around and pointed to a spot on the east side of the reef. "It's right 180
over there, somewhere." ❷   183

"Show me," Doris said.   187

"Let me rest a minute," Jane said. "I got caught in the current and it 202
scared me to death."   206

Doris said, "Let's sit in the boat a minute, and you can catch your 220
breath."   221

So the teachers swam back to the boat. They climbed in, and Jane   234
sprawled out in the bottom <u>of</u> the boat. The sun was a white disk 248
directly overhead. It seemed to burn holes into Jane's eyes. Jane rolled 260

over on her side. "I really saw it," she said. "It looked big and dark. I 276
don't know why, but I got very scared when I saw it. I felt like I was 293
seeing something that was trying to hide." 300

"Oh, I can't wait," Doris exclaimed. "Let's go see it. Right now." 312

"OK," Jane said. She stood up in the boat. Her hands were 324
trembling, and her knees felt wobbly. She pointed to the east side of the 338
reef. "It's over there, about 150 feet from the other side of the reef." ❸ 352

Jane decided they should swim to the other side of the reef and then 366
dive down. Jane didn't want to let the currents take them past the 379
ship. Before they went down, Jane said, "I think it's about 100 feet 392
deep or more, but don't go all the way down. We don't have enough 406
air. Don't go below sixty feet." 412

Down they went through a cloud of bubbles. Down. The water was 424
getting darker. Jane couldn't see the bottom, yet she knew that her 436
eyes would get used to the dark in a minute or so. Down. She could 451
hear her heart pounding, and she could feel the mask pressing against 463
her face. The sound of the bubbles coming from her mouth was very 476
loud—lub-u-glub-u-lub. Down. "Something is wrong," Jane said to 485
herself. Then she realized that more than one thing was wrong. The 497
water was too warm. When she had passed over the ship before, the 510
water was cold. And now there was no current. Were they in the 523
wrong place? ❹ 525

Jane peered down. She couldn't see the bottom. She looked at the 537
depth gauge on her wrist. "I've got to see the bottom," she thought. 550
Down. Down. Jane kept looking and swimming. But she wasn't 560
looking at her depth gauge or listening to the sound of her heart. She 574
was now fifty feet down. Doris was above her, trying to signal her, but 588
Jane was looking down and swimming slowly toward the bottom. ❺ 598

Suddenly Jane stopped. She could see the bottom now. It was very   610
far down. "This can't be the right place," she thought. "I had better go 624
up." When she looked up, she realized that she had gone deeper than   637
she had intended. The sun was green. Doris was a shadow above her.   650
Jane looked at her watch and realized that she did not have enough air 664
to stay underwater very long. If she returned to the surface   675
immediately, however, she might get the bends. ❻   682

1 th wh

A	B
then	swishing
when	bash
whistled	batch
chill	which
whether	switch

2 agreed decided hours

northeasters breathe smart

3
1. fierce
2. pleaded
3. advice
4. nervous

4
surround turned distance seafood

mouthpiece meant business weather

figure wanted valve wasted sprawl

signaled above worth worry enough

carrying struck warn spare bobbing

television tried spraying morning

report problem goose being knot

5
furthermore   difficulty   realization

1. furthermore 2. difficulty 3. realization

situation   extensive

4. situation 5. extensive

a. The situation created extensive problems.
b. Furthermore, he had the realization that he could succeed.
c. The students were amazed by the difficulty of the assignment.
d. She had a sad realization that her car needed extensive repairs.

6 A New Diving Plan

Jane had gone down too deep, and if she returned to the surface too   14
fast, she might get the bends. But she didn't have enough air to go up   29
slowly. She went up until she was about twenty feet below the surface.   42
She signaled to Doris, who was above her. Jane pointed to her tank   55
and shook her head from side to side.   63

She said, "I'm running out of air," but underwater, what she said   75
sounded like this, "Ibib-rur-n-obobub." ❶   79

Doris shook her head up and down and gave the OK signal with her   93
right hand as if she understood. Then Doris swam to the surface. Jane   106
waited and waited. She began to get nervous. She had only about a   119
minute's worth of air left. "Where is she?" Jane wondered. Then she   131
saw Doris swimming toward her. Doris had gone back to the boat to   144
get a spare air tank. She was carrying that tank and swimming   156
toward Jane.   158

Jane took the tank, placed the mouthpiece in her mouth, turned on   170
the air valve, and began to breathe air from the new tank. Jane gave   184
the signal for "thanks," and she meant it. ❷   192

That evening Jane said, "We're not going at this diving business in a   205
very smart way. When we go back, we'll have to string some spare   218
tanks at the end of the anchor line. When we need them, they'll be   232
there, and we won't be in danger." ❸   239

Doris agreed. The two women worked out their plan for the next   251
day. They decided that they would go out unless the northeast wind   263
was fierce. Doris said, "If we don't get out there tomorrow, we may   276
never get another chance."   280

The next morning was gray and cold. The teachers went down to 292
the dock. The boats were bobbing in the waves. The woman at the 305
dock said, "I won't rent a boat to you today. No way." 317

So the day was wasted. Jane and Doris walked along the beach. 329
They drove to a seafood stand for lunch. They walked along the beach 342
in the afternoon. Then they went back to their motel room and 354
watched television. They didn't talk much. ❹ Slowly night came, and it 365
was time for bed. But Jane didn't sleep well. The wind whistled 377
through a crack under the door. In the distance waves were breaking 389
on the beach, swishing and spraying. 395

The next morning was gray and windy. Jane looked out the window 407
and tried to go back to sleep. There would be no diving today. It 421
would be another day of walking around, killing time, and waiting. 432
"Let me see the sun," Jane pleaded. But there was no sun that day. 446

The next morning was gray, but the wind had stopped. "Get up," 458
Jane yelled. "It's calm. We can go diving." 466

Jane wanted to get to the reef really fast. In the back of her mind 481
she was afraid that the wind would start blowing again. The woman at 494
the dock said, "I don't know. The weather report says that there may 507
be some more winds today." 512

"Come on," Doris said. "There's no problem. The water looks 522
smooth as glass, and tomorrow is our last day. We won't sink your 535
boat." ❺ 536

"OK," the woman said, "but remember, I warned you. You never 547
know about these northeasters. They can come up in the wink of an 560
eye. My advice to you would be to forget it. Don't go out there, but if 576
you want to go—" 580

Jane smiled at Doris. Jane felt goose bumps forming on her arms 592
and neck. "This is it," she said. "Today is the day we find that sunken 607
ship." 608

"Yes," Doris replied. "Today is the day." 615

An hour later, the boat was near the coral reef again. Jane didn't 628
have any trouble finding the place where she had anchored the boat 640
before. Now all she had to do was figure out where that sunken ship 654
was. 655

When Doris and Jane went over the side, a line of blue-gray clouds 668
was far to the north. The clouds were moving toward the little boat 681
and the two divers. Those clouds were being pushed by a wind of forty 695
knots. ❻ 696

1

igh

A	B
right	frightened
fright	fighting
brightness	sighted

2

latch   which   ouch   fresh   thrash
through   while   thought   chance
navigation   clearly   charge   motioned
carved   investigation   afraid
announced   route   nearest   apart

3

1. wispy
2. suspended
3. anchor
4. swayed
5. slime

4

approached   barnacles   swirled   glanced
surface   buoys   spotted   hanging
panic   sucking   forehead   quit
quiet   directed   peaking   staring
caught   yanked   shadow   heavy
lying   laying   horizon   finished

5

inflexible   temperature   remarkable

1. inflexible   2. temperature   3. remarkable

celebration   commented

4. celebration   5. commented

a. His comments about the team showed how inflexible he was.
b. The family arranged for a remarkable celebration.
c. I commented on the low temperature for today.
d. Her injured arm was totally inflexible.

6   The Gray Ghost Ship

Jane and Doris set the diving flags in the water. They hung an air   14
tank on the line leading to the anchor. "Now we should be able to stay   29
down until we find that ship," Jane said when the last flag was in the   44
water.   45

The plan was for the women to take the route that Jane had taken   59
when she spotted the sunken ship. The women would anchor the boat   71
in the same spot they had before. They would dive there and let the   85
current take them through the gap in the reef and past the ship. One   99
of them would then swim down to the ship while the other went to the   114
anchor line. When the diver who went to the ship finished the   126
investigation, the other diver would swim part way down with a fresh   138
air tank and meet the other diver. ❶   145

"Here we go," Jane announced. Both divers were in the water   156
hanging on to the side of the boat. They didn't spot the line of   170
blue-gray clouds to the north. Jane slid her mask over her face. Down   183
she went. Doris was there next to her, moving through a mass of   196
bubbles.   197

Down they went through the warm water. Down. Then the pull of   209
the current began sucking at their legs. "Don't panic," Jane said to   221
herself. She turned to Doris and smiled, but Doris seemed to slip past   234
her in the current. Down <u>and</u> to the east. Through the gap in the reef.   249
Down, down. Cooler water now, and not as much downward pull. ❷   260

Scan the bottom. Darkness and bubbles. "I wish the sun were out,"   272
Jane thought to herself. "It's so dark down here I can't see anything."   285

"What's that?" A dark line—dark black against the almost-black 295
bottom. The mast. There it is, Jane motioned, but Doris was looking 307
the other way. Jane grabbed Doris's leg. "Look. Look," she exclaimed. 318

Jane pointed to herself and then pointed down. "I'm going down." 329
And she did. Through the cooler water. Ouch. Her ears hurt, and she 342
felt a sharp pain in the middle of her forehead. The mask seemed to 356
be pushing her face out of shape. Down. ❸ 364

Suddenly she could see the ship. It was covered with wispy plants 376
that swayed and swirled in the current. The ship looked like a dark 389
gray ghost. "Maybe I don't want to go down there," Jane thought. She 402
looked up. Doris was a dark figure suspended in the water far above 415
her. "I've come this far," Jane thought, "so I won't quit now." ❹ 427

Down. Jane could now see parts of the ship clearly. There was a rail 441
made of heavy carved timbers, covered with barnacles. There was 451
part of a cabin with a door. The deck seemed to be covered with slime 466
and long strings of seaweed. As Jane approached the door of the 478
cabin, she reached into the pouch in her belt and pulled out an 491
underwater flashlight. She turned it on and directed the beam into the 503
cabin. There were stairs covered with slime. There were some boxes 514
and what looked like a broken chair. And there was a pile of—bones. 528
Part of a skull was peeking through the slime. The eye sockets seemed 541
to be staring at Jane. ❺ 546

She dropped the flashlight and swam. Her arms and legs went as 558
fast as they could go. A string of seaweed caught on one of her arms. 573
She yanked it off. She swam up and up and up. Then she looked back. 588

Below her was the dark shadow of the ship with the even darker mast 602
lying next to it. She stopped and began to talk to herself. "Be calm. It 617
was only a skull, only some bones." She began to swim fast again. 630

Doris met her about fifty feet from the surface. Doris gave her a 643
fresh tank of air. Jane stayed there for five minutes. From time to time 657
she glanced down at the ship below, but she could no longer see it 671
because the sky was getting darker and darker. 679

When they reached the surface, Jane told Doris, "I'm not going 690
back down there." ➏ 693

Doris pointed to the horizon and said, "Jane, look." Jane looked at 705
the sky. 707

1

al

A	B
alter	salty
falter	almond
calling	install

2

while   weather   whether   thrash

slightly   bright   tightly   wheeling

together   faintly   agreed   faster

seemingly   feast   cloudy   first

gently   emerging   placed   salvage

3

1. protection
2. suggest
3. glance
4. breaker
5. venture
6. emerge

4

afternoon   patterns   flounder   mound

huge   hours   inspection   jerking   worse

jagged   ruffled   horizon   plumes

wilder   towing   aboard   spare   bluff

responded   rolled   forming   continued

gallons   whistled   designs   during   flight

impossible   whipped   evening   believe

neither   slime   already   storm   yards

5

injury   announcement   investigation

1. injury   2. announcement   3. investigation

procedures   consistent

4. procedures   5. consistent

a. The judge gave approval for a police investigation.

b. The announcement about the new procedures was not consistent with the earlier announcement.

c. They ran an investigation on what caused the injury.

d. We were surprised that they hadn't made the announcement yet.

e. Their approval of the plan was consistent with the way they voted earlier.

6   Trapped in the Storm

There was a line of dark clouds to the north, and there was a line of   16
whitecaps on the horizon under the clouds.   23

"We're in for it now," Doris exclaimed.   30

"What are we going to do?" Jane asked. "Those waves are going to   43
hit us in a few minutes."   49

The women swam back to their boat, towing the spare air tank.   61
They climbed aboard. Jane started the engine, and the boat began to   73
move slowly along the reef. Jane explained, "I don't know where to go.   86
We've got to find some protection from that storm, but I don't see any   100
protection." ❶   101

"Let's keep moving along the reef," Doris suggested. "Maybe we   111
can find a place where the reef is high enough to protect the boat."   125

Jane glanced back. The clouds were closer, and the whitecaps   135
seemed to be bigger and wilder. The old scow continued to move   147
slowly along the west side of the reef. Jane glanced back at the clouds   161
again.   162

"Look," Doris said. Doris was pointing ahead. "There seems to be   173
a coral bluff ahead."   177

Jane could barely see it. It looked like a gray-white mound emerging   189
from the sea. The boat was about half a mile from the mound. ❷   202

"I wish this boat would move faster," Jane shouted. Before Doris   213
could respond, however, a gust of cold wind swept past the boat,   225
making ruffled patterns in the water. The boat turned slightly when   236
the wind hit <u>it</u>.   240

"Here it comes," Doris shouted. Jane could hardly hear Doris's   250
voice above the wind. Already whitecaps were forming on the other   261
side of the reef. The wind was blowing the tops of the waves into a fine   277
spray. Jane felt the side of her face getting wet. She licked her lips.   291
They were salty. ❸   294

The waves were now starting to roll over the low places along the   307
reef. As the waves rolled under the boat, the boat began to rock from   321
side to side. The rocking, which was gentle at first, became more   333
violent. From time to time one of the waves would splash against the   346
side of the boat and send warm water streaming into the boat. Doris   359
was bailing. The boat was only about a hundred yards from the   371
coral bluff now; however, the boat was moving quite slowly as it   383
climbed over the waves, rolling from side to side. ❹   392

"If it gets any worse," Doris yelled, "we'll have to turn the front of   406
the boat so that it faces into the wind. We're going to flounder if we   421
keep going in this direction."   426

But the boat continued along the coral and Doris continued to bail.   438
Just before the boat was alongside the coral mound, a huge breaker hit   451
the side of the boat and dumped about twenty gallons of seawater into   464
the boat. "Bail," Jane shouted as she began to splash water from the   477
boat with her hands.   481

Now the boat was behind the mound. Huge breakers were smashing   492
against the other side of the mound, sending plumes of spray into the   505
air. But the boat was in a protected place. Doris tied a rope around   519
part of the mound. Then she and Jane sat in the front of the boat,   534
close to the coral, as the surf pounded and the wind whistled through   547
the designs in the coral.   552

The wind blew for more than two hours. During that time the 564
women waited. From time to time they tried to talk, but it was almost 578
impossible to hear what was said above the wind and the surf. ❺ 590

Then almost as suddenly as the storm had started, the wind died 602
down. Huge waves continued to roll over the reef for another hour, 614
but the waves became smaller and calmer. They were no longer being 626
whipped into jagged shapes by the wind. 633

At around five o'clock that evening, the waves were small enough 644
for the women to venture back to the dock. Jane said, "I sure won't 658
forget this day for a long, long time." ❻ 666

1

oa

A	B
foam	croak
float	soap
boasted	bloat
loaded	

2

explained   changing   speedboat

astound   carved   observed   lanterns

already   arrangements   excited

3

1. statue
2. figurehead
3. salvage
4. claim
5. marine

4

darkness   grain   better   oxygen

placed   afraid   nearly   probably

believe   dead   slime   covered

company   profits   split   suggested

proof   explore   writing   important

early   guess   instruments   restaurant

5

individual   combination   obviously

1. individual   2. combination   3. obviously

disagreement   participants

4. disagreement   5. participants

a. I am obviously in strong disagreement with that plan.
b. Individual participants went to their different meeting rooms.
c. She obviously had a combination of good looks and a sense of humor.
d. There were only three participants in the final events.
e. Every year some students forget the combination to their locker.

6   # Exploring the Ship

Jane and Doris made it home safely from the reef. When the women   13
returned to their motel, Jane was very tired but still excited from her   26
adventures. She and Doris had dinner at the motel restaurant. As they   38
waited to be served, they began to talk. The more they talked, the   51
faster and louder they talked. They made plans about going back to   63
the sunken ship. About a hundred times, Jane said, "There is no way   76
I'm going back inside that ship. I just won't do it." She explained that   90
the storm frightened her, but not nearly as much as that ship had—   103
down in the dark sea, covered with slime and filled with bones. ❶   115

"OK," Doris said. "Let's go back early in the morning and put up a   129
salvage-claim flag. Then we'll make a deal with some salvage company   140
to go out there and explore the ship. We'll split the profits with them."   154

"Hey," Jane said. "That's a good idea. Let's do that."   164

And they did. The next morning they rented a speedboat—not that   176
old scow that they had been using. The speedboat cost them fifty   188
dollars, which was most of the money they had. The women agreed   200
that it was better to have a fast boat, even if that meant paying more   215
money. ❷   216

The ride out was a lot of fun. Doris drove the boat, and Jane sat in   232
the back, feeling the spray made by <u>the</u> boat as it cut a path along the   248
surface of the water. Jane watched the little waves zip by. Then the   261
women placed a red salvage flag along with the diving flags over the   274
spot where the sunken ship was resting.   281

Jane took a picture of Doris and the salvage flag. "That's just for   294
proof," Jane said. "We have just claimed a sunken treasure. I don't   306
believe it."   308

"Me neither," Doris agreed.   312

By noon, the women had made arrangements with a man from a   324
marine salvage outfit. His name was Mike. By two o'clock that   335
afternoon, Mike, Doris, Jane, and two other men were anchored   345
above the sunken ship. They were in a boat that looked like an old   359
tugboat. Mike was in diving gear. He and one of the other men   372
explained that they would go down and explore the ship. ❸   382

By four that afternoon, the divers returned to the surface. Mike's   393
mask bubbled up from the sea. He pushed the mask back and smiled.   406
"Well, you found a sunken ship, all right," he explained. "But I'm   418
afraid there's no gold on this ship."   425

"Oh, no," Doris said. She turned to Jane, and each woman shook   437
her head.   439

"But," Mike added, "there are some things on board that are worth   451
some money."   453

"What?" Jane asked.   456

"Well, there are a lot of little things. This ship was probably built   469
around 1780. It was probably carrying grain and other supplies. There   480
are some bottles in the hold that are probably worth twenty dollars   492
each. I would guess there are a hundred bottles down there."   503

Jane and Doris looked at each other and smiled.   512

"And there are some old navigation instruments. A couple of them   523
seem to be in fair shape. They're probably worth more than two   535
hundred dollars each." Mike listed other things—a statue, a carved   546
figurehead, some writing instruments, some old lanterns. ❹   553

Doris and Jane didn't get rich. Their trip to Florida cost them more   566
than one thousand dollars. But each woman got two thousand dollars   577
for her share of the salvage from the sunken ship. On the flight back   591
home, Jane felt pretty proud. "We may not be rich," she observed, "but   604
we did it. Instead of sitting and thinking about it, we did it. I think   619
that's the most important part." ❺   624

1   **un**

A	B

unreal   unable

unseen   unlimited

unbelievable   unfortunate

uncertain

2   bright   easily   interesting   contained

distance   gigantic   although   falter

fifteenth   branches   approaches   flights

matches   floating   frightened

3   1. tunnel
2. fluttered
3. snaked
4. drizzly
5. canopy

4   sequoia   foliage   building   cousin

swirled   darkness   drifted   develop

survive   through   swayed   Pacific

November   create   covered   among

suggested   neither   extended

constructed   parent   rapidly

5   The Redwood Tree

This is the story of a redwood tree that is living today in   13
northern California. That redwood, like many others, has had an   23
interesting life.   25

Its life began with a seed contained in a cone. A redwood cone is   39
about as big as a quarter. The cone starts to grow in early summer. By   54
late summer it is full-sized and bright green with many seeds inside.   66
The cone is not yet full grown, however. As fall approaches, the cone   79
begins to change color, turning brown. Small flaps on all sides of the   92
cone open, and as they do, the tiny seeds fall out. The seeds are so   107
small that ten of them would easily fit on the end of your finger. If you   123
wanted a pound of these seeds, you would have to collect about 120   136
thousand of them. ❶   139

It seems strange that a seed so small can grow into the world's   152
tallest tree, but it's true. Redwoods are the tallest trees, although a   164
cousin of the redwood—the giant sequoia—has a thicker trunk than   176
the redwood. Some giant sequoias have trunks so thick that people   187
have constructed tunnels through them, and these tunnels are so big   198
that cars can pass through them. The giant sequoia, however, does not   210
grow as tall as the redwood. To get an idea of how tall the bigger   225
redwoods are, imagine what it would be like to climb a flight of stairs   239
as high as these redwoods. Imagine climbing five flights of stairs.   250
Imagine how far down it is when you are five stories high. A big   264
redwood is much taller than a five-story building, however. So   274
imagine going up to the tenth floor, the fifteenth floor, the twentieth   286
floor. From up here you can see a long distance, and it's a long, long   301
way down. However, if you were on the twentieth floor of a building,   314
you would not be near the top of a big redwood. You would probably   328

be tired from climbing twenty flights of stairs; however, to reach the   340
top of a big redwood, you would have to climb another fifteen flights   353
of stairs. That's right. A very tall redwood is about as tall as a   367
thirty-five-story building. A person standing down at the base of the   378
tree would look like an ant. The base of the redwood's trunk is so big   393
that eight people could stand next to each other and hide behind the   406
trunk. And that gigantic tree develops from a seed smaller than a   418
grain of wheat. ❷   421

It was on a sunny November day that the seed of the redwood tree   435
in this story fluttered from the cone. The parent tree stood on the   448
bank of a small creek that snaked among the giant redwoods. The   460
weather had been cold, and a drizzly rain had been falling for days.   473
During the rain, the flaps of the redwood cone swelled up and closed.   486
But now the sun emerged, and a brisk wind swirled through the tops   499
of the redwoods, bending their tops to the south. As the top of the   573
parent tree swayed in the cool wind, the cones began to dry out, and   587
the flaps began to open. Below, the forest was deeply shaded by the   600
foliage of the giant redwoods, which formed a canopy of green that   612
extended as far as one could see. In the distance was the sound of the   627
Pacific Ocean.   629

Late that afternoon, a sudden gust of wind pushed through the   640
forest, bending branches of the redwoods. When that wind hit the   651
parent tree, six of the cone's forty seeds fluttered down and drifted   663
down, down, into the dark forest below. One of those seeds would   675
develop into a giant. The others would not survive. ❸   684

1

A	B
citing	exciting
act	exact
ample	example
tended	extended
plain	explain
posed	exposed
change	exchange

2 un

A	B
untold	unthinking
unbelievable	uneasy
unable	unfinished
unfortunate	unaware

3
1. litter
2. mole
3. severe

4

slightly boasted crunch installed

astounded alternate cloudy always

seeming inspection alter person

flight white hours exceptionally

produce survive branches coated

5

wrist midst obviously developed

neither fertile receive canopy event

adventure continued occasionally lodged

quite quiet pinpoints remained

exposed feast contained strength

creating worse jagged ruffled weigh

edge fortunate rattle square

6   The First Winter

During a good seed year a large redwood will produce over twelve 12
pounds of seeds, which is nearly a million and a half seeds. And the 26
year that our redwood seed fluttered from the cone was an 37
exceptionally good year. The parent tree produced over fifteen pounds 47
of seeds that year, enough seed to start a forest that would be six 61
square miles in size. However, only a few redwood seeds survived. In 73
fact, only three of the seeds from the parent tree survived their first 86
year, and only one lived beyond the first year. ❶ 95

Obviously, our seed was lucky. It was a fortunate seed because it 107
was fertile. If a seed is not fertile, it cannot grow, and about nine of 122
every ten redwood seeds are not fertile. Our seed was also fortunate 134
because it landed in a place where it could survive. If it had fallen on a 150
part of the forest floor covered with thick, heavy litter, it probably 162
would not have grown. If it had fluttered to a spot that became too 176
dry during the summer, it would have died during that first year. ❷ 188

Our seed landed in a spot where moles had been digging. They had 201
made small piles of fresh brown dirt, and our seed landed on the edge 215
of the dirt. Later that winter another fortunate event took place. The 227
top fifty feet of a nearby tree broke off during a severe <u>windstorm</u>. 240
When the top, which weighed more than three elephants, crashed to 251
the forest floor, it tore the branches from the trees that were in its 265
path. The fallen top left a large hole in the green canopy that shaded 279
the forest floor. This event was fortunate for our seed because it would 292
receive sunlight. Some trees are capable of growing only in bright 303
sunlight, while other trees survive only in the shade. Redwoods are 314
unusual trees because they can survive in either shade or sunlight; 325
however, they don't grow well in deep shade. ❸ 333

To give you an idea of how much faster redwoods grow in the 346
sunlight, let's say that we planted two seeds, one in the deep shade, the 360
other in the sunlight. When we look at the trees fifty years later, we 374
observe that the tree exposed to the full sunlight is over one hundred 387
feet tall. The base of its trunk is almost three feet across. The tree 401
grown in the shade, however, is only about six feet tall, and its trunk is 416
not as big around as your wrist. ❹ 423

During the winter that our seed was resting on the mole diggings, 435
the weather was cold and rainy. Most of the rain came in the form of a 451
fine mist that would feel like tiny pinpoints of cold against your face. 464
Occasionally, however, large drops of rain would rattle through the 474
northern California forest, creating tiny streams on the forest floor. 484
Our seed was much smaller than a drop of water, and it was pushed 498
around by the water quite a bit during the first part of the winter. At 513
one time it seemed as if a heavy rain would wash it away from the 528
mole diggings. However, it became lodged in a small crack between 539
two mounds of dirt. And there it remained, ready to grow when days 552
became warmer in the spring. ❺ 557

1 **un**

A	B
unfaithful	uneven
unexpected	unfastened
unequal	unfailing
uneventful	unfinished

2 **ly**

A	B
occasionally	quietly
fortunately	unbelievably
obviously	slightly
exceptionally	easily

3
1. swell
2. torch
3. charred
4. smoldering

4

screech smallest cheap section watch

toasted brightened approached amount

straighten received crushed squirrel

wonder whisper seedling convert

5

visible connected height unfortunate

ignited exciting motionless thought

impossible celebration pancake strength

stretched changed bounding manufacture

flooding created sapling though

blazed developing emerged through

6 Seedling to Sapling

In April something exciting happened on the floor of the redwood   11
forest, just as it happened every year. Some of the redwood seeds   23
began to develop into baby trees, which are called seedlings. ❶   33

The forest floor was soaked by the winter rain, and the rain was still   47
falling; however, the days were becoming warmer. In early April our   58
seed began to change. At first it began to swell slightly as the inside of   73
the seed changed. The hard inside of the seed changed into a white   86
pulp that looks and feels something like pancake batter. Parts of this   98
white blob then began to become harder and take on a form. One end   112
of the blob began to take on the shape of a tiny green plant. The other   128
end became pointed and began to look like a tiny root. The root end   142
pushed out through one end of the seed and began to worm its way   156
down into the soft ground. ❷ When the seedling was less than an inch   169
long, it started to straighten up. The top of the seedling was still inside   183
the seed, and the seed was in the soft mud. The only part of the   198
seedling that was visible above ground was the stem that connected   209
the root to the seed. The seedling looked something like a person   221
bending over in shallow water, with only the person's back above the   233
water. The seedling looked like this: 239

<u>As</u> the seedling grew a longer root, it had enough strength to pull its   253
top from the seed. The empty seed remained in the mud, and the top   267
slowly began to stand up. It was only about a half inch tall, with two   282
little leaves stretched out to the side like two little green arms. A   295
squirrel could have stepped on that seedling and crushed it. But not   307

far from that unbelievably small seedling was the parent tree, standing 318
over 400 feet tall. ❸ 322

During the seedling's first summer, it grew to a height of about 334
three inches. On sunny days, the sun's rays came through the hole in 347
the forest's canopy and flooded the ground around the seedling with 358
sunlight. Trees, as you know, need sunlight to survive. They take the 370
incoming sunlight and convert it into food. Without sunlight they 380
starve because they can't manufacture food. Our seedling was 389
fortunate because it received a fair amount of sunlight through the 400
hole created by the falling treetop. ❹ 406

Things went well for the seedling for six years. By the end of the 420
sixth year our young redwood was no longer a seedling. It was now 433
what is called a sapling—a young tree. And it was growing quite 446
rapidly. You might think that redwoods are very slow-growing, but 456
they actually grow faster than most trees. At the end of its sixth year, 470
our redwood was nearly twelve feet tall, and it was reaching straight 482
up to the top of the forest, which was still a long, long way above the 498
sapling. But the sapling was now ready to grow nearly three feet a 511
year. ❺ 525

That fall, however, something unfortunate happened. Late one 533
evening lightning struck a nearby tree. A burning branch fell and 544
ignited the litter on the forest floor. Soon a hot, orange fire blazed 557
through the forest. That fire didn't reach even the bottom branches of 569
the bigger trees, because those branches were more than one hundred 580
feet above the forest floor. However, the fire burned the smaller trees 592
to the ground. It swept over our redwood sapling, and within a few 605
seconds, the sapling was a torch. Within a few minutes, the sapling 617
was a charred stick smoldering in the forest. ❻ 625

1 oi

A	B
oil	noise
point	pinpoint
voice	soil

2 ly

A	B
quickly	completely
certainly	uncertainly
occasionally	severely
frequently	gently
unbelievably	obviously

3

1. original
2. shade
3. toppled
4. sprouts

4

suggestion   although   investigation

thousand   furthermore   cloaked

5

burls   smolder   charred   continued

creating   once   burnt   shaped

disease   germs   natural   original

survived   telephone   knotty   extended

seasons   towering   ago   causes   single

6   Toward the Towering Green Canopy

No fire fighters came to put out the fire in the redwood forest   13
because that fire took place long ago. In fact, it took place more than   27
two thousand years ago. At that time there were no houses or roads in   41
the area now known as northern California. Nobody put out the fire.   53
So the fire burned. After it flashed through the forest, the flames died   66
away; however, parts of the bigger trees and large fallen branches   77
continued to smolder for nearly a month. A fire smoldered at the base   90
of the redwood's parent tree, creating a charred hole that was big   102
enough for a person to sit in. Many other large trees also had   115
smoldering bases.   117

But when the heavy rains came in the late fall, the smoldering fires   130
died out and the forest was once more calm with the sound of gentle   144
rain falling on the charred forest floor. ❶ The forest remained calm   155
until the next spring when the trees again began to grow. Our   167
redwood was among the first to start growing. Although it had been   179
burned to the ground, it was not dead. Its roots were alive, and those   193
roots sent up three shoots. These shoots were quite thick and very   205
fast-growing. By the middle of July, the tallest of the three was nearly   218
six feet tall, growing right next to the charred trunk of the tree that   232
had been burnt.   235

Fires often kill young <u>trees</u>, but fires don't often kill young   246
redwoods because the redwoods simply send up new sprouts.   255
Furthermore, there is no insect or disease that kills redwood saplings.   266
While germs and different kinds of bugs kill other types of trees, no   279
natural enemy kills the redwood. ❷   284

So our redwood continued to grow. Within three years, it was taller 296
than it had been before the fire. By now, one of the original sprouts 310
had become the main trunk and it was growing quite rapidly, while 322
the other sprouts were hardly growing at all. Six years after the fire, 335
the two slow-growing sprouts were dead. Only the main sprout 345
survived. Our sapling was now taller than the roof of a single-story 357
building. Twenty-five years after the fire, our redwood was fifty feet 368
tall, still growing at the rate of about three feet a year. Its trunk was 383
now as big around as a telephone pole, and it had several large burls 397
on it. Redwood burls are knotty growths on the trunk and the 409
branches. They look like big lumps. Smaller burls are as big as your 422
fist. Larger ones may be three feet across and extend a foot out from 436
the tree. These burls are masses of buds. If you take part of a burl and 452
place it in water, the buds will sprout, and a bunch of tiny redwood 466
shoots will begin to grow from the burl. ❸ 474

The largest burl on our redwood was right under one of the side 487
branches. It was about as big as two fists held together. By now, our 501
redwood was starting to look like a forest tree. Young redwoods are 513
shaped like Christmas trees. If they grow in a forest, however, the 525
bottom branches don't receive any sun, because the higher branches 535
of the tree block much of the sunlight. This causes the lower branches 548
to die. As the tree continues to grow, the higher branches keep 560
shading the lower branches, and the lower branches keep dying. Soon 571
the trunk of the tree may be free of branches for some distance. When 585
our redwood was fifty feet tall, only the top twenty-five feet of the 598
trunk had living branches. The bottom twenty-five feet of the trunk 609
had either dead branches or no branches. 616

The seasons followed each other—rain, warmth and sunlight, and 626
more rain. By the time our redwood was eighty years old, it was over 640
225 feet tall—which is about as tall as an 18-story building. The base 654
of its trunk was six feet across. Its trunk was bare of branches for over 669
ninety feet. And its top was near the green canopy created by the 682
towering older trees. **❹** 685

1

ure

A	B
treasure	pleasure
picture	nature
mature	assure
sure	pressure

2

exceptionally actually noisy installed

severely uncertainly occasionally crouched

foiled unexpectedly emerge unbelievably

furthermore unfortunately boiling survive

approaching latches alternate particularly

3

1. mature
2. leveled
3. deafening

4

thorough through tough thought

though sugar toppled producing

producer height reached frightening

flared swirling gigantic toothpicks

including swayed great burnt

natural towering continuing knotty

change racing parent exchanged

5   Another Fire

When our redwood was eighty years old, it was producing seeds; 11
however, less than one of every hundred seeds was fertile. Our 22
redwood did not become a good seed producer until it was over two 35
hundred years old. Then it continued to produce fertile seeds until its 47
death. 48

After our redwood reached the height of 225 feet, it began to grow 61
more and more slowly. It had become a mature tree. When it was two 75
hundred years old, it was growing only a couple of inches a year, but it 90
was already more than three hundred feet tall. By the time it was four 104
hundred years old, it was growing at the rate of less than an inch a 119
year. ❶ 120

It was during our redwood's 420th year that a terrible fire swept 132
through the forest. This fire was not like the one that had leveled the 146
small trees years before. This was a fire that rolled over the tops of the 161
tallest trees in the forest, sending up flames more than 400 feet into a 175
sky that was dark with smoke. The roar of the fire was deafening. Its 189
speed was frightening. It began in a pile of dry litter near the base of a 205
young tree. The fire flared up in a few seconds. Within a minute it was 220
climbing the smaller trees and then the larger ones. When it reached 232
our redwood, the fire was a rolling, swirling mass that was hot enough 245
to melt metal. With a rush it burned all the green needles from our 259
redwood. It burned the branches and burned the trunk. ❷ 268

That fire smoldered for three months. A few trees toppled during 279
the fire, particularly the very old ones. The parent of our redwood was 292
one of those that toppled. The parent tree was more than two 304

thousand years old and had lived through five great fires. But most of   317
the big trees remained standing. They looked like gigantic charred   327
toothpicks sticking up from the black forest floor.   335

Not all of the trees in the forest were redwoods. Some were sugar   348
pines, and there were a few oaks. The fire swept over all these trees.   362
And when the following spring came, the older oaks were dead and   374
the older sugar pines were dead. But the mature redwoods, including   385
ours, were still alive. ❸   389

The fire never reached the part of the tree trunk that was alive. The   403
living part of a tree trunk is a very thin layer just under the bark. The   419
rest of a tree trunk or a branch is not alive. The wood inside is not   435
alive. It is dead matter with a thin layer of living matter around it. The   450
oaks in the forest were dead because their bark was about an inch   463
thick. The fire burned through their bark and burned the layer of   475
living matter just under the bark. The same thing happened to the   487
sugar pines. But the mature redwoods have very thick bark. The bark   499
on the trunk of our redwood, for example, was about eight inches   511
thick. ❹   512

1   **un**   **ly**

A	B
ridiculously	unfamiliar
particularly	uncertain
tightly	unnatural
actually	unexpectedly
exceptionally	

2   treasure   exaggerate   examine   sure   broil

occasionally   probably   stalled   situation

voiced   nature   boasted   moist   injure

sprouts   mature   brighten   insure

3   adapt

4   through   thought   thorough   though

tough   colony   colonies   earth   canopy

Atlantic   continent   realize   adopt   consider

ordinary   continued   dense   century

terrible   surroundings   loose   danger

destroyed   narrower   disturbed   sugar

endure   amazing   cause   normal   possible

5 A Green Toothpick

To realize how amazing the mature redwoods are, you have to   11
remember that most other older trees become very fixed in their ways   23
and would not adjust to the changes a fire would cause. Most young   36
trees, whether they're redwoods or sugar pines, can adapt well to   47
different situations. If you were to pile up dirt one foot deep around 60
the base of a sugar pine sapling, the tree would adjust and keep on   74
living. However, if you piled up dirt only four inches deep around the 87
base of a mature sugar pine, you would probably kill the tree.   99

Mature trees often become so set in their ways that they die if the   113
trees next to them are cut down. When these other trees are cut down, 127
sunlight reaches the base of the mature tree, and the tree dies. ❶ Now 140
consider the mature redwood. Remember, our redwood was 420 years   150
old when the fire burned every needle from it. You would think that a 164
tree so old could not survive. But the redwood is no ordinary tree.   177
And our redwood did survive.   182

The forest looked very strange the next spring. The charred trees   193
that had looked like black toothpicks now looked like green   203
toothpicks. Little green sprouts shot out from the trunk of every   214
mature redwood—from the ground to the top of every tree. Sprouts   226
also shot out from what was left of the top branches. The trees looked 240
very strange, almost as if somebody had painted the trunks and the   252
remaining branches green.   255

The shoots grew very fast. By the end of the summer, some of them   269
were almost ten feet long. They continued growing rapidly during the   280
next several years. The shoots near the bottom of the trees became   292
shaded and died off. Those near the top of the trees slowly took the   306
shape of a cone. Within twenty years after the fire, the mature   318

redwoods looked quite normal again, with long, bare trunks and green, full, cone-shaped tops. ❷ Once more a canopy of green shaded the forest floor. The canopy was not as dense as it had been, which meant that some of the younger trees that sprouted from the ground after the fire had a chance to grow more rapidly than young trees did before the great fire.

Century after century went by. When our tree was seventeen hundred years old, it lost its top during a terrible windstorm. This happened the year before Columbus sailed across the Atlantic. The top forty feet of our redwood crashed to the forest floor, tearing branches from the surrounding trees and leaving a large hole in the canopy of green. That hole made it possible for some of the younger redwoods to grow. One seedling that sprouted the next year came from a seed of our redwood. That seedling was growing in the loose dirt dug up when the top of our redwood crashed to the forest floor. The seedling looked ridiculously small next to our huge redwood.

Our redwood did not grow its top back quickly. Over two hundred years passed before the redwood was as tall as it had been before the windstorm. By now, British colonies were being settled on the other side of the continent. ❸

Things remained peaceful in the redwood forest for the next three hundred years. Three smaller fires swept through the forest, and one left a large hole in the base of our redwood. Over the years a lot of animals used that hole, mostly squirrels and rabbits. It was big enough for three people to sit in, but it didn't really harm the tree. The wood from redwoods doesn't rot even if it is exposed to the rain. Water will rot most other woods. Boards made from pine or fir must be treated if they are to be exposed to the weather. Not so with boards of redwood. ❹

1

ly   un

A	B
suddenly	uneventful
severely	unstable
particularly	uncontrolled
rarely	unfortunately

2

exaggerate   unfailingly   assure   jointly

groans   exceptionally   unexplainable   creature

certain   hoist   lecture   surrounding

location   choicest   loaning   termites

3

1. polite
2. remarkable
3. outskirts
4. brittle

4

county   country   beautiful   contains

continues   becomes   forever

protected   gravel   narrower   edge

mature   destroy   contact   shallow

furniture   excellent   fault   dangerous

shrink   material   fences   building

square   bothered   national   rarely

5 | # The Redwoods Today

As you've seen, redwoods are remarkable. Fire can't destroy them.   10
Even if young trees are cut down, they sprout up again. Redwoods are   23
not bothered by termites or any insect that destroys other trees. The   35
wood from redwoods is as remarkable as the trees. The wood will not   48
rot if it comes in contact with wet earth. Even after the wood has been   63
soaked for years, it won't rot. The wood is soft and easy to work with,   78
so it makes good furniture and excellent siding for houses. ❶   88

The redwood seems like a perfect tree, except for two faults. The   100
first fault is that the roots of redwoods are very shallow. They rarely   113
go down more than ten feet. The roots fan out to the sides like great   128
hooks or claws that hang on to the soil. When redwoods grow in   141
forests, the roots of one tree lock under the roots of surrounding trees.   154
When no trees surround the mature redwood, however, it becomes   164
unstable. The first strong wind that hits the tree might blow it over. ❷   177

Because redwoods have shallow roots, the trees are dangerous near   187
cities. Let's say that a huge redwood—200 feet tall—is growing next to   201
some houses on the outskirts of town. And let's say that there are no   215
surrounding trees. One night there is a great storm, and the redwood   227
comes down.   229

The second problem is that the wood in older redwoods <u>becomes</u>   240
brittle. It may split or crack. If that happens, parts of the tree may   254
come down during a storm. ❸   259

Because of these two problems, the redwood forests began to shrink   270
up during the past 60 years. The great redwoods came down to make   283
furniture, fences, and other building material. But even as early as   294

1921, the State of California began giving money so that redwood parks could be formed. The old redwoods within these parks would be protected.

Our redwood does not live in one of these first parks. It lives near Arcata, California, in an area called Redwood Creek. And our redwood was lucky, because in 1968, the whole Redwood Creek area became part of a new park—Redwood National Park. The park contains 172 square miles of mature redwoods. ❹

Our redwood is not the tallest tree along Redwood Creek. There is one that is more than four hundred feet tall. But our redwood is one of the biggest trees. It's not easy to find because there is no road that leads to it. To find it, you have to park your car on the gravel county road and walk along the edge of the creek, through the ferns and the soft litter on the forest floor. Look at the bigger trees and you'll see one with a base so big that you could hide three cars behind it. You'll see a cone-shaped hole near the bottom of the tree. And when you look up, the trunk seems to go up forever. But if you look closely, you'll see a place near the top of the tree where the trunk suddenly becomes narrower, marking where the top had broken off long ago. And when you stand there in the silent forest looking at our redwood, you'll probably feel proud. You will be certain of one thing, however— you're looking at one beautiful tree. ❺

Lesson 33

1

conditioner Bruce office manage

furthermore grouchier occasionally

exceptionally simply curling

unbelievable pinched choice

2

1. insurance
2. freeway
3. bothersome

3

sore phony polite insects world

vice president newspapers freeways

something usually timer everything

oven concrete simple neighbors

peaceful humming ocean groves

bananas coconuts jungle canopy

wearing pretend sour listen

4 Bruce the Grouch

Bruce Celt had a good job as vice president of an insurance   12
company. Furthermore, he had a nice home. However, he was not   23
happy. He didn't like to drive in his car on the freeways. He didn't like   38
the food that he ate. He read the newspapers only occasionally   49
because everything that happened in the world seemed bad.   58

Every day Bruce Celt went to work, and every day he worked hard.   71
He worked through the lunch hour because he didn't like eating out.   83
Sometimes he ate an apple or an orange. After work he left the office,   97
but he didn't smile on his way out. He simply drove down the freeway.   111
Honk, honk. Stop and go, and stop again. Honk. Every day it was the   125
same. ❶   126

Bruce lived alone. By the time he got home, his eyes were sore, and   140
he had a pain in his head. Usually he parked his car in his garage and   156
went into his house and sat. Occasionally he looked outside and   167
watched what his neighbors were doing. But his neighbors didn't   177
interest him. Sometimes he would sit outside in his yard, but the air   190
was filled with smoke, and somebody was always trying to talk to   202
him. For example, one of his neighbors would say, "Hey, Bruce, have   214
you seen my new car? It's nice. Come on over, and let's go for a spin in   231
it." Bruce would try to be polite, but <u>he</u> couldn't help himself. He was   245
a grouch.   247

After the sun went down, he would turn on the lights. But he didn't   261
like lights because they seemed phony. They weren't sunlight. Usually   271
he ate a frozen dinner. He took it from the freezer and popped it into   286
the oven. When the timer on the oven went ding, he pulled out the   300
dinner and ate it.   304

After dinner Bruce would go for a walk. He would try to listen to   318
the sounds of the birds and the insects. All he could hear, however,   331
was the roar of cars on the freeway. Bruce usually walked for an hour.   345
Then he would return to his home and go to bed. ❷   356

He was unhappy with his bed. It was too soft and too big.   369
Furthermore, sleeping was not easy for Bruce. He would lie in bed   381
and listen to the sound of the air conditioner. Occasionally he would   393
hear the sound of the motor in the freezer. And as he lay there, Bruce   408
would find himself making the same wish night after night. "I wish I   421
lived a life that was simple. With all my heart I wish that I could live   437
with plants and animals, not with cars and concrete, not with   448
television sets and freezers." ❸   452

But then something very strange happened. One night Bruce was   462
sadder and grouchier than he had been for a long time. Things seemed   475
very bad at the office. He couldn't stand another frozen dinner. His   487
neighbors seemed exceptionally bothersome.   491

And that night he said to himself, "I'm going to wish as hard as I   506
can wish. I'm going to wish myself out of this place. I shouldn't have   520
to spend the rest of my life being so unhappy. I'm going to wish harder   535
than I've ever wished before."   540

So Bruce pressed his eyes shut as hard as he could and he wished.   554
He made a picture of a place in his mind, and he wished for that   569
place. It was a peaceful place—an island with trees and sand and   582
warm ocean water. "Take me there," he wished. "Please, get me out of   595
here." ❹   596

Bruce didn't remember falling asleep that night. He only   605
remembered wishing and wishing and wishing. When he woke up the   616
next morning, however, he couldn't believe his eyes. He wasn't   626
sleeping on his soft bed, and he wasn't in his bedroom listening to the   640
humming of the air conditioner. In fact, he wasn't in his house; he was   654

on a sandy beach. Not fifty feet from where he sat was the ocean. Its 669

gentle waves came curling along the beach. In back of him were 681

groves of tall trees. He could see bananas and coconuts beneath the 693

trees. He could hear the sound of jungle birds in the canopy of green. 707

"This is unbelievable," Bruce said to himself. He pinched himself on 718

the arm, but the trees, the sand, the ocean, and the exciting sounds 731

did not go away. "I can't believe it," Bruce said to himself, and he 745

stood up. He was wearing a pair of shorts and nothing more. There 758

were no footprints in the sand. ❺ 764

1

re

A	B
rebuild	require
regain	remember
reopen	reply
reappear	responsible
restate	remaining
	receiving

2

fertile   particularly   original   especially

swirled   slowly   excited   survive

future   except   thirsty   moisture

3

1. deserve
2. breadfruit
3. bored

4

prove   approval   problems   somersaults

earth   parrots   crickets   fourth   edge

bubbled   fortunate   restless   wonder

worry   tackle   unfortunately   coconuts

healthy   realize   although   handfuls

shoving   among   grove   single

5 A Dream Come True

Bruce walked slowly along the beach, stopping many times to look   11
at the crabs and the seashells. He felt the warm morning breeze in his   25
face. "I hope this is true," he thought. "I hope this is really true." Bruce   40
wanted to jump up and down and yell, "Yippee." He wanted to turn   53
somersaults in the sand. But in the back of his mind he kept thinking,   67
"Maybe this isn't really happening. So don't get your hopes up."   78

Bruce stopped at the edge of the water and swirled his hand in it.   92
Then he licked his fingers. Salty. The water was salty, so the water was   106
ocean water. ❶   108

By the evening of his second day on the island, Bruce was getting   121
used to the idea that he was not dreaming. By then he had walked all   136
the way around the island and proved to himself that it was an island.   150
He had eaten coconuts and bananas from the trees. He had also eaten   163
breadfruit and berries. He had fallen asleep in the sun on the beach,   176
and he had a sunburn to prove it. Later he had slept in the shade of a   193
big coconut tree. He had watched parrots and monkeys. He had   204
breathed clean air and listened to the sounds of the waves, the   216
crickets, and the bees. He had gone swimming in the ocean.   227
Fortunately, he had found fresh water near the shore. It came from a   240
refreshing spring. The water bubbled from the rocks and ran down the   252
hill in a little stream. It was the best water Bruce had ever drunk. ❷   266

After his third day on the island, Bruce felt less fortunate and a   279
little more restless. He didn't enjoy watching crabs on the beach as   291
much as he had on the first two days. The parrots in the trees didn't   306
seem as exciting. While the sun seemed a little too hot, the shade   319
seemed too dark. ❸   322

And that evening when the sun was setting, he found himself 333
saying, "I wonder what I'm going to do now?" He didn't want to go to 348
sleep because he wasn't tired. However, there was no television to 359
watch, no books to read, no lights to turn off. 369

The fourth day was even less exciting than the third. "I wished for 382
this, so I guess I deserve it," he said to himself. "But there is nothing 397
to do here. If only there were some problems in this place. If only 411
there were something to worry about. I wish there were other people 423
on this island—even if I didn't like them." ❹ 432

No sooner had Bruce made the wish than he saw a group of women 446
and men walking down the beach. "That's strange," Bruce thought. 456
"I've looked over this island from one end to the other, and I haven't 470
seen a single footprint, except the ones I've made. Where did these 482
people come from?" 485

"Hello," Bruce called. He waved. 490

They waved back. Then one of them said in a high voice, "Unk, 503
unk." 504

Bruce walked over to the people. Bruce pointed to himself. "My 515
name is Bruce," he said. "Bruce." 521

A tall woman wearing a long robe replied, "Unk," and pointed to 533
her mouth. 535

"If you're thirsty," Bruce said, "let me give you some water. Follow 547
me." He led the others to the spring in the grove of trees. But when he 563
got to the spot where the water had been bubbling up from the rocks, 577
there was no water. There was no stream. 585

"Unfortunately, there is no water," Bruce said. "However, we can 595
always drink coconut milk." He looked around for coconuts on the 606
ground. He couldn't see any healthy ones. There had been hundreds 617
of them, but now they all looked rotten. ❺ 625

1 **un   ly   re**

A	B

return   repeat

reply   remodel

require   report

remember   receive

2 thi<u>r</u>sty <u>e</u>xpecting situ<u>a</u>tions glan<u>c</u>ed

s<u>u</u>rvive silent<u>ly</u> <u>e</u>xcept we<u>d</u>ged

3 1. disturbed

2. logical

4 strangely realized immediate solve

fighters although probably branches

unafraid insurance extended collecting

decided pry pried forehead

bored signs ankle among

scoop handfuls shoving tasted

5   More Problems to Tackle

One man pointed to his mouth and said, "Unk, unk." 10

Bruce said, "You're probably hungry. Well, we certainly should be 20
able to find some breadfruit or bananas. Follow me." The others 31
followed, but all the trees seemed to be bare. Bruce was becoming 43
disturbed. Where had all the bananas and breadfruit gone? What had 54
happened to the water? And what would happen if he didn't find 66
water pretty soon? Bruce knew that he would probably die within five 78
days without water. He knew that he could go a long time without 91
food. In fact, he had read about people who had gone thirty days 104
without food. However, people can't live very long without water. ❶ 114

Bruce turned to the other people, and suddenly he found himself 125
talking to them. He was explaining the situation, even though he 136
knew that they didn't understand what he was saying. "Let's look at 148
our problem," Bruce said slowly. "We have no fresh water. It is 160
impossible for us to drink water from the sea because the water is 173
salty." 174

Bruce glanced at the strangers. They were standing silently, 183
watching him. Strangely enough, Bruce was unafraid. In fact, he felt 194
excited about solving a problem. For an instant he remembered 204
situations in which he had solved problems for his insurance company. 215
For an instant Bruce realized how much he had missed those 226
problems. 227

"We don't have to worry so much about food," Bruce said aloud, 239
"<u>because</u> we can survive a long time without food. Our water problem 251
is more immediate." ❷ The strangers stared, and Bruce paced back 261
and forth in front of them. "We can solve this problem if we're 274
logical." 275

Bruce pointed to the sea. "We could boil seawater and collect the 287
steam, which would turn into fresh water. Or we could dig for water. 300
In either case, we will need tools." 307

Bruce turned to the strangers. "What do you want to do?" 318
"Unk." ❸ 319

Bruce decided that it would probably be easier to dig for water than 332
to boil seawater. He and the others walked to the place where the 345
spring had been. Bruce found a rock with a sharp edge that he used to 360
make a point on the end of a stout branch. Then he walked to the pile 376
of rocks where the spring had been. He wedged the point of the stick 390
between two rocks; then he pushed down on the stick and pried a rock 404
loose. Bruce picked up the rock and tossed it aside. "See?" he said. 417
"Use this to dig. Dig." ❹ 422

"Unk," one woman said. Soon everybody was working with long, 432
stout branches. Some of the people pried up rocks, while others 443
heaved them aside, making a hole where the stream had been. "If we 456
dig deep enough, we should reach fresh water," Bruce explained as he 468
wiped his hand across his forehead. The work was heavy, and the day 481
seemed exceptionally hot, but Bruce was not bored. He was solving a 493
problem, and that was exciting. ❺ 498

The hole became deeper and deeper. At first the bottom of the hole 521
was dry. By the time the hole was waist-deep, the rocks were damp, 524
and there were signs of moisture in the hole. When the hole was 537
neck-deep and only two people could work in it at a time, there were 551
more signs of water. The rocks that were being heaved from the hole 564
now were soaking wet. ❻ 568

Finally, the two people working in the hole were standing 578
ankle-deep in fresh water, and the hole was beginning to fill. Some of 591
the other people didn't want to wait for the water to reach the level of 606
the ground. They jumped into the hole and began drinking the water, 618

which was still muddy. Bruce was among them. He jumped into the 630
hole and managed to bend over and scoop up handfuls of water. The 643
hole was only about ten feet across, but there were five people in it, 657
shoving, pushing, and trying to drink. But the water tasted great to 669
Bruce. He smiled, laughed, splashed water on the other people, and 680
drank until his sides hurt. He felt unbelievably happy and refreshed. ❼ 691

1 re ly un

A	B
exceptionally	responsible
refreshed	uncertain
particularly	fortunately
unfortunate	repeated

2

moisture soaking easier sharp

explained replied occasionally

expect painted thirsty

unbelievably stout injure

3

1. flexible
2. shortage
3. suitable
4. procedure

4

disappeared ordinary surface stalk

sharpened average constructed serious

waded waddled severe branches

solved choice furthermore feathers

probably practice difficult fitted

instead feast stray rapidly

removed announced collected

search plenty completed

5

Finding Food

That night, when the well was full of fresh water and the people   13
were no longer thirsty, Bruce thought about the things that had   24
happened. He tried to figure out how his life had changed when the   37
things on the island had changed. Here's what he figured out: To live,   50
you need some things. You need food and water. When the island had   63
plenty of food and water, Bruce didn't have to do anything to stay   76
alive. He didn't have to hunt for food, and he didn't have to hunt for   91
water. But when the food and water disappeared from the island,   102
Bruce had to do something. He had to figure out a way to get water.   117
He dug a well, but before he dug the well, he had to make tools. Bruce   133
hadn't made tools during his first three days on the island because he   146
hadn't needed them to stay alive. ❶   152

Bruce and the others had solved the water problem. The next   163
problem they faced was the lack of food.   171

"We can make tools for hunting the animals in the jungle," Bruce   183
said, "or we can make nets for fishing in the sea." He looked at the   198
jungle and then at the sea. "I think we'll start with the tools for   212
hunting birds and rabbits."   216

The tools were bows and arrows. Bruce made five bows from stout,   228
flexible branches. ❷ The bowstrings were vines tied to each end of <u>the</u>   240
branches, and the arrows were long, straight sticks, sharpened on one   251
end against a flat rock and fitted on the other end with parrot feathers.   265

Now it was time to practice shooting with the bows and arrows.   277
After an hour's practice, some of the strangers were quite good. Bruce   289
was probably about average at hitting a target made of grass. ❸   300
Things were far more difficult when they went hunting in the jungle,   312

however. They searched for five hours, and in the end the hunters 324
had killed only two rabbits and one bird. 332

Even before the hunt was over, Bruce said to himself, "I think we 345
should try to get food by fishing instead of by hunting." The hunters 358
had spent most of their time trying to find the stray arrows that they 372
had shot. Although the hunters had started out with twenty-one 382
arrows, they had only three left when the hunt was completed. ❹ 393

"This won't be a big feast," Bruce announced, "but it will probably 405
be a good one." To cook the dinner, Bruce made a fire. He made it the 421
way the Native Americans would build fires. He looped the bowstring 432
around a stick and twirled the stick back and forth by moving the 445
bow. One end of the stick was pressed against a rock. That end began 459
to get hot as the stick turned rapidly. Bits of wood placed on the rock 474
next to the hot end of the stick began to smoke. Suddenly, the wood 488
bits burst into flame. The strangers shouted, "Unk, unk," and smiled. 499

After dinner Bruce was still hungry. Something had to be done 510
about the shortage of food. He said, "We'll probably have better luck 522
fishing than hunting." And he was right. The group made nets from 534
vines collected in the coconut grove. Four people waded into the 545
ocean, tossed the net over a school of fish, pulled the net toward the 559
shore, and caught two fish. They repeated the procedure and caught 570
three more fish. ❺ 573

That evening Bruce again thought of the events. "First we solved 584
the water problem, which was the most serious problem," he said to 596
himself. "Now we have solved the food problem." As Bruce lay there 608
near the fire with a long stalk of grass between his teeth, he thought, 622
"I just wish that the other people could speak English. I'm tired of 635
listening to 'unk, unk.' " 639

At that moment, one woman walked over to Bruce and said, "That 651
was a particularly good fish dinner." ❻ 657

Lesson 37

1

returning   temperature   chattered

remarkable   judged   unusually

repeated   mature   severely   celebration

Centa   survival   extreme

2

1. tingly
2. site

3

breaking   delighted   shelter   gathered

group   younger   discovered   hollowing

serious   huddled   covering   shivering

already   remain   blazed   bear   suitable

probably   strangers   dancing   protect

jogged   feasting   located   replies   feathers

coals   learned   reporting   particularly

rethink   blowing   concluded   surroundings

4   Fighting the Cold

For some unknown reason all the strangers could speak English.   10
Bruce was delighted. "This is remarkable. It calls for a celebration,"   21
he announced. There was a great celebration with racing, dancing,   31
singing, telling stories, and a lot of feasting.   39

Bruce slept well that night. When he woke up in the morning, he   52
was shivering. ❶ It was snowing, and the air was unusually cold.   63
Bruce judged the temperature to be below zero. The ocean was gray.   75
The waves were breaking loudly, and the whitecaps were rolling far up   87
the beach. The trees looked different because they had lost their   98
leaves. Small drifts of snow were starting to build up here and there.   111

"What's this?" Bruce said. Two people standing near him were   121
shivering, too. One of them was a woman named Centa. Bruce had   133
learned her name the day before.   139

Centa said, "If we can't find some way to stay warm, I'm afraid we   153
will all die. Already some of us are getting sick." ❷   163

Bruce thought for a moment. His teeth chattered every time he tried   175
to say something. At last he said, "Let's build up the fire." The people   189
gathered wood and threw it on the fire. The fire blazed up in big,   203
orange flames. Showers of sparks and smoke rose into the air.   214

"We need a shelter," Bruce said, standing close to the fire and   226
rubbing his hands together. "We'll never survive this cold unless we   237
build a <u>shelter</u>."   240

"What is shelter?" Centa asked.   245

Bruce explained, "A shelter is a place that is warm and dry. We   258
could build a place that would protect us from the wind and cold.   271
Maybe we could dig a cave in the side of a hill, or we could construct   287
a shelter out of branches and vines and dry grass." ❸   297

Bruce, Centa, and the others jogged off to find a suitable site for the 311
shelter. Centa found a steep hill that faced away from the sea. 323

"Bring the digging tools over here," Bruce said. "We'll hollow out 334
this part of the hill. After we've made a little cave, we'll cover the front 349
of it with some material that will break the wind." 359

Three people began hollowing out the side of the hill while Bruce 371
and Centa started to make a covering for the front of the cave. ❹ 384
"Let's weave long branches together," Bruce suggested. "Then we can 394
cover them with leaves and grass and whatever else we can find." 406

One young woman kept the fire going. From time to time people 418
working on the shelter would run over to the fire and warm up. Then 432
they would return to their work. The group worked very fast. Before 444
an hour had gone by, they had hollowed out the side of the hill. By 459
then Bruce and Centa had made a covering for the front of the cave. 473

Bruce and Centa fitted the "door" they had made over the front of 486
the cave. Then Bruce used a tool to drag hot coals to the shelter. "We 501
don't want a big fire in our shelter," he told the others. "If the fire is 517
too big, it will make a lot of smoke, and we'll have trouble 530
breathing." ❺ 531

As everybody huddled together inside the cave, Bruce announced, 540
"The next thing we have to do is make warm clothes. We can use the 555
skins from the rabbits we hunt. Maybe we can also use feathers from 568
the birds." 570

Unfortunately, the problem with rabbits and birds, as Bruce 579
realized, is that they are small. To make a coat from the hides of 593
rabbits, a person might need as many as twenty or thirty rabbits. The 606
hide of one large animal like a bear, however, would make two or 619
three coats. ❻ 621

The next morning the wind was blowing particularly hard. As   631
Bruce sat in the shelter waiting for the wind to die down, he began to   646
rethink the things that were happening to him. He concluded, you   657
need some things to stay alive. You need air, warmth, water, and food.   670
Unless you have all of those things, you die. If you don't want to die,   685
you've got to do something. You've got to build something or change   697
your surroundings in some way. ❼ If you don't have enough warmth,   708
you've got to do something so that you can stay warm. If you don't   722
have enough water, you've got to do something that will give you   734
enough water.   736

Lesson 38

1

dis

A	B
dishonor	displease
disjoin	distract
displace	dislocate
	distance

2

ch<u>oi</u>ce appr<u>oa</u>ched <u>ner</u>vously <u>dis</u>gusted

3

1. chores
2. comment
3. hoist
4. chimney

4

whispered sneak spotted squealing calm

hooves thread cloth yarn pounded

braced fan-shaped clothes obviously

remained fibers splitting reported create

howling hollowing pleasantly notice tingly

surprised gather collected narrow tangles

5   Life Problems

Bruce looked outside. He could hear the wind howling. It made him 12
shiver just listening to it. He remained in the shelter and began to 25
think again. He thought, "Air, warmth, water, and food are survival 36
problems. If you have more than one survival problem at the same 48
time, the first problem you solve is the problem that would take your 61
life first. If you have a water problem and a food problem, you solve 75
the water problem first, because the water problem will take your life 87
first. If you have a water problem and an air problem, you obviously 100
would solve the air problem first, because the air problem will take 112
your life first." ❶ 115

Centa went to the door of the shelter and looked outside. "I think 128
the wind is dying down," she reported. 135

Bruce said, "Good. This is our chance to gather the material that 147
we need to make warm clothes." 153

Bruce, Centa, and one of the men left the shelter. Bruce braced 165
himself for the cold, and at first he was pleasantly surprised. The air 178
didn't seem as cold as he had thought it would be. However, as he 192
jogged along with the others toward a place where dead vines lay in 205
tangles on the ground, he began to notice the cold. His legs were 218
becoming tingly. The tips of his ears and fingers began to hurt. "Let's 231
keep moving," he said to the others. "It <u>is</u> very cold out here." ❷ 244

Bruce collected vines, while Centa picked up the skins of the 255
rabbits they had eaten the day before. The other man peeled bark 267
from some of the trees. 272

Then they returned to the shelter with their materials. Bruce looked 283
over the materials, and he said, "We can pound the bark with rocks 296
and make cloth out of it." Bruce showed two others how to do it. As 311
they pounded away on the bark, Bruce told another woman, "Pull the 323
fibers from the vines. We can use those fibers as thread or yarn." So 337
the woman began pulling the fibers from the vines. 346

Bruce said, "I'll use them as thread to lace the rabbit skins together, 359
but first I'll need a needle." ❸ 365

Centa ran to the beach and found some fan-shaped shells. She took 377
one of the shells and hit it gently with a rock, splitting it into long, 392
narrow pieces that were pointed at one end. "This will work as a 405
needle," she said, handing one of the pieces to Bruce. 415

Bruce tied the vine fiber around the fat end of the needle and 428
pushed the needle through one of the rabbit skins. As Bruce worked, 440
Centa commented, "We'll need a lot more skins before we can make 452
clothes from these skins. Let's make cloth clothes first; then we'll go 464
hunting for some larger animals." 469

"Yes," Bruce said. "If we find larger animals, we can make clothes 481
faster." ❹ 482

Early the next day, when the sky was growing light gray, Bruce and 495
two other people went hunting. On the far side of the island, a long 509
distance from their shelter, they found tracks made in the snow by a 522
large animal and examined them. Following the tracks, they soon 532
came to a hill near the beach. A large wild pig and two baby pigs were 548
standing there. "Don't kill the baby pigs," Bruce whispered as he and 560
the other hunters began to sneak up the hill. ❺ The large pig spotted 573
them and began to run away. A woman shot an arrow, hitting the pig 587
in the side. The pig turned around and began to squeal loudly. Bruce 600
shot an arrow that struck the pig in the chest, and the pig fell over. 615

Bruce felt sick as he walked over to the pig. It disgusted him to kill   630
animals. He wouldn't have killed the pig if he'd had a choice, but what   644
was he to do?   648

The little pigs ran nervously around the mother pig, squealing   658
loudly. They did not run away when Bruce and the others approached.   670
❻ One hunter picked up both of the baby pigs. He held one under   683
each arm. As soon as he picked them up, they stopped squealing, and   696
they seemed to calm down.   701

Bruce and the others tied the large pig's front hooves together with   713
a vine. They also tied the back hooves together. Then they slid a   726
branch between the pig's legs. They hoisted the branch and carried the   738
pig back to their shelter. ❼   743

1 **dis**

A	B
dislike	dislocate
disjoin	distract
distrust	disbelief
	distaste

2 obviously arrangement chores

exception unbelievable piece mounted

occasionally nearly attached specific

chowder investigation starting

particular charred relaxed probably

3
1. examine
2. chowder
3. husks
4. verses
5. remodel

4 chimney scraped skinned preparing commented

bowl plenty tackled tusks started

giant caught busy sang chorus

comfortable sense vines solved unfortunately

5   Problems of Comfort

Bruce said, "We will try to keep the young pigs and raise them. But   14
that means we will have to find food to feed them. And we must build   29
a shelter for them."   33

For the rest of the day, the people took turns making a shelter for   47
the pigs next to the shelter for the people. There was a pen in front of   63
the pigs' shelter. The pigs could stay in their yard or go inside their   77
shelter.   78

Bruce and Centa dug up some plants that had survived the snow.   90
They threw the plants inside the pen. "These will give the young pigs   103
something to eat," Bruce commented. ❶   108

Later that day Bruce and the others were huddled inside the shelter.   120
The large pig was cooking over a small fire. It had been skinned. The   134
skin had been scraped and was hanging on one wall of the shelter.   147

There was a lot to do—feed the pigs, hunt for food, get water and   162
wood, make clothes, and make the shelter more comfortable. Work   172
would be done faster if each person had a specific job.   183

Different people were given different jobs. One woman was given   193
the job of preparing the pigskin by pounding it with rocks until it was   207
soft. One man did the chores around the shelter. Other people were   219
given the job of fixing up the shelter. They were to make it bigger and   234
to build a chimney so <u>that</u> the shelter would not be smoky. Bruce and   248
Centa were to take care of the hunting and fishing. They would go out   262
and find food for the others. ❷   268

The day after the three pigs were found, Bruce and the others   280
rigged up a way to catch fish without getting wet. They reworked their   293
fishing net so that it looked like a giant bowl that was attached to a   308
long pole. Standing on the shore and holding the pole, Bruce and   320

Centa could move the net along under the water. Fish swam into the   333
open end of the net.   338

In one day Bruce and Centa caught thirty-six fish. The biggest was   350
nearly three feet long. ❸ They also made three crab traps. They dug   362
deep holes on the beach, lined the walls of the holes with sticks, and   376
waited. Bruce said, "When the tide comes in, these holes will be   388
underwater. Then the tide will go out. Some crabs should fall into the   401
holes, and they won't be able to get out."   410

That evening the people had bowls of crab chowder. The bowls were   422
made of coconut husks, and the spoons they used were seashells.   433
There were bits of seaweed and other plants in the crab chowder. After   446
the chowder came fish, and after the fish everybody relaxed.   456

Bruce looked around at the shelter that the others had made larger.   468
There was a chimney above the fire. The chimney was made of mud   481
and of rocks tied together with vines. ❹   488

As the people were sitting around, Bruce thought, "Obviously we   498
solved the problems of life first. Those were the problems of water,   510
food, and warmth. After we solved these problems, we started to solve   522
problems of comfort. We didn't have to raise pigs to stay alive;   534
however, raising pigs is easier than hunting for them. We didn't have   546
to make the new nets, but it is much more comfortable to catch fish   550
from the shore with the new net. And we didn't have to remodel the   574
shelter, but the chimney makes it more comfortable in the shelter." ❺   585

Bruce looked at the pigskin mounted on the wall. Then he said to   598
himself, "We solved the life problems first. Then, after we solved the   610
last life problem, we began to solve problems of comfort. That makes   622
a lot of sense. ❻ If we didn't solve all of the life problems first, we   637
wouldn't have to worry about the problems of comfort. Unfortunately,   647
we would be dead."   651

Just then one young woman said, "Let's sing songs." That sounded 662
like a good idea, so everybody sang. One of the older men made up a 677
song about the shelter. Everybody sang it. 684

> "Oh, the shelter is warm, 689
> the shelter is good. 693
> We've got plenty of food 698
> and plenty of wood. 702
> Our shelter is fine. 706
> Our shelter is fine. 710
> When we're in our shelter, 715
> we have a very good time." 721

Different people made up verses. Then everybody repeated the 730
chorus of the song. ❼ 734

Late that night Bruce woke up. He hadn't thought about this before, 746
but he realized now that he didn't mind talking to people on the 759
island. He didn't mind his job; in fact, he didn't think about his job 773
much. There were things that had to be done, and Bruce was excited 786
about doing them. There were problems to solve, and he tackled them. 798
He didn't have time to think about whether he was happy or sad. He 812
was too busy to be a grouch. ❽ 819

Lesson 40

1

A	**B**	**C**
un	distinct	disappeared
ly	discovery	displeased
re	disbelief	discomfort
dis		disagreement

2

1. extension
2. argument
3. deadlocked
4. hammock

3

achieved figure remodeling completed

loose combination referred original

rattle consisted thoughtfully kitchen

procedures particularly warmer

charge collected obviously switched

continued connecting entire leaned

specific occurred examine announced

arrangement prepared exceptional

unbelievable agreement individual

caution comfortable unfortunate

usually decision involved

4 The Trees Are Dead

The days were cold for about two months. The weather then became obviously warmer. Spring was coming, and by now the shelter had been remodeled three times.

The first remodeling occurred about three weeks after the weather had turned cold. This remodeling was achieved by digging another hole next to the original one and then joining the two holes, forming a shelter that was about twice the size of the original one. The second remodeling began almost as soon as the first had been completed. It consisted of a large extension with a flat roof and a large fireplace. The people referred to this area as the porch. It became the workroom. Animal skins and tools hung on the grass-and-wood walls. The last remodeling consisted of a second story, which was dug out of part of the hill above the original cave and connected with it by a roof and a ladder. ❶ The second story became the sleeping area, and the entire downstairs became a combination workroom, kitchen, and dining area.

Everyone had specific jobs, but some people had switched jobs with other people. It turned out that one older man was very good at making clothes, so he switched jobs with the man who had been making them. Also, the procedures for taking care of the animals had changed. By now there were four young pigs, two wild dogs, over thirty monkeys, and ten rabbits in a large, <u>open</u> pen. The monkeys were not doing well. They couldn't seem to stand the cold weather. The woman in charge of the animals collected plants and seeds for them to eat, made sure that they had plenty of water, and cleaned the animals' shelter. ❷

One day, when the weather was particularly warm, Centa and   293
Bruce were out checking their traps. Bruce pointed to the trees.   304
"Unfortunately, I think these trees are dead," he said. He took his ax   317
and chopped through the bark of the tree. He examined the layer that   330
was just beneath the bark. "See," he said. "If this tree were alive, it   344
would have a bright green layer beneath the bark. The layer on this   357
tree is gray, which means that the tree is dead." ❸   367

Bruce and Centa checked the other trees. All were dead. Finally   378
Bruce said, "We probably won't have coconut, banana, or breadfruit   388
trees this summer. Furthermore, all of the animals that live off the   400
trees will have no food, so they will either die or leave the island."   414

Centa said, "What are we going to do if we don't have food this   428
summer?"   429

Bruce said, "We may be able to live off the sea animals. But we will   444
have trouble keeping the land animals if we can't find plants for   456
them." Bruce leaned against a dead tree and continued thoughtfully,   466
"Maybe we should think about building a boat and leaving the   477
island." ❹   478

That evening Bruce sat on his hammock in the shelter and thought,   490
"When people move from place to place, they do so because they   502
figure that the new place will be better than the old place. The old   516
place probably doesn't give them enough comfort. Things are too   526
hard in the old place. They don't know what things will be like in the   541
new place, but they figure that there is a place where things are better.   555
So they go out to find that place. If the old place gives them the   570
comfort they want, there is no reason for them to move. If the old   584
place doesn't give them the comfort they want, they may think about   596
moving to another place. If the old place has a life problem, they must   610
move from the old place, because if they don't they will die." ❺   622

The days were getting warmer now. Some grass was beginning to 633
grow, so the group decided to turn the animals loose and let them 646
hunt for their own food. Each animal had a rattle around its neck that 660
was made from little bones and coconut shells. You could hear the 672
animals even if you could not see them. However, most of the animals 685
stayed near the shelter. ❻ 689

Lesson 41

1
agree
agreed
agreement
argue
argument
argued

2 dis ly re un

A	B
displeased	dissatisfied
replied	exceptionally
exactly	disagreement

3
whether cheered unbelievable scratched

unusually cautioned announced original

survived choice maintain future exactly

4
1. decision
2. solution
3. enforce

5
involved deadlocked possible almost

decided property obviously excited

occasionally meant particularly favor

protected risk exceptionally decisions

individuals agreements unfortunately

6 Their First Real Argument

The people had their first real argument that spring. The group disagreed about whether they should remain on the island or move. To move, the group would have to build a boat and sail across the sea. Obviously, there was some risk involved in moving. The question was whether there wasn't as much risk in remaining on the island.

Centa didn't want to move. She spoke for the others who agreed with her. She said, "There is some grass on the island, which means that there will be some food for the animals. We will probably discover that we can survive here."

Bruce was in favor of building a boat. He spoke for those who agreed with him. He said, "Even if we don't use the boat, we should be ready to move if we have to. I think we should build the boat and then see what happens." ❶

"No," Centa argued. "Building a boat will take a lot of time. We should use that time for planting seeds and growing crops."

Bruce said, "I don't agree with you. It is possible that most seeds won't grow after the cold winter. Furthermore, some seeds need years and years to grow into plants that will have fruit."

The argument continued for days. At last Centa said, "We've got to figure out some way to settle this argument. Since there is an even number of us, we are deadlocked. Half want to build a boat; half don't. If there were one more person, we could never be deadlocked." ❷

Then everybody began to argue about how to settle the disagreement. Some people said that Bruce should have two votes. Centa and the people on her side said that Centa should have two votes. But the people on Bruce's side said, "No way."

On the third day of the argument, Bruce stated, "We should figure 311
out a fair way to settle this argument." Everybody agreed, and here's 323
their solution. They found a flat stone and on one side of it scratched 337
an X. They placed the stone inside a coconut shell. Then they shook 350
the shell and turned it over. They had agreed that they would build 363
the boat if the stone landed so that the X was showing. If the other 378
side was showing, they would not build the boat. ❸ 387

The side without the X showed. Everybody on Centa's side was 398
excited and cheered. 401

One woman on Bruce's side of the argument was displeased. She 412
said, "I don't care what the stone says. I'm going to build a boat. The 427
rest of you can do anything you want." 435

Bruce said, "No. We agreed that we would all do whatever the stone 448
said. That means we are all going to do it." ❹ 458

Bruce was thinking there were many laws in the city where he had 471
lived—traffic laws, laws about how to do business, laws that protect 483
people and their property. On the island there were no laws at first. 496
Bruce and the others had just made one—a law about how the group 510
makes decisions. This law told every person that, even though each 521
person has some rights, the group has rights, too. Individuals can not 533
do what they want if it hurts the group. 542

"I changed my mind," the woman said. 549

"No," Bruce said. "If we live together, you can't change your mind 561
about some things. What if you decided to kill all of the animals? 574
That would hurt the rest of us, so we couldn't let you do that. What if 590
you decided to take somebody's clothes? That wouldn't be fair to that 602
person. So we can't let you make that choice." 611

"Who's going to stop me?" the woman asked. 619

"We will," Bruce said. "The rest of us must enforce the rules." ❺   631

"That's not fair to me," the woman replied.   639

Bruce said, "Well, it's not fair to us if you break your agreements."   652

The woman walked away and acted angry for many days. She did   664
her job, but she was pretty dissatisfied and grouchy about it.   675

Lesson 42

1

un   re   dis

A	B
removed	unbelievably
uncertain	discovered
responded	replied

2

excellent   surface   thorns

pressure   enforce   peacefully

shaped   solution   decision   advice

3

1. prevented
2. barge
3. minnows
4. evaporate
5. remarked

4

patches   paddles   smoldering   exceptionally

hundred   tiller   occasionally   narrow

quite   cove   quiet   prevented   quit

signaled   caught   argued   piece   obviously

stretch   attached   constructing   hooked   smiling

5   **Visitors**

As the days got hotter, Bruce and the others planted seeds. First   12
they had to make new tools for plowing up the land. Then they   25
planted the seeds they had found during the winter. After the seeds   37
had been planted, the people waited. Some plants came up, but   48
unfortunately they had bitter stems and bitter roots. Everybody   57
agreed that there would not be a good food crop. The grass on the   71
island grew in little patches; however, these patches were far apart.   82
Between them was bare ground. There were a few bitter plants   93
growing among the dead trees, but there weren't many of them. There   105
were some other plants that grew exceptionally slowly. ❶   113

Then one day one man came running to the shelter. He yelled, "A   126
boat! There's a boat coming to the island!" Bruce and the others ran   139
down to the beach. The boat was over thirty feet long and very   152
narrow. The people on the island jumped into the water and swam out   165
to meet the boat. The people in the boat were smiling and waving   178
their paddles.   180

When the boat was on the beach and everybody had greeted the   192
people in the boat, a woman from the boat said, "We have come to   206
look for fish—we have no fish near our island." ❷   216

"We have lots of fish," Centa said.   223

The woman said, "We will give you gold for your fish."   234

Bruce said, "We don't have <u>any</u> need for gold. Do you have   246
anything that we need?"   250

"All we have with us is a boat full of bananas. That is the only thing   266
that grows on our island."   271

Bruce and the others smiled. "Bananas?" Bruce asked. "We will   281
trade for bananas. We will give you one fish for every five bananas." ❸   294

"That is fair," the woman said as she started to count out five 307
hundred bananas. Bruce counted out one hundred fish, and the trade 318
was made. 320

When the visitors left the island, they said they would come back 332
within two weeks with at least two thousand bananas. After the boat 344
left, Centa said, "We must start catching fish. We will need four 356
hundred fish for the trade." 361

"We will need a place to keep those fish alive," Bruce remarked. "If 374
we kill them, they will all be rotten by the time two weeks have 388
passed." That made sense to the others. 395

Centa said, "I discovered a narrow cove on the north end of the 408
island that will make an excellent sea cage." ❹ 416

The little cove was shaped like the letter U. "This cove is perfect," 429
Bruce said. "If we stretch a net across the mouth of the cove, the fish 444
will be prevented from swimming away." 450

After fixing the sea cage, the people began constructing more nets. 461
They made nets for catching small fish that would be used as bait for 475
large fish. The people made fishhooks from the thorns that they 486
removed from dead bushes. They attached minnows to the thorns, 496
and they attached the thorns to a line. A piece of wood attached to 510
the line worked like a bobber; when it went underwater, it signaled 522
that a fish had been hooked. ❺ 528

The people continued to fish night and day; however, after one week 540
had passed, the group had caught only sixty-five fish. Bruce announced, 551
"We've got to figure out how to catch fish at a faster rate. And I think I 568
have an idea. The fish are not near the shore; therefore, they must be out 583
in deep water. We've obviously got to go out and get them." 595

"How are we going to do that?" one woman asked. 605

"We'll build a little fishing barge," Bruce replied. "We'll make the   616
barge big enough for two people who will go out and catch fish.   629
They'll store the fish on the barge and return when the barge is loaded   643
with fish." ❻   645

Two people began to argue. One woman thought that it was a good   658
idea to build a barge. But one man said, "There are more of us than   673
there are of them. When those people come with the bananas, we'll   685
take what we want."   689

Centa responded, "The people won't want to trade with us after we   701
do that."   703

Bruce said, "Let's take a vote. And let's give Centa two votes so that   717
we don't have a deadlock." ❼   722

Everybody agreed, and they voted. There were more votes for   732
building the barge. That afternoon they chopped down trees, gathered   742
vines, and tied the tree trunks together with the vines. They worked   754
all night. Occasionally some people would rest for three hours while   765
the other people worked. Then they would switch; those who had been   777
resting would work while the others rested.   784

Lesson 43

1

thought

through

tough

enough

ought

brought

2

st<u>ee</u>ring <u>re</u>turning till<u>er</u> <u>re</u>gain

probab<u>ly</u> <u>di</u>spleased <u>un</u>likely balan<u>c</u>ed

3

1. shad
2. bargain

4

floated fortunately unfair

remarked evaporate smolder

finally smiling handfuls

spotted cheat branches

pointed argument weigh weighs

weighed weight attractive

5   **A Smart Trade**

By noon the next day, they had completed the barge. It wasn't a   13
very attractive barge, but it floated. The bottom of the barge was   25
made up of seven logs tied together. Each log was about twenty-five   37
feet long. In the back of the barge was a tiller for steering. There was a   53
small sail made of grass and vines and bark. And in the middle of the   68
barge was a large box. The box was about twelve feet long, six feet   82
wide, and three feet high. It would hold many, many fish. ❶   93

Bruce and a man named Jonas went out on the barge with nets and   107
fishing lines. They planned to be gone for as long as a week, returning   121
in time to trade for bananas.   127

Fortunately, the barge didn't have to go far before the men spotted   139
schools of fish. Most of the fish were more than three feet long. Jonas   153
threw handfuls of small minnows into the water. Just then Bruce had   165
a fish on his line. It pulled so hard that it began to move the barge.   181
"Drop your bait and help me with this fish," Bruce yelled. Jonas   193
pulled in his line and grabbed onto Bruce's line. Finally, the contest   205
was over, and the men had a fish that was ten feet long. It probably   220
weighed more than two hundred pounds. ❷ It was not a shad; it was a   234
big, blue tuna fish.   238

That <u>was</u> the first tuna fish the men caught, but not the last one.   252
Before the sun went down they had thirty shad and twelve tunas.   264
Most of the tunas were six feet long; however, one was even larger   277
than the first one they had caught.   284

Finally, the barge box was filled with tuna fish, but Jonas and   296
Bruce did not have hundreds and hundreds of fish. They had only   308
forty-two fish.   310

Jonas remarked, "We made a deal with the woman to trade one fish 323
for five bananas. But most of these fish must be worth one hundred 336
bananas each. Some of them must be worth five hundred bananas." ❸ 347

A week later the woman and her friends returned to the island. 359
They came in three boats; each boat was loaded with bananas. When 371
Bruce and Centa met them on the shore, Bruce was holding a pan full 385
of minnows. Also in the pan was a fish that was about twelve inches 399
long. This was the size of fish the woman had traded for when she 413
came to the island before. 418

After Bruce and Centa greeted the woman and the others, Bruce 429
held up the fish that was twelve inches long. ❹ Bruce said, "Do you 442
remember what we said we would trade for?" 450

"Yes," the woman said. "We said that we would give you five 462
bananas for every fish." 466

"Good," Bruce said. "This fish is worth five bananas. Is that right?" 478

"Yes," the woman said. She was smiling. 485

Bruce held up one of the minnows. "And this fish is worth five 498
bananas," he said. 501

The woman stopped smiling. "Are you trying to cheat us?" she said. 513
"That fish is not even a fish. I won't give you five bananas for that 528
little thing." 530

"You are right," Bruce said. "We must be fair." Bruce walked over 542
to a scale that he had made from two branches. The branches formed 555
a T. Bruce placed the first fish on one end of the T. Then he placed a 572
rock on the other end, and the scale balanced. Bruce picked up the 585
rock and said, "Why don't we call the weight of this rock one fish?" ❺ 599

"That is fair," the woman said. "So you would have to place many 612
of those tiny fish on the scale to balance the weight of the rock." 626

"That is right," Bruce said. Then he signaled the others to bring out 639
the largest of the fish from their sea cage. Bruce pointed to the big 653
tuna. He said, "This fish weighs as much as seven hundred of these 666
rocks. So we have to treat this fish as if it were seven hundred fish." 681

At first the woman looked displeased. Then she smiled and said, 692
"That is fair, and that is a lovely fish." 701

1 | **re un dis**

A	B
unfortunately	unnoticed
regain	displeased
uneventful	uncertain
reflection	require

2 | sp<u>oi</u>l <u>sh</u>ade am<u>ou</u>nt occasional<u>ly</u>

<u>c</u>l<u>ea</u>ning particular<u>ly</u> probab<u>ly</u> sev<u>er</u>al

<u>c</u>ertainly s<u>al</u>ted f<u>ur</u>thermore barge<u>s</u>

3 | 1. demand
2. disapprove

4 | shore excellent announced smolder

frowned trouble evaporating firewood

demand fresh stacked pieces bargain

shad price severe simple similar

5 Another Sharp Trade

Bruce and the woman decided to trade again. After the three boats   12
left, Centa said, "We should go out for the tuna and shad again. The   26
fish may move away from here, and we won't be able to trade for   40
bananas."   41

Bruce agreed. Before two people could leave on the fishing trip,   52
everybody helped build a shed for storing the dead fish. They called it   65
the shad shed. One woman said, "We built the shad shed in the shade   79
so that the tuna would not spoil." ❶   86

Jonas and another man went out in the barge for two days. When   99
they returned, they had fifty fish on the barge. Everybody spent most   111
of the day cleaning the fish, removing bones and the insides, and   123
feeding the insides to the pigs and the wild dogs. The people stacked   136
the fish in the shad shed and made a hot fire in the shed. When the fire   153
was blazing hot, they threw wet grass on the fire so that the fire would   168
smolder and produce a great amount of smoke. After smoking the fish   180
for more than twenty-four hours, they rubbed salt all over the fish.   192
They got the salt by evaporating seawater. They smoked the fish   203
again, this time for over a week. The smoke and the salt kept the bugs   218
away from the fish. ❷   222

Several days before the boats were to return to the island with   234
bananas, some of the people <u>complained</u>. An old woman said, "We   245
put a lot of work in on this batch of fish. We had to clean them and   262
store them. Then we had to salt them and smoke them so that they   276
would keep. Yet we agreed to trade for the same price we traded for   290
before. That's unfair to us."   295

Bruce replied, "That's an excellent point. I have a plan, and for this   308
plan we need small shore fish." ❸   314

A week later Bruce and Jonas met the boats from the other island. 327
Centa and the others were sitting in the shade near the shad shed 340
eating smoked fish. Next to Bruce were the small shore fish, which 352
were rotting and smelled particularly bad. They were covered with 362
flies and other bugs. 366

After the boats were on the shore, Bruce announced, "We're ready 377
to trade." 379

The woman looked at the fish next to Bruce and said, "Those fish 392
are rotten. We certainly won't trade for them." 400

Jonas said, "Well, the only other fish we have are smoked fish, and I 414
don't think it would be fair to trade those at the fresh fish price." ❹ 428

The woman was displeased and frowned. Bruce called for Centa to 439
bring over some pieces of smoked fish. Centa passed these pieces to 451
the people who had come to trade. "This tastes unusually good," the 463
woman said. 465

"Yes," Centa said. "And since they are smoked, you certainly don't 476
have to worry about them rotting. They will keep." 485

The woman frowned again and said, "Yes, some of the fish in the 498
last batch began to rot before we could eat them. However, we 510
wouldn't have that trouble with these fish." 517

Bruce said, "Do you think it would be fair to trade one smoked fish 531
for nine bananas?" ❺ 534

"No, I disapprove," the woman said. "One fish for six bananas." 545

Centa laughed. "That's not fair," she said. 552

Centa, Bruce, and the woman bargained for a long time. At last 564
they agreed that one fish for seven and a half bananas was a fair price. 579

Things were going particularly well on the island. Trading boats 589
came to the island every month during the summer. By the end of the 603
summer there were plenty of bananas for the winter. Life was almost 615
uneventful. ❻ 616

Centa, Bruce, and Jonas had caught enough fish to last for a long 629
time. These fish were smoked and salted and hung in the shed. 641
Furthermore, during the summer the women and men had found 651
other animals. Now the people on the island had more than fifty 663
animals. Also they had cut down many dead trees, and there was lots 676
of firewood for the winter. 681

Occasionally, Bruce would think about what had happened. The 690
people on his island could catch fish. There was a demand for fish on 704
the woman's island. The people on her island had lots of bananas. 716
There was a demand for bananas on Bruce's island, so the people 728
traded. The people on Bruce's island got bananas, and the people on 740
the other island got fish. Bruce said to himself, "The price of things 753
goes up when there is a demand for those things. If somebody needs 766
fish, the price goes up. If they have plenty of fish, the price goes 780
down." ❼ 781

1 un   re   ly   dis

2 **pre**

A	B
pretest	prepare
preview	prevent
precaution	preserve
predetermine	

3 <u>s</u>alted   su<u>rv</u>ival   <u>ex</u>perienced

<u>un</u>usual   <u>c</u>ertainly   suddenl<u>y</u>

4 1. exceptionally
2. carnivorous

5 particularly   company   solve

griping   hammock   stared   realize

started   comfortably   blankets

warmth   glanced   though

trimming   thought   neighbor

6 A Changed Man

One evening Bruce was lying in his hammock thinking. After he   11
had thought about the island and the things that happened, he began   23
to think about his home in the city and his job. He thought, "People   37
paid me to do my job because there was a demand for insurance.   50
People wanted insurance. They paid for the insurance. But it takes a   62
lot of money to run an insurance company. A lot of people must put   76
in a lot of work to give people insurance. I helped people get   89
insurance, so the people had to pay me for my work." ❶   100

Bruce thought about his home and his car. He said, "Most of the   113
problems I had to solve were not problems of survival. I had to solve   127
problems of comfort. I had a car, but I didn't need a car to live. I had   144
air conditioning and other things; however, I didn't need those things   155
to live. I needed them to be more comfortable. But you don't think   168
about comfort until your survival problems are solved. All of my   179
problems of survival had been solved. I had enough to eat, I had a   193
house that was warm when the weather got cold, I had warm clothes,   206
and I certainly had good water to drink." ❷   214

As Bruce lay there in his hammock, he began to wish that he was   228
back in his home. He said to himself, "If I were <u>back</u> there, I would   243
look at things differently. I wouldn't be as grouchy; I would realize   255
that my life was exceptionally easy. I didn't have to work fifteen hours   268
a day. On the island I work fifteen hours a day, and I am happy.   283
Maybe I would be happy in my old home if I worked more. Maybe I   298
wouldn't try as hard to live comfortably. Maybe I would spend more   310
time doing things and less time thinking about how bad things are. I   323
probably made things worse by griping about how bad they were." ❸   334

The next morning he woke up and rolled over. He ran his hand   347
across his pillow and threw back the blankets before he opened his   359
eyes. Then he noticed the hum of the air conditioner.   369

He opened his eyes quickly and sat up. He was back in his home. It   384
was quiet and clean. He sat there for a moment trying to figure out   398
what had happened. Then he ran to the telephone, dialed the   409
operator, and asked her the date.   415

She told him, "August fourteenth."   420

"What year?" he asked.   424

She told him the year, and then Bruce knew it was the same day   438
that he had gone to the island. Perhaps the whole thing had been a   452
strange dream. Bruce glanced out of the window. A neighbor woman   463
was trimming her bushes. Bruce waved and smiled; she waved back. ❹   474

"It was all a crazy dream," Bruce said to himself. "But I'm glad to   488
be back."   490

He ran to his dresser and opened it. He was thinking, "I'm going to   504
get dressed and go outside. I'm going to talk to my neighbors and   517
walk around." Suddenly he stopped and stared at something on the   528
dresser. It was an ax made out of a tree branch and a sharp rock. He   544
picked it up and looked at it. It had initials scratched on the   557
handle—B.C.   559

"Bruce Celt," Bruce said to himself. "This is my ax. I made it on the   574
island."   575

Bruce felt a little dizzy. Did it really happen, or was it a dream? ❺   589

After a minute Bruce said, "I guess I'll never know how it   601
happened, but I'm glad it did happen. I found out a lot of things on   616
that island. I found out a lot about people and why things are the way   631
they are."   633

And from that day on, Bruce was a changed man. First of all, he 647
didn't hate his job. He always worked to do a better job. And he was 662
no longer a grouch. People who knew him said that he was a good 676
friend. He saw a lot of things about his city that he didn't like. But he 692
didn't gripe about them. Instead he did things to make them better. ❻ 704
He followed this motto: 708

We all need each other to solve our problems of life 719
and our problems of comfort. 724

Bruce knew that people must work together. He knew that 734
everybody has a job and that all jobs are important. Some people 746
bring you food and water, some bring you warmth, and others help 758
you live more comfortably. 762

1   **aw**   **au**

A	B
law	awful
haul	crawl
saw	draw
claw	fault

2   **tri**

triceratops

tricycle

triangle

3   **re**   **un**   **pre**   **dis**

4

eastern   armor   prehistoric

snout   carnivorous   emerged

vegetable   extended   measure

5

1. grazing
2. reptiles
3. mammal
4. thrash
5. herd
6. predator

6

ornithomimid   scene   leopard   occasional

rhinoceros   territory   dinosaur   crocodiles

hippopotamus   watermelon   spine

adulthood   shoulders   glide   buried

incredible   fierce   wiggled   indicates

unbearable   full-grown   shield

7   A Prehistoric Plain

The white-hot sun beat down on the great plain. The plain was 12
covered with grass and occasional trees, and you could see heat waves 24
rising from the ground. The grazing animals, moving slowly across 34
the plain, looked as if they were melting in the heat waves. The heat 48
was almost unbearable, although the animals didn't seem to mind it. 59
The temperature was more than 110 degrees. ❶ 66

A few of the animals were mammals, but most were reptiles. From 78
time to time, some flying reptiles would glide over the grazing animals 90
looking for a baby or a weak animal they could attack. Everywhere 102
there were insects, some as big as your fist. 111

If it weren't for the types of animals on the plain, the scene would look 126
quite similar to one you might see in eastern Africa today. Thousands of 139
animals were grazing in herds, each herd moving in its own territory at 152
its own pace. And each herd was taking its turn at the water hole. 166

Also, like today, there were predators on the plain. The predators 177
today are carnivorous mammals like lions and leopards. But back then 188
the predators on the plain were reptiles, including gigantic dinosaurs. ❷ 198

One of the most incredible types of predators lived in a large swamp 211
twenty miles north of the plain. These predators looked like the crocodiles 223
you might see in Africa today. They were different in one respect, 235
however. Though today's crocodiles <u>are</u> only ten feet long, the ones that 247
were in the swamp when our story took place were as long as fifty feet. 262
This means that they were longer than a line of five elephants. Their 275
mouths were so big that a baby hippopotamus could probably fit inside. ❸ 287

The ocean north of the great swamp also contained many fierce 298
animals. Some of them were sharks that looked just like sharks you 310
would see today. Others looked like large dinosaurs with flippers 320

instead of legs. Some of the fish you see today were in the ocean back 335
then—the dogfish, the garfish. 340

Several eggs were buried in the sand near a high cliff at the edge of 355
the plain. One of the eggs was ready to hatch. It didn't look much like 370
a chicken's egg. It was much bigger than any egg you have ever seen. 384
In fact, it was probably bigger than a watermelon, and its shell was 397
about half an inch thick. Suddenly the egg wiggled and moved under 409
the sand as the animal inside tried to get out. The animal's pushing 422
made a crack in the shell, and as it pushed again, the crack became 436
larger. The animal thrashed and kicked for over a minute before its 448
head emerged from the shell. Its head looked like an armor shield, 460
with three horns—one at the end of its snout and two larger horns on 475
its brow, one above each eye. The armor plate of the skull was formed 489
by thick bone, and the plate extended behind the head, covering the 501
upper part of the animal's spine. ❹ 507

This animal was known as a triceratops. The *tri* in its name 519
indicates that it had three horns. A triceratops was a dinosaur and 531
one of the largest grazing animals on the plain. You could see many 544
full-grown triceratops moving across the plain—they looked like 553
tanks. Of the animals that are alive today, the one that looks most like 567
a triceratops is the rhinoceros; however, a big rhinoceros would look 578
tiny next to a triceratops. ❺ 583

The triceratops that emerged from the egg already weighed seven 593
pounds. If none of the predators killed it before it reached adulthood, 605
it would grow up to weigh 20,000 pounds—the weight of several 617
elephants—and it would measure more than twenty feet high at the 629
shoulders. As an adult, it would eat more than 2,000 pounds of grass 642
and other forms of vegetable matter each day. But growing up on the 655
plain was not easy, and the chances of our triceratops reaching 666
adulthood were pretty poor. ❻ 670

1 **tri**

triangle

triceps

trimester

2 A   B   C

au   tau<u>gh</u>t   crawl

aw   dra<u>w</u>ing   caution

cau<u>gh</u>t   sprawl

3 dif<u>fe</u>rently atten<u>tion</u> rhino<u>c</u>eros

fr<u>igh</u>tened <u>ex</u>tinct instinctivel<u>y</u>

<u>di</u>sturbance ov<u>er</u>grown mo<u>tion</u>less

4
1. foul-tasting
2. programmed
3. roamed
4. keen
5. taut
6. extinct

5

brontosaurs triceratops ornithomimid

tongue galloping Tekla vision

muscles designed straight squirmed

hippopotamus grazing territory

blazing shoulders ostrich lizard

scrambled predator successful

shallow caused search inhabited

Lesson
47

6 Triceratops Meets Ornithomimid

There were twelve triceratops eggs buried in the sand near the cliff. 12
The first to hatch was Tekla. She squirmed free of the egg, dug her 26
way to the surface, and looked at her world for the first time. She felt 41
warmth and hunger. Her mouth was filled with sand. She moved her 53
tongue, trying to spit out the foul-tasting sand. 61

Tekla would never know her mother. She didn't have to learn how to 74
walk. Unlike mammals, she was programmed to walk from the moment 85
she was born. She was also programmed to search for food and to fight; 99
she would have no fear of most animals. Only faintly would she realize 112
that she was a triceratops, and not one of the other animals that 125
roamed the plain. She would know only that she felt more comfortable 137
around other triceratops than she did around the other animals. Like 148
most grazing animals, she had a keen sense of smell and sharp vision. ❶ 161

Still trying to remove the sand from her mouth, she rolled on the 174
hot sand. It felt good on her back. She looked up at the sun, white and 190
blazing. The sun felt good. Suddenly, however, Tekla sensed danger. 200
Instinctively she scrambled to her feet and faced into the wind. 211
Danger, danger, something screamed inside her. Danger. She put her 221
head down and stood motionless with her muscles taut and her heavy, 233
huge feet planted firmly in the <u>sand</u>. ❷ 240

She seemed to be looking straight ahead, but grazing animals are 251
designed differently from predators. Predators have eyes on the front 261
of their heads so they can look straight ahead. They look straight 273
ahead when they attack, and they must attack to survive. Grazing 284
animals, however, have eyes that are on the sides of their heads. A 297
grazing animal like a cow or a horse may seem to be looking only 311
straight ahead, but its right eye can see everything on its right side. 324

And its left eye can see everything on its left. The animal can even see 339
its own back end. ❸ The eyes are designed to protect the grazing animal 352
from attack. It doesn't have to worry about looking straight ahead as 364
much as it has to worry about predators attacking from behind. 375

Run, run, something screamed inside Tekla. Instinct was telling 384
Tekla what to do. She had never seen an ornithomimid, the predator 396
who loved to eat dinosaur eggs. She had never smelled an 407
ornithomimid, yet she knew instinctively what to do. She ran from the 419
cliffs toward the other grazing animals on the plain. She could run 431
quite fast, nearly as fast as a horse. ❹ Tekla looked like a fat little 445
rhinoceros, her stubby legs galloping through the heat waves toward 455
the distant line of grazing animals. She was very frightened. Her heart 467
was pounding, but her mind had one thought—escape. 476

And she did escape. Her brothers and sisters were not as lucky. The 489
ornithomimid sniffed around in the sand. That sand was once a 500
beach, and the cliff had been on the edge of the beach. When the 514
great brontosaurs lived on Earth, Tekla's plain was a large, shallow 525
body of water, and it was inhabited by thousands of brontosaurs. By 537
the time Tekla was born, the great brontosaurs had been extinct for 549
more than sixty million years. ❺ The water had dried up, and all that 562
remained were the cliffs, the great sand beach, the bones of some 574
brontosaurs buried deep under the sand, and the shells of sea animals 586
that once inhabited the plain. 591

The ornithomimid looked something like an overgrown ostrich 599
with a long lizard tail and sharp teeth. It wasn't usually successful at 612
finding eggs in the sand because they were often buried quite deep. 624
But the disturbance that Tekla caused caught the attention of the 635
ornithomimid. Quickly it ran over to the spot where the pieces of 647
Tekla's shell remained on the sand. The ornithomimid sniffed the shell 658
and then began to dig in the sand. ❻ 666

1

A	B	C
aw	l<u>aw</u>	c<u>au</u>tion
au	bec<u>au</u>se	dr<u>aw</u>
	cr<u>aw</u>l	f<u>au</u>lt

2

exposing thund<u>e</u>red emerg<u>i</u>ng f<u>e</u>ared

<u>un</u>like absolut<u>e</u>ly crun<u>ch</u>ing s<u>ur</u>vived

scr<u>ea</u>med sile<u>n</u>ced sev<u>e</u>ral ex<u>c</u>ite ac<u>c</u>ept

3

1. leisurely

2. aroused

3. feast

4. scavengers

5. ignore

6. slither

4

tyrannosaur heavy occasional building predator

frozen lizard finished instincts distance

constantly instinctively instantly stripped

5   Ornithomimid Meets Tyrannosaur

The ornithomimid dug in the sand, exposing three eggs. One of 11
Tekla's brothers was emerging from his shell. Snap, went the jaws of 23
the ornithomimid, and Tekla's brother never saw the sun or ate the 35
rich grasses on the plain. The ornithomimid ate three eggs. Suddenly, 46
the ornithomimid stopped and stood up. It looked almost frozen as it 58
sniffed the air. Then it began to run. It ran faster than a horse, but not 74
fast enough. 76

Another animal thundered behind it—the most feared animal on 86
the plain. It was a tyrannosaur. Like an ornithomimid, it stood on two 99
heavy legs with a long lizard tail behind it. Unlike an ornithomimid, a 112
tyrannosaur was taller than a two-story building. A tyrannosaur was 122
a predator able to kill nearly any other animal on the plain. It was 136
forty feet from the tip of its nose to the end of its tail. Its head was 153
very big. A tyrannosaur looked strange with its tiny front legs that 165
were much smaller than its head. ❶ 171

Although the ornithomimid was swift, the tyrannosaur overtook it 180
after the two animals had run less than fifty feet. The jaws of the 194
tyrannosaur closed on the upper back of the ornithomimid with a 205
crunching sound that could be heard far across the plain. The 216
ornithomimid thrashed and screamed for a moment, but another bite 226
from the tyrannosaur's jaws silenced it. 232

The tyrannosaur leisurely picked at the dead <u>ornithomimid</u> as 241
several of Tekla's sisters and brothers freed themselves from their eggs. 252
None survived, however. The smell of blood and food had aroused 263
many predators, some large and some small. Some would wait for the 275
scraps left by the larger animals. Others were bigger and bolder. They 287
were ready to steal the kill from other animals—but not from a 300

tyrannosaur. ❷ By the next morning, little remained of Tekla's 309
brothers and sisters except a few pieces of egg shell. And very little 322
remained of the ornithomimid. After the tyrannosaur had finished 331
feasting on the better parts of the ornithomimid, it went off to sleep. 344
Scavengers closed in. Within three hours they had stripped the 354
ornithomimid to the bone. Other scavengers moved in. During the 364
night, they feasted on the bones. And the next morning when the sun 377
rose over the night fog that settled on the plain, all that marked the 391
place where the ornithomimid had fallen were a few large bones and 403
footprints—thousands of them. ❸ 407

    That morning found Tekla far from the cliffs. Her instincts had told 419
her to run with the other grazing animals on the plain. So she did. She 434
found herself near a group of about twenty triceratops. They moved 445
slower than most of the other grazing animals, and they ate 456
constantly. They were quite calm—much like a herd of cows on a hot 470
day. From time to time, they lay down. During the hottest part of the 484
day, they slept. Tekla slept with them. They seemed to half ignore and 497
half accept her. After resting with them for about an hour, she began 510
to trot around. Some of them lifted their heads and looked at her for a 525
moment, but then they returned to their afternoon sleep. ❹ 534

    Tekla felt playful, but there wasn't much to play with. She sniffed a 547
snake that was about twenty feet long. The snake slowly began to 559
slither away. Tekla stepped on the snake's tail. Instantly, the snake 570
turned and struck at her. Instinctively, Tekla ducked her head. The 581
snake struck the large plate on Tekla's head. ❺ Before the snake could 593
strike again, Tekla turned and ran back to the sleeping triceratops. 604
She nibbled on grass and strolled around the snoozing animals. She 615
felt content. There were occasional sounds of animals fighting in the 626
distance, but the grazing animals were calm. And so was Tekla. 637

1 un   re   pre   tri   dis

2 beetles related discovery crouched

glancing experiencing carnivores floated

herbivores occasionally extinct fierce

3
1. foliage
2. prance
3. resume
4. unison
5. scramble

4 crocodile period metasequoia

dignified ginkgo Cretaceous similar

dragonflies warmth mammal grove

history ruled inhabit earth

frequently business realize

flesh listened aware wading

5

Asleep on the Plain

The sky became dark as clouds of insects floated over the plain in 13
the late afternoon. Some insects were flies that looked exactly like the 25
flies you see today. Others were dragonflies. Though they were similar 36
to today's dragonflies, they were much bigger. There were butterflies, 46
fleas, and flying ants. There were grasshoppers and flying beetles. 56
Tekla was covered with insects, but they didn't bother her very much. 68
Occasionally, she felt a sharp bite. She would roll over so that some of 82
the insects would fly away. The grass waved in the breeze. ❶ In the 95
distance was a grove of trees. 101

Two types of trees in that grove are alive today. One is related to the 116
redwood. It is called the metasequoia. Its foliage is like that of the 129
redwood, except that its needles fall off in the fall. Until 1946, 141
scientists had thought that the metasequoia had been extinct for over 152
a hundred million years. However, the tree was discovered growing in 163
a remote part of China. The other tree that grows today is the ginkgo. 177
It has leaves shaped like fans, and it makes a good shade tree. Some of 192
the trees in the grove might have looked similar to trees you see today, 206
but they were different and have been extinct for more than a hundred 219
million years. ❷ 221

Tekla didn't know anything about her place in the history of the 233
world. She lived in what we call the last part of the dinosaur age. The 248
dinosaurs were on Earth for more than one hundred fifty million 259
years. The last part of the dinosaur age is called the Cretaceous 271
period; the end of the Cretaceous period marked the end of the 283
dinosaurs. ❸ Tekla didn't know that there would be humans on Earth 294
eighty million years after the end of the Cretaceous period. She didn't 306
know that the world would be ruled by a mammal, the human, who 319

would control more power than the most fierce tyrannosaur that ever 330
lived. She didn't know that animals like horses, cows, and elephants 341
would someday inhabit Earth. What she did know was that the sun 353
felt good, that the bite of some insects hurt, and that she was thirsty. ❹ 367

The other triceratops were thirsty, too. They awoke, resumed 376
eating, and then began moving slowly toward the water hole that was 388
about three miles away. Tekla tagged along, stopping frequently to 398
look at lizards or other animals. When they reached the water hole, 410
the young triceratops splashed and pranced around in the shallow 420
water. The adults went about the business of drinking in a more 432
dignified way. Experiencing water for the first time, Tekla felt its 443
warmth and listened to the sounds it made as she thrashed about. ❺ 455

The water hole was teeming with animals. Some were wading and 466
drinking. Others crouched along the shore, drinking and glancing 475
about to make sure that no predators were near. 484

Tekla didn't realize that the different types of animals around her 495
were similar to animals of today. There were those animals that ate 507
the flesh of other animals—the carnivores. And there were those, like 519
Tekla, that ate plants—the herbivores. ❻ She wasn't aware that there 530
were carnivores that made their home in the warm water of the water 543
hole. She didn't know that one of those carnivores was about ten feet 556
from her. It was a crocodile hidden under a bed of floating weeds, 569
with only its two eyes and the end of its snout above the surface of the 585
water. Tekla didn't notice that the crocodile's tail was beginning to 596
move, making the animal slide forward in the water. ❼ 605

Lesson 50

1

re ly tri pre dis

2

<u>re</u>opened usual<u>ly</u> moti<u>on</u>less ch<u>ar</u>ged

intelligent <u>th</u>undered experien<u>ce</u> rev<u>ea</u>l

<u>re</u>leased probab<u>ly</u> bo<u>th</u>ered meas<u>u</u>red

3

1. alert
2. visible
3. secluded
4. gash
5. daggerlike

4

movement capable instead unison

dangerous scramble crocodile flee

instinctively narrow instincts jaws alert

shoulder drastic instantly compared

5 | # A Narrow Escape

The movement in the water sent off an instinctive alarm in Tekla. 12
She turned toward the movement and lowered her head. Almost in 23
unison the other triceratops stopped drinking and stood motionless. 32
Some of the younger ones began to back out of the water, still facing 46
Tekla. 47

Suddenly, a huge open mouth shot from under the water. The mouth 59
was bigger than Tekla. Tekla quickly backed up, almost falling down. 70
The huge crocodile jaws closed on her head. Instantly the jaws 81
reopened. They had closed on Tekla's three horns, and the horns had 93
punched holes in the roof of the crocodile's mouth. ❶ As soon as the 106
crocodile released her, Tekla scrambled from the water hole. Within a 117
few moments, she was calm again. She didn't feel the blood running 129
from the front of her neck where the crocodile's lower teeth had dug in. 143

Tekla didn't react very much to the pain because she was a reptile, 156
and pain doesn't serve reptiles the way it serves most intelligent 167
animals. Intelligent animals learn more quickly. Pain helps them 176
learn. When they do something and then feel pain, they soon learn 188
that what they did leads to pain. ❷ Humans probably react more to 200
pain than any other animal that has lived on Earth. On the other 213
hand, pain didn't help triceratops learn, because they were not 223
capable of learning very much. They had brains that were tiny 234
compared to their overall size, <u>and</u> they were capable of learning very 246
little. But triceratops had instincts that helped them get along in the 258
world. Tekla's instincts told her how to walk, what to eat, when to feel 272
frightened, when to run, when to fight, and when to mate. ❸ 283

The days went by, and Tekla grew. Every day during her first year, 296
she gained weight. When she was one year old, she was about 308

one-fourth the size of a full-grown triceratops; she weighed about 318
5,000 pounds. She stood five feet tall and measured seven feet from the 331
tip of her middle horn to the end of her long tail. 343

That first year went by quickly. Tekla did the same thing day after 356
day. She ate. She became alert if the sound of a tyrannosaur was 369
heard across the plain. She stood shoulder to shoulder with the other 381
triceratops facing a tyrannosaur when one came near the herd. But 392
tyrannosaurs never bothered the herd. ❹ Instead, they chose to run 402
down lone dinosaurs as they tried to flee across the plain to the water 416
hole. These attacks were not always successful, especially if the other 427
dinosaur was a large, healthy adult. 433

Tekla's first year was not marked by drastic changes in seasons. One 445
part of the year was drier than the others. Another part of the year 459
was a little cooler with more rain; however, all seasons were fairly 471
warm and wet with heavy clouds usually visible in the sky. 482

Shortly after Tekla's first birthday, she left the herd. Four adult 493
female triceratops were going back to the sand near the cliffs to lay 506
their eggs. Tekla tagged along. When the adults got near the cliff, they 519
split up, each going to a secluded spot. Tekla began to follow one of the 534
females. She turned and attacked Tekla. She charged her with her head 546
down. ❺ Tekla tried to get out of the way, but the middle horn caught 560
her hind leg. She turned and began to run. The adult's horn had made 574
a deep gash in her leg, and the leg seemed to drag when she ran. 589

Suddenly, Tekla sensed something more dangerous than the female 598
triceratops. She stopped and looked around, trying to locate the 608
danger. Then she saw it. Standing above a grove of small trees, it 621
looked like a green mountain. Its mouth was open in a half-smile, 633
revealing two rows of daggerlike teeth. It was the biggest tyrannosaur 644
Tekla had ever seen. 648

1

hesitation pretended differently roamed

measured prance blindly instantly

2

1. faked
2. viciously
3. vegetation
4. knee-deep

3

chorus kangaroo tremendous closest

smiling defend full-grown behave

juvenile grazing confused butted

though adult predator plodded

drew herbivore occasion unison

thundered shoulder bumped

4

Surviving the Attacks

The huge tyrannosaur hopped forward like a kangaroo. Then it   10
began to walk toward Tekla. Tekla backed up, out of the path of the   24
tyrannosaur. The great dinosaur forgot Tekla. It decided to go after   35
the adult triceratops now in its path.   42

The tyrannosaur ran around to attack the triceratops from behind,   52
but the triceratops turned around quickly. The tyrannosaur faked   61
with its head several times and then quickly jumped to one side.   73
Again the triceratops turned to face the predator, but as quickly as it 86
turned, the tyrannosaur jumped to the other side. Before the   96
triceratops could turn again, the great smiling jaws of the tyrannosaur 107
came down on its back. The sound of the breaking bones carried   119
across the plain. The tyrannosaur struck again, this time from behind. 130
The triceratops was still on its feet, but it could hardly move. The   143
tyrannosaur moved to the side of the triceratops, butted it viciously 154
until it fell over, and then struck again for the kill.   165

By now, Tekla was far from the cliffs, running as well as she could   179
across the plain. Her instincts told her to return to the herd. There   192
was safety in the herd. ❶ Five or more triceratops could defend   203
themselves against a tyrannosaur; however, a single triceratops,   211
though it was huge and had great horns, could not hope to survive a   225
battle with a full-grown tyrannosaur.   230

By the time Tekla reached her fourth birthday, she was full-grown.   241
She didn't behave much differently from the way she had behaved   252
when she was a juvenile. She didn't, <u>however</u>, move around as much   264
now. She plodded along with the herd as it roamed the plain, eating   277
nearly all the time. Now Tekla ate more than 2,000 pounds of   289
vegetation a day. She measured nearly thirty feet from the tip of her 302

nose to the end of her tail. She weighed nearly 20,000 pounds. Every 315
time she stepped on the plain, she left a footprint that was about two 329
inches deep. ❷ 331

Her size had changed and so had some of her instincts. When Tekla 344
had been a juvenile, her instincts had told her to hide in the face of 359
danger. Now, her instincts told her to fight. When a tyrannosaur drew 371
near the herd, Tekla took her place with the other triceratops, her 383
head down and her large horns pointed at the predator. Perhaps twice 395
a week some large tyrannosaurs would come near, but none ever 406
attacked the herd. Usually the tyrannosaur would prance and jump 416
and make passes at the triceratops. Sometimes it pretended to charge 427
the herd, hoping that one of the herbivores would break away from 439
the group. But on each occasion, the triceratops herd stood its 450
ground, and the tyrannosaur would soon leave to find a meal 461
elsewhere. ❸ 462

Shortly after her fourth birthday, Tekla had her first battle with a 474
tyrannosaur. It happened at the water hole. There were many animals 485
along the edge of the hole, most of them grazing animals. Suddenly, a 498
tyrannosaur charged through a grove of trees toward the water hole. 509
In unison, the animals stopped drinking. They stood alert for an 520
instant, and then they ran. The triceratops thundered from the hole. 531
Hundreds of birds took to the air with a chorus of wing flapping that 545
could be heard a mile away. Small reptiles sped from the water hole. ❹ 558

The animals moved in two waves, one going left and one moving 570
right, leaving a path for the charging tyrannosaur. Tekla and three 581
other triceratops were knee-deep in the water. They were caught in the 593
middle of the confused animals that were all running blindly from the 605
water hole. Before Tekla and the others could leave, they saw they 617
were right in the path of the tyrannosaur. 625

Instinctively, the four triceratops stood shoulder to shoulder and   634
faced the tyrannosaur. Without hesitation, the huge predator jumped   643
to one side of the group and tried to bite the back of the closest   658
triceratops. All the triceratops tried to turn and face the tyrannosaur,   669
but they just bumped into each other. One of them, a young male,   682
began to run from the water hole. Instantly, the tyrannosaur charged   693
after him. ❺   695

1 **sub**

submerge

submit

substandard

subtract

2 moaning   semicircle   wildly   released

thrashing   infection   heaving   breathed

either   leisurely   experienced   flail

3
1. ribs
2. shrill
3. trample

4 strength   knocked   silent   injured

struck   flicking   message   normal

lowered   powerful   locomotive   seriously

finished   occasionally   scavengers

fallen   settled   meanwhile

5 The Tyrannosaur Attacks

Fight, Tekla's instincts told her. Fight. Without fear, Tekla charged   10
after the tyrannosaur, who now had its jaws firmly planted in the   22
male's back. The male was trying to turn to face the tyrannosaur, but   35
the tyrannosaur had a firm hold on his back. Tekla lowered her head   48
and charged with all her strength. Like all dinosaurs, her back legs   60
were bigger and more powerful than her front legs, and she pushed so   73
hard against the soft ground near the water hole that she made   85
footprints over a foot deep. ❶ She pushed with all her strength.   96
Faster—move faster, her instincts told her.   103

Her two large horns struck the tyrannosaur in the side. One broke   115
the tyrannosaur's lowest rib. The other entered the side of its belly.   127
Both horns went in their full length.   134

Tekla had hit the tyrannosaur so hard that the ground shook. The   146
tyrannosaur released its grip on the young male, let out a shrill roar,   159
and fell over, kicking wildly. ❷ The two other triceratops charged   169
from the water hole. Almost as quickly as the tyrannosaur had fallen   181
over, it stood up again, wildly flailing its tail, and jumping around like   194
a huge kangaroo. Tekla stood her ground with her head down. As the   207
tyrannosaur lowered its head to strike at Tekla's neck, she charged   218
again, this time planting her two large horns in the tyrannosaur's soft   230
belly. At the same time, the two triceratops that had been in the water   244
hole charged forward—one on either side of the tyrannosaur. The   255
tyrannosaur went down as the six horns tore into its sides with the   268
force of a locomotive. Meanwhile, the injured male triceratops stood   278
and watched. It tried to move forward, but it was seriously injured. It   291
would die before the sun set.   297

The tyrannosaur was on its back, roaring and thrashing its tail 308
from side to side. The tail struck one of the triceratops and knocked it 322
over. One of the other triceratops charged and struck the fallen 333
tyrannosaur in the neck. Another charged and drove its horns into the 345
predator's side. 347

Just when it seemed as if the tyrannosaur was finished, the giant 359
animal rolled to one side and snapped at Tekla with frightening speed. 371
Its huge jaws caught her front shoulder, right below her armor plate. 383
The tyrannosaur released its grip when the other triceratops charged 393
and struck it in the side of the head. 402

Suddenly, the plain was silent. The tyrannosaur lay on its back, 413
flicking its tail from time to time. The four triceratops stood in a 426
semicircle facing their fallen enemy. The birds settled along the shore of 438
the water hole, and many dinosaurs returned, acting as if nothing had 450
happened. Some of them walked near the fallen tyrannosaur without 460
even looking at it. It was almost as if a message had gone out to all the 477
animals that the danger had passed and things were back to normal. ❸ 489

The four triceratops stood over the tyrannosaur for about a minute. 500
Then Tekla and two others turned away and returned to the water 512
hole. The injured male didn't follow. It stood there bleeding, its head 524
down and its sides heaving every time it breathed. Long after Tekla 536
and the other triceratops left the water hole and returned to grazing, 548
the injured male stood there. At last it lay down as some of the smaller 563
predators and scavengers moved in for the great feast that night. ❹ 574

The grass around the two fallen dinosaurs had been trampled when 585
the sun came up the next morning. Only a few of the larger bones of 600
the tyrannosaur and the male triceratops marked the spot where the 611
battle had taken place. The animals had forgotten yesterday's battle. 621

Tekla had several cracked bones and an infection, but she didn't 632
remember the battle. She knew only that she should eat and rest. ❺ 644

Lesson

53

1 **sub**

A	B
submarine	subtract
submerge	submit
	substitute
	sublet

2 required   interest   insurance

experienced   accurately

3
1. stampede
2. offspring
3. urge
4. concealed
5. scent

4 focus   ancient   occurred   veered   inherit

occasion   gallop   sprinted   tumbled   hurry

secluded   mated   strongest   sixteenth   lion

groves   electric   straight   ginkgo   buffalo

scrambled   skeleton   fought   instinctive

5   The Battle to Survive

When Tekla was five, she mated with a large male triceratops.   11
Three males had fought over her. Their instinctive fighting to see who   23
would mate was insurance that only the strongest would produce   33
offspring, and those offspring would inherit their parents' strength. ❶   42

In the spring, Tekla experienced some new instincts. She had a   53
strong urge to be alone. If another triceratops drew near her, she   65
would lower her head and move her horns from side to side, a sign   79
that she was ready to attack. The other triceratops kept their distance.   91
A few days after Tekla had experienced the urge to be alone, the urge   105
took on a new focus. Instinct told her, "Go to the cliffs. Go to the   120
cliffs." And so, late one afternoon she left the herd and walked to the   134
ancient beach near the cliffs. Her instincts told her to find a secluded   147
spot and dig a deep hole. She dug the hole with her front feet. Then   162
she walked around the hole three or four times, making sure that she   175
was safe. "Hurry," her instincts told her. It was time to lay eggs. ❷   188

She laid seven large eggs. Then she covered the hole and returned to   201
the herd. She had done everything that was required of a mother   213
triceratops. She would never know her babies. She would have no   224
interest in them. They were on their own, just as Tekla had been from   238
the day she was born.   243

Every year for the next twelve years, Tekla returned to the sand   255
beach to lay eggs. Every year after laying the eggs, she returned to the   269
herd. ❸ During those twelve years, she had one more fight with a   281
tyrannosaur. She and five other triceratops killed a large female. Tekla   292
left the battle with the tip of her left horn broken off.   304

Tekla's last fight occurred shortly after her sixteenth birthday. She   314
was grazing on the edge of the herd. The herd made a practice of   328

grazing in the open, far from the groves of trees which could hide the 342

predators. On this occasion, however, the herd had moved close to a 354

grove of ginkgo trees. There was almost no breeze, so Tekla couldn't 366

smell the danger that the grove concealed. ❹ 373

Suddenly, the herd stopped grazing; it was as if an electric shock 385

had been sent through the herd. Then the triceratops began to run. 397

Tekla hadn't caught the scent of the predator, but she caught the panic 410

of the herd. Like stampeding cattle, they began to gallop from the 422

grove of trees. Almost as quickly as they began to stampede, one large 435

tyrannosaur, and then another, sped from the grove. Part of the 446

triceratops herd split, moving off to the right. The rest kept running 458

straight ahead. Tekla also ran straight ahead, but she was far behind 470

the other triceratops. Behind her was one large tyrannosaur that 480

could easily outrun a triceratops. 485

And it did. As the other tyrannosaur ran after the triceratops that 497

veered to the right, this tyrannosaur sprinted after Tekla, overtaking 507

her about three hundred yards from the grove of ginkgo trees. It tried 520

to break her back with its powerful jaws, but the two animals were 533

moving too fast for the tyrannosaur to direct its jaws accurately. It 545

caught some of Tekla's flesh in its jaws as it fell on her back. Both 560

animals tumbled to the ground with a terrible crash. Tekla scrambled 571

to her feet, began to run away, and then suddenly stopped to face the 585

predator. 586

Nobody is sure why grazing animals sometimes run from predators 596

and at other times fight. Sometimes water buffalo will run from lions, 608

even though a water buffalo can easily kill a lion. The triceratops herd 621

ran from two tyrannosaurs, although they could easily have killed 631

both of them if they had stood their ground. Tekla had run because 644

the other triceratops had run. Now, however, her instincts told her 655

that she must fight. ❺ 658

1

pre   re   ly   un   dis   sub

A	B
reconstruction	submerge
abruptly	remains
unsuccessful	carefully
seriously	removing

2

mo<u>ti</u>onless   p<u>a</u>rtner   s<u>ur</u>viving   w<u>ea</u>kened

3

1. pounced
2. preserved
3. silt
4. fossilized
5. buckles
6. paleontologist
7. transform

4

paralyzed   inflicted   Wyoming   sun-bleached

chiseling   sidestepped   locusts   seeped

scar   wonder   skeleton   died

agreed   replied   attempt   washed

ringing   blinked   through   respond

warning   limestone   wounded

5

Tekla's Last Battle

Tekla fought with all her might. She charged the tyrannosaur and   11
planted her horns in its belly. She lifted her head and tossed the   24
tyrannosaur to the side. The predator, seriously wounded, walked away   34
from her and stood motionless for a moment, as Tekla waited with her   47
head down. The tyrannosaur sidestepped Tekla's next charge and   56
pounced on her back. It was all over for Tekla. She thrashed around,   69
trying to roll over, but the huge carnivore held fast. Its jaws had come   83
down like a mammoth vice on her spine, breaking the bones. Tekla felt   96
dizzy. She tried to move her hind legs, but they wouldn't respond. Her   109
rear half was paralyzed. She turned her head and watched the   120
predator, but she didn't attempt to fight any more. A warm feeling   132
spread over her, as if the sun had become brighter and brighter. Things   145
looked lighter to her. The plain in the distance seemed washed out,   157
almost white. The noises of the plain became faint ringing sounds.   168

She didn't remember her early years on the plain, the hundreds of   180
times she had roamed through the grass, the water hole. She simply   192
blinked several times. Then she saw no more. She felt very warm as   205
the plain faded farther and farther away. Her huge head dropped to   217
the ground, and she was dead.   223

The tyrannosaur didn't feed on her. It was bleeding from the deep   235
wounds Tekla had inflicted. ❶ It walked around Tekla several times.   245
Then it stood motionless, with its mouth half open. The other   256
tyrannosaur returned from <u>an</u> unsuccessful chase. It caught the smell   266
of blood. Quickly, it hopped around Tekla. Then without any   276
warning, it attacked the wounded tyrannosaur, closing its jaws around   286
the huge animal's throat. Within a few minutes, the weakened   296
tyrannosaur was dead, lying next to Tekla.   303

Later that afternoon, after the surviving tyrannosaur had eaten its 313
fill and the smaller predators had moved in to finish off the fallen 326
dinosaurs, a strange thing happened. A great cloud of locusts swept 337
over the plain, eating everything in their path. The grazing animals, 348
the scavengers, and even the predators moved quickly to the north, 359
leaving the remains of Tekla and the tyrannosaur to the locusts. If it 372
hadn't been for those locusts, very little might have remained of Tekla. 384
As it turned out, however, her bones and the bones of the tyrannosaur 397
were preserved. They lay sun-bleached on the plain for more than fifty 409
years. ❷ Then a great flood came, and the place where Tekla had 421
fallen became the bottom of a lake. Each year, more and more silt and 435
sand covered the bones. After thousands of years, a solution of 446
limestone had seeped into the bones, transforming them into solid 456
rock. Tekla's bones were now fossilized. 462

Eighty million years passed. During that time, the lake dried up, 473
the dinosaurs disappeared from Earth, and the crust of Earth 483
buckled, forming new cliffs and mountains. Tekla's bones were near 493
the edge of one of those cliffs. ❸ 500

One day over eighty million years after Tekla's death, two 510
paleontologists were digging for fossil remains in northern Wyoming. 519
They were chiseling small bones from the face of a cliff. One of them 533
chiseled around the bones of Tekla's tail. "I think we've found 544
something," the paleontologist said to his partner. It took the 554
paleontologists more than a month to remove the remains of Tekla 565
and the tyrannosaur from the limestone cliff. The paleontologists 574
carefully laid out each bone until they had reconstructed the skeletons 585
of the two animals. They couldn't find the tip of Tekla's left horn. 598

When they had completed the reconstruction of the two animals, 608
one paleontologist said, "The triceratops has a broken back. It also has 620
an old bone scar. I wonder if the tyrannosaur killed this triceratops." ❹ 632

"I don't know," the other paleontologist said. "The tyrannosaur has 642
broken bones in its neck. I don't see how a triceratops could inflict 655
that kind of wound. And there are no signs of horn wounds on the 669
tyrannosaur's skeleton." 671

"Yes," the first paleontologist said as he looked at a row of fluffy 684
clouds above a nearby mountain. "We'll never know what happened, I 695
guess. But I sure would have liked to have been there and seen just 709
how those animals died." 713

"Me, too," the other paleontologist agreed. "But I guess we'll never 724
know." ❺ 725

1

2

fantastic   unbelievable   interested   world

sorting   famous   bathtub   ounce

authoritative   fascinating   concerned   thrown

3

1. champion
2. set a record
3. official

4

Setting Records

Most people are interested in champions. They want to know who is the best at doing different things. They are interested in the biggest, the oldest, the longest, and the most. They enjoy talking about champions and records, and they sometimes argue about who is the best at doing this or doing that. To settle arguments, people need an official, authoritative list of records. There is just such a list. It is *The Guinness Book of World Records,* a book that set a record of its own. It has become the fastest-selling book in the world. ❶

The Guinness Book of World Records is fascinating because it lists some of the most fantastic records ever set. Some of these are accidents of nature. Who was the tallest person, what was the largest animal, what was the oldest living thing? These were not records that anyone tried to set. These things just happened.

Some people are apparently so interested in being a champion that they aren't too concerned about what record they set, so long as they set a record or win first prize. ❷ Some of the records they have set are amazing. The Guinness book records them all.

Take sports—not just ordinary, everyday sports such as swimming, baseball, and track. Here are a few unusual sports records.

Catching a grape in the mouth: longest distance on level ground, grape thrown from 327 feet.

Bathtub racing: 36 miles in one hour, 22 minutes, 27 seconds.

Crawling (at least one knee always on the ground): longest distance, 31½ miles.

Hoop rolling: 600 miles in 18 days.

Pogo-stick jumping: 64,649 jumps in 8 hours, 35 minutes.

Riding on horseback in full armor: 146 miles in 3 days, 3 hours, 40 minutes. ❸

There are also, if you are interested, records for balancing on one foot, custard-pie throwing, and a record for onion peeling that almost makes you cry!

Some of the records suggest interesting questions. The one for nonstop joke telling, for instance. It was set by someone who cracked jokes for eight hours straight. The question is: How many listeners were still laughing at the end of the eight hours?

1

ea

head

spread

bread

instead

2

ly

re

dis

sub

tri

3

university   intelligent   absolutely

replied   disgustedly   administration

4

1. physics
2. fault
3. property
4. detect
5. schedule

5

constantly   abruptly   producing   failure

researchers   devices   laboratory

mathematical   laser   escalator   irritating

focused   deliver   professors   machine

involved   clothespins   conducted   series

detector   instruments   stranded   locomotive

laugh   campus   experiment   transform

6   Milly, the Joker

Although Dr. Milly Jacobson was only twenty-eight years old, she   10
was a professor of physics at State University. She was tall, intelligent,   22
and friendly. She was good at playing tennis, at bowling, and at   34
shooting pool. She had one serious fault, however. She constantly   44
played jokes on the other professors. And some of her jokes were very   57
corny and quite irritating to those involved. ❶   64

For example, one day she came into her laboratory and said to   76
Dr. Fred Frankle, "Freddy, what's one plus one?"   84

"Two," Fred Frankle replied.   88

"And what do the letters *t-o-o* spell?"   95

"Too," Fred Frankle replied.   99

"And what's the last name of the person who wrote stories about   111
Tom Sawyer?"   113

"Twain," Fred replied.   116

"Good," Milly said. "Now say all of the answers you gave."   127

Fred thought for a moment. He then said, "Two, too, twain."   138

"Very good," Milly said and began to laugh. "Tomorrow I'll teach   149
you how to say *locomotive*."   154

Fred shook his head and said disgustedly, "Milly, don't you ever get   166
tired of playing those corny jokes on people?"   174

"I'm sorry," Milly said, walking toward her laser machine. "I just   185
can't help it." She began to laugh again. "Two, too, twain," she said   198
softly to herself. She abruptly stopped smiling and faced Fred. "Oh, by   210
the way. Did you hear about the robbery near campus this morning?"   222

"No," he said.   225

"Two clothespins held up a pair of pants," Milly said and began to   238
laugh again.   240

"Come on, Milly," Fred said. "We've got work to do." 250

Milly went to her desk and took out a <u>folder</u> containing charts. 262
Next to each chart was a long mathematical formula. For the past 274
year, Milly had been working with laser beams trying to discover 285
some of the basic properties of metals like silver, lead, iron, and gold. 298
❷ She had conducted hundreds of experiments and had carefully 307
recorded the results of each. For these experiments, she would place a 319
bit of metal on a screen. Then she would turn a laser beam on the 334
metal. Some laser beams are pure red light, and since they are 346
absolutely pure, the beams do not spread out as they move from the 359
laser gun to a nearby target. If a beam is one millimeter wide when it 374
leaves the laser gun, it is one millimeter wide when it strikes the 387
target. And when it strikes the target, it is capable of producing so 400
much heat that it can transform a piece of metal into gas. Milly was 414
using different recording devices to measure how the gas form of 425
silver was different from the gas form of lead. ❸ 434

In the last experiments she had run, she had noticed something very 446
strange. She had set the laser gun so it would deliver a series of very 461
short bursts of light and focused it on bits of gold. This experiment 474
had given a strange reading on the metal detector. The reading was 486
unlike readings for lead, zinc, or any other metal. 495

She prepared another experiment with gold. After placing a bit of 506
gold on the target, she again set the laser gun so it would deliver a 521
series of short bursts. She checked the other recording instruments. 531
Then she turned to Fred Frankle, who was writing notes in a 543
notebook. "Say," Milly said, "did you hear about the power failure in 555
the administration building yesterday?" 559

"No," Fred replied. 562

Milly said, "The dean was stranded on the escalator for three 573
hours." Milly began to laugh. 578

Fred shook his head. "Some day," he said, "you're going to be   590
serious about something, and nobody will believe you. You're like the   601
little child who hollered 'wolf' too many times." ❹   609

"I know," Milly said. "I should stop joking around, but it makes the   622
day so much more fun."   627

1

ea

dealt

instead

wealth

thread

deaf

2

associa<u>tion</u>   <u>ex</u>pression   rese<u>r</u>vation   <u>c</u>igars

3

1. researcher
2. physicist
3. jokester
4. bonds
5. provides

4

conventions   exchange   surprised

exploding   performing   complicated

molecules   behavior   probably   cue

professors   responded   receiving

supposed   involved   earlier   daylights

opportunity   accompany   buzzer   schedule

5   Convention

Every year there are several large conventions for people who do   11
research in physics, and every year Dr. Milly Jacobson went to one of   24
those conventions. This year she planned to attend the convention of   35
the International Association of Physicists. This convention allows   43
researchers to exchange information about their latest projects, and   52
provides an opportunity for a researcher in a branch of physics to talk   65
to other researchers in that same branch. Milly's behavior at these   76
conventions probably would surprise you. She played a number of   86
jokes at home at State University, but when she went to a convention,   99
she became a full-time jokester. ❶   104

Before she left for the convention of the International Association   114
of Physicists, she packed her handshake buzzer and her loaded cigars.   125
She also took along her pride—a pool cue with an exploding tip that   139
she invented herself. She had placed an exploding cap in the tip of the   153
cue, so that when somebody tried to shoot a ball with the cue and the   168
end of the cue would strike the ball—bang! ❷   177

Milly was scheduled to present a paper on the experiments she had   189
been performing with the laser beam and different metals. She wasn't   200
ready to report on the strange readings she was receiving when she   212
used short bursts of laser light on gold. However, she had prepared a   225
paper on some of the earlier work she had done with the laser beam.   239
The paper was very involved and complicated. It dealt with the kinds   251
of bonds that hold the molecules of metals <u>together</u> and how the   263
bonds of different metals responded to the laser beam. ❸   272

The convention of the International Association of Physicists was   281
held in New York City. Fred Frankle was to accompany Milly. She   293

told him, "Don't worry about reservations, Freddy. I've taken care of 304
everything." Indeed she had. 308

Fred and Milly arrived at the airport; they went to the gate for the 322
New York flight; they stood in line waiting for the agent at the gate to 337
take their tickets and check them in for the flight. 347

When it was Milly's turn, she handed the agent two tickets, one for 360
herself and one for Fred. The agent looked over the tickets. She then 373
looked up and said, "Which one of you is Dr. Frankle?" 384

"I am," Fred replied. 388

"Well, I'm very sorry, sir," the agent said. "But this ticket is not for 402
the New York flight. It's for Bismarck, North Dakota." 411

"Bismarck!" Fred shouted. "I'm supposed to go to New York." 421

By now Milly was laughing so hard that tears were forming in her 434
eyes. She reached in her purse and pulled out another ticket. "Here," 446
she said, handing the ticket to the agent. "I think this is the right one." 461
It was Fred's ticket to New York. ❹ 468

"Milly," Fred said as he and Milly approached the gate. "One of 480
these days I'm going to get really mad at you. You scared the daylights 494
out of me. I could just see myself going to Bismarck, North Dakota." 507

"Oh," Milly said, laughing. "You should have seen the expression 517
on your face. I wish I had a picture of it." 528

"Well, I just hope you behave yourself at the convention. Don't 539
make a fool out of yourself like you did last year." ❺ 550

"I'll be good," Milly replied. She was lying. 558

1

A	B
deaf	weather
deal	wheat
dealt	steal
death	pleasure

2 appl<u>au</u>ded Vir<u>g</u>inia phys<u>i</u>cist Terran<u>c</u>e publi<u>cati</u>on

3
1. harmless
2. formal
3. delicately
4. prominent

4

warn restaurant snickered serious arrived

couple collar effects wonderful lobby

embarrassing association audiences stroked

ushers researchers gentleman broadly

5

Living It Up

Milly and Fred arrived in New York City shortly after seven in the 13
evening. They took a bus directly to their hotel. In the lobby they met 27
several physicists they knew. One was a very serious man named 38
Dr. Osgood Terrance, who always spoke as if he were in front of a 52
class of students. 55

"Well," he said, "Dr. Jacobson and Dr. Frankle. It certainly is a 67
pleasure to see you again. I noticed from the program that Dr. Jacobson 80
is delivering another paper. I'm certainly looking forward to it." ❶ 90

Milly, who was facing Dr. Terrance, pointed straight ahead and 100
said, "Did you see that? A man picked up somebody else's bag over 113
there." When Dr. Terrance turned around, Milly pinned a large 123
red-and-white button on the back of his collar. The button said KISS 135
ME IN THE DARK. 139

Fred started to object, but Milly said, "Shhh. It's a harmless joke." 151

So the very formal Dr. Terrance chatted for a few moments and then 164
walked across the lobby as people turned around and snickered. ❷ 174

After going to her room, Milly took her exploding cue stick and 186
went to the hotel's pool room. She beat a couple of physicists and a 200
truck driver in a game of eight ball. Then she secretly loaded the tip of 215
the cue stick with three caps, handed it to one of the physicists, and 229
said, "Here, try this cue stick. I think you'll get a bang out of it." 244

He did. He was trying to make a very delicate shot. He stroked the 258
stick <u>back</u> and forth several times. Then, very delicately, he hit the cue 271
ball. BOOM. The physicist dropped the cue stick and jumped about a 283
foot off the floor. Everybody laughed, but the physicist who tried to 295
make the shot didn't look very happy. 302

Before going to bed, Milly shook hands with a very prominent   313
physicist. Of course, she had her handshake buzzer in her hand. She   325
pinned another red-and-white button on the back of a woman from   336
California. Then she went to her room and retired for the night. She   349
was having a wonderful time. ❸   354

The next morning at nine o'clock she gave her talk. About seventy   366
people were in the audience. A professor from Virginia introduced   376
her. "Dr. Jacobson," he began, "is one of the leading laser researchers 388
today." He then listed some of the papers Milly had written for   400
publication and told something about her latest research. ❹   408

The people in the audience clapped, and Milly stood up. She said,   420
"I am passing out a paper that summarizes what I have learned about   433
the effects of laser beams on different metals." Three ushers passed   444
out copies of the paper to everyone in the audience. "Please do not   457
open the paper yet," Milly said as the papers were being passed out.   470
"We'll go through it together." The members of the audience held   481
their copies and waited. Printed on the cover of each copy were these   494
words: 495
EVERYTHING I HAVE LEARNED ABOUT THE EFFECTS OF   503
LASERS, BY DR. MILLY JACOBSON.   508

"OK," Milly said after all the papers had been passed out. "You can   521
thumb through your copy now." As the members of the audience   532
thumbed through the pages, they began to laugh. Every page was   543
blank. A young physicist from Texas yelled out, "You've learned just   554
as much about lasers as I have." Everybody laughed. Others in the   566
audience made comments.   569

Then Milly delivered her real paper, and after going through it, she   581
answered questions from the audience. She was very well received. The   592
audience applauded for over a minute, and Milly smiled broadly. ❺   602

She was having a great time. Just as the audience was getting up to
leave, Milly said, "Ladies and gentlemen, I would like to warn you
against eating in this hotel's restaurant." Everybody stopped and
looked at Milly. "They have some very embarrassing things going on
there. Yesterday evening I looked at my table and saw the salad
dressing."

"Oh, no," some of the people shouted. "That's corny." But Milly
loved it.

INFORMATION PASSAGE

Fresnel	vandals	technology
lenses	columns	engineers

Lighthouses

Lighthouses have a bright light that warns ships and boats about getting too close to dangerous areas. At one time, lighthouses were the only means for alerting ships about dangerous places. Today, lighthouses are not necessary because ships have radar and depth finders. Some ships also use messages from Global Positioning System (GPS) to provide information about exactly where the ship is on a map. If the GPS message shows the ship in a particular location, the ship is within 10 to 20 feet of where the message indicates it is. ❶

The early lighthouses were designed so that they were about 40 miles apart. The light from one lighthouse cannot be seen for more than about 20 miles because Earth is curved, but the light travels in a straight line. If a ship is 20 miles down the coast from one lighthouse, the ship's captain can probably see the light from the next lighthouse.

If the engineers who built lighthouses made them taller, the light would be visible from a greater distance. The problem with making them taller is that fog is common along a coast line. Often there are low clouds not more than 100 feet above the ocean. If the light from a lighthouse came from much more than 100 feet above the ocean, it would often be in the clouds, and the light would not be visible to ships. In some places, lighthouses are only about 30 feet tall. A short lighthouse tells you there are frequent fogs in the area. ❷

The most powerful lenses for lighthouses were built in France and were designed by a man named Fresnel. The Fresnel lens has a very complicated design. It has columns of glass with fins on them. A lighthouse in Oregon had one of the largest Fresnel lenses ever built. This lens, which was over six feet tall, was damaged by vandals in the 1990s. Several experts in glass and lenses decided to make replacements for the columns that were damaged. They worked for three years on this project. Even though they had equipment and technology far more advanced than Fresnel had, they could not make parts as good as those of the original lens. ❸

Lesson 59

1

A	B
pleasant	deal
please	dealt
dream	instead
health	creature

2

pre   sub   un   re   ly

3

college   taught   slightest

seriously   pretended   acid

4

1. impish
2. undergraduate
3. graduate student
4. doctoral degree
5. related to
6. incurable

5

apologized   entertainers   respond

advantage   practical   wrong

faked   conducted   striking

attracted   professional   equals

affect   routine   clue

6 The Same Old Routine

Milly had a ball during the remaining two days of the convention of $\quad$ 13
the International Association of Physicists. She attended sessions $\quad$ 21
during the day and was generally very serious, except when she shook $\quad$ 33
hands with her handshake buzzer or pinned one of her red-and-white $\quad$ 44
buttons on another physicist. In the evenings, however, she played one $\quad$ 55
joke after another. By the end of the last evening of the convention, she $\quad$ 69
had attracted a crowd of people who followed her around, waiting to $\quad$ 81
see what her next joke would be. Most of the people in the crowd were $\quad$ 96
physicists, but some were people who found Milly more entertaining $\quad$ 106
than the professional entertainers in the hotel. One reason they found $\quad$ 117
Milly so funny was that, though she had an impish twinkle in her eye, $\quad$ 131
she didn't look like the type of person who would play practical jokes. ❶ 144
For Milly, the convention was more fun than a circus. She had so much $\quad$ 158
fun that she began to plan her tricks for the following year's convention $\quad$ 171
of the International Association of Physicists. $\quad$ 177

Milly found it a little dull to return to the routine in her laboratory $\quad$ 191
and her classroom. She taught two courses—one for undergraduates $\quad$ 201
who were taking their first college course in physics, and another for $\quad$ 213
graduate students who were studying for their doctoral degree. She was 224
pleasant and entertaining when she taught. She told stories that related 235
to whatever the students were studying. $\quad$ 241

Milly made it a rule never to play practical jokes on her students. $\quad$ 254
From time to time she <u>would</u> break the rule with her graduate $\quad$ 266
students, but she never joked with undergraduates. She didn't want to 277
take advantage of them because she felt they were not in a position to 291
get even if she played a joke on them. The other physicists, on the $\quad$ 305
other hand, were Milly's equals. They could get mad at her or laugh at 319

her or play a joke on her if they wished. And sometimes they did. ❷   333

For example, after Milly returned from the convention, she had very   344

strange results when she performed a laser experiment on a piece of   356

zinc. The reason was that the piece of zinc was not pure zinc. Fred   370

and one of the other physicists, Dr. Helen Mark, had treated the zinc   383

with acid. As Milly conducted the experiment and recorded the   393

results, Fred watched her, laughing to himself. ❸   400

Milly quickly figured out what was wrong, but she didn't give the   412

slightest clue that she had. Instead, very seriously she performed   422

several other experiments with the treated zinc. For one of these   433

experiments, she placed a piece of the zinc in a box. What Fred didn't   447

know was that Milly had also placed a large rubber snake in the box.   461

The snake was on a large spring, so the snake would pop out of the   476

box when the lid was opened.   482

Milly placed the box on the laser target and faked an experiment.   494

Then she pretended to open the box and look inside. Finally, she   506

called Fred over and said, "Freddy, I can't understand what's   516

happening with this zinc. Look inside that box; you're not going to   528

believe what you see."   532

"OK," Fred said, smiling. He opened the box, and the snake flew   544

out, striking him on the chin. He dropped the box lid and jumped in   558

fright. His face turned quite red as he said, "We were just trying to   572

teach you a lesson, but I think you're incurable." ❹   581

Milly apologized for her joke; then she returned to her experiments.   592

For some reason, she decided to put a piece of gold in the box and see   608

if the metal detector would still give strange readings. It did. Then she   621

filled the box with dirt and shot a series of short laser bursts at it. The   637

metal detector reacted the same as it had when there was no dirt in   651

the box. Milly began to reason this way: If the box and the dirt don't   666

affect the reading on the metal detector, the laser can be used to   679

detect gold when it is underground. If the beam goes in the direction $\quad$ 692
of gold, the metal detector will respond in that strange way. I can find $\quad$ 706
gold with my laser. ❺ $\quad$ 710

Lesson 60

compare   scientifically   creature   designed

greyhound   cosmopolitan   measuring

cheetah   accurate   capable   distance

spine-tailed   falcons   maximum   marine

machine   difference   feats

1. fascinated
2. attained
3. surpass
4. achieved
5. incredible

Speed Records

For some reason, people are fascinated with records. We like to know the record size of fish that are caught, the record weight of animals, and record feats of strength. The question of record speeds is one of the more popular record topics.

Let's start with human records. The fastest recorded time for a person to run 100 meters (about 328 feet) is 9.77 seconds, which would be an average speed of about 23 miles per hour. ❶

The human being is much slower in the water. The record time for swimming 100 meters is 47.8 seconds, which is only about 5 miles per hour. This speed is very slow when we compare it with that of the male killer whale, the blue whale. ❷ This creature can swim about 30 miles per hour, but it is certainly not the fastest marine animal. The fastest fish to be scientifically clocked was a cosmopolitan sailfish, which attained a speed of 67 miles per hour. At this speed, the sailfish would swim 100 meters in about 3 seconds. ❸

Measuring the speed of land animals is much easier than measuring that of creatures in the water. The fastest racehorse achieved an average speed of about 45 miles per hour over a course approximately one-quarter of a mile long. The fastest dog is the greyhound, which has been clocked at 41 miles per hour.

The fastest land animal in the world is probably the cheetah. Experts have not been able to accurately check the top speed of a healthy cheetah. Most agree, however, that it can run over 60 miles per hour over short distances. ❹

There are animals that are much faster than the cheetah—these animals fly. The spine-tailed swift has been clocked at about 105 miles per hour. At this speed, the bird could fly about 100 meters in about 2 seconds. There are reports of other birds that can surpass the spine-tailed swift in speed, but none has been proven. Falcons, for example, are supposed to dive at a speed of almost 200 miles per hour. But the maximum speed ever recorded for these birds has been 40 miles per hour. ❺

Machines, of course, can go faster than any creature. The fastest car reached a speed of 763 miles per hour; the fastest plane reached a speed of 4,520 miles per hour; and the fastest rocket flew at 158,000 miles per hour.

There is an incredible difference between the speed of the human being and that of some machines. The fastest person could run 100 meters in 9.77 seconds. The fastest airplane can travel that distance in about five-hundredths of a second!

Lesson
61

1

treated   treasure   please

pleasure   retreat

2

carefully   discovered   sprawling   garbage

3

1. sarcastic
2. apparatus
3. maintenance department
4. data
5. calculate
6. computer program
7. identify

4

surrounds   repeating   experiment

recording   response   truckload   shovel

dandelions   vehicle   beautiful

conclusions   equipment   arrived   gravel

campus   developed   effect   hasty

phoned   machine   entire   types

5   # The Gold Detector

Milly Jacobson had discovered that the metal detector responded in   10
a strange way to gold, even when there was dirt around the gold. She   24
repeated the experiment with the piece of gold in the box of dirt,   37
carefully recording the metal detector readings. She tested the gold to   48
make sure it hadn't been treated. Then she got a garbage can, phoned   61
a dirt-and-gravel company, and told the woman on the phone,   71
"Deliver one truckload of dirt and one truckload of gravel to the   83
physics laboratory at State University."   88

When the two truckloads arrived, Fred Frankle said, "Milly, what   98
are you up to now?"   103

"I think I've discovered something very important," Milly said.   112

"I'll just bet you have," Fred said sarcastically. He was sarcastic   123
because he thought that Milly was setting up another one of her   135
jokes. ❶ He said, "I'll tell you, Milly. I don't think the dean is going to   150
be very happy when he sees these two piles in front of the physics lab."   165
The piles did look rather ugly. The State University campus was very   177
beautiful, with large sprawling trees shading a lawn that was almost   188
free of weeds and dandelions. The lawn was carefully edged next to   200
the sidewalks that connected the different buildings on the campus.   210
And there they were—a huge pile of dirt and another of gravel—on   224
the lawn in front of the physics lab, with some of the dirt and gravel   239
spilling onto the sidewalk.   243

Milly looked at the piles, shook her head, and said, "I guess they'll   256
be mad, but I think I'm on to something very big. I'll arrange to have   271
this stuff removed when I'm done."   277

"Good luck," <u>Fred</u> said sarcastically.   282

Milly loaded the garbage can with dirt and hauled it into her lab.　295
She dug down and placed a very tiny bit of gold in the dirt. Then she　311
covered the gold. Checking her equipment, she said to herself, "Now　322
we'll see what happens with a very small piece of gold when a lot of　337
dirt surrounds it."　340

The metal detector showed a weaker response than it had shown　351
before, but the response was basically the same. It was a gold　363
response.　364

Next, Milly took her laser apparatus outside. This was not an easy　376
thing to do. The laser gun, weighing more than four hundred pounds,　388
was not designed to be moved. It took three students, Milly, and Fred　401
over half an hour to set the machine up outside, facing the two piles.　415
During the entire time Fred kept repeating, "This better not be　426
another joke." ❷　428

Milly got a shovel from the maintenance department and dug down　439
to the bottom of the dirt pile. She placed a fairly big piece of gold in　455
one spot and a tiny piece about three feet to the side of the large piece.　471
She covered the gold with dirt, aimed the gun at the pile, and fired　485
short bursts at different parts of the pile. She repeated the experiment　497
six times, recording the readings from each part of the pile. Then she　510
sat under one of the large sprawling trees near the piles and studied　523
her results. The results showed that she could locate each piece of　535
gold in the pile and that she could tell if one piece was bigger than　550
another. ❸　551

She repeated the experiment with the pile of gravel. "Perhaps gravel　562
will have a different effect on the gold," she thought. It didn't. She　575
placed bits of other types of metal in the gravel pile and repeated the　589
experiment to see what effect these other metals would have. They　600
didn't affect the results. The metal detector responded to the bits of　612

copper and iron that were close to the surface of the pile, but it didn't 627
respond in the same way it did for gold, which could be identified in 641
any part of the pile. 646

"Don't jump to any conclusions," Milly warned herself as she 656
returned to the lab and examined the data again. ❹ For over three 668
hours Milly went over the data. She did a series of calculations on 681
each experiment she had performed. She developed a computer 690
program and used the computer to test her results. It was almost 702
seven in the evening when she realized that her conclusion had not 714
been hasty. ❺ She tossed a stack of papers in the air and screamed, "I 728
can find gold." She ran out of the lab. 737

Three maintenance men were standing next to the piles in front of 749
the lab. One of them began to ask Milly as she ran from the lab, "Do 765
you know who dumped these piles of—" 772

"Gold," Milly shouted. She ran up to the top of the dirt pile. "I did 787
it. I found gold." 791

One maintenance man turned to the other and said, "She *must* be 803
the one who had these piles dumped here." 810

Lesson
62

1 **less**

soundless

motionless

meaningless

purposeless

2 **sub   dis   un   tri   pre**

3 geology   foundation   available   convince

additional   certainly   ain't   experimental

4
1. recreational vehicle
2. mounting
3. salary
4. request
5. recommend
6. grant
7. approval

5 personally   pleasure   please   guide

suggested   shrugged   awarded   secretary

involve   machine   foothills   argued

equipment   objected   couple   double

hiring   dozen   indicated

6 **Some Hasty Preparation**

Milly was on the phone early the next day, and she stayed on the   14
phone for most of the morning. She called a friend in the geology   27
department at the University of California and asked her where she   38
would suggest looking for gold. Her friend suggested the foothills near   49
Sacramento, California. Then she called a recreational vehicle place   58
in Sacramento and rented a four-wheel-drive pickup truck. She asked   68
the man if he would recommend someone to guide her to the foothills   81
and help her find gold. He gave her three names.   91

Milly called the first two, but they were not available to guide her.   104
The third said that he could guide if it didn't involve too much   117
walking. "I'm a very old man. I'm all right for a couple of miles," he   132
said, "but my feet and legs give out after that."   142

Milly asked him if he would be able to dig for some gold if she   157
could locate it. "That depends," he replied. "There is digging and   168
there is digging. If there ain't too many rocks and if the gold ain't too   183
deep, I can do it." ❶   188

Next Milly called the campus machine shop. "I have a rush job. I   201
need a mounting for my laser gun, so I can put it in the back of a   218
pickup truck. I have the plans."   224

The man at the machine shop told her there was no way he could do   239
the job before next Tuesday, but Milly argued and argued and argued.   251
She told him she would pay him double if he could complete the job   265
by the following morning. At last the man agreed. ❷   274

After spending most of the <u>morning</u> on the phone, Milly went to   286
the office of the physics department. She handed the secretary a pile   298
of forms. Each form was a request for money. One was for the   311

truckload of dirt and the truckload of gravel. One was for a round-trip 324
plane ticket to Sacramento, California. Others were for shipping and 334
mounting the laser, renting the four-wheel-drive truck, hiring the 343
guide, and for additional equipment Milly needed for her trip. The 354
secretary thumbed through the stack of requests, looked up, and said 365
flatly, "I'll have to get the dean's approval on these." She carried the 378
forms into the dean's office. 383

After a moment, a voice said loudly, "What is all this?" Then the 396
dean rushed out, carrying the forms. 402

"Dr. Jacobson," he said angrily, "what do you think you're doing? 413
Who is supposed to pay for these things? Certainly not your grant." 425
Milly's research with the laser was paid for by the Federal Science 437
Foundation. The Foundation awarded her a grant, but the grant 447
indicated how the money was to be spent. And the money was not to 461
be spent on four-wheel-drive trucks or plane trips to California. 471
"There's no way I can approve these expenses," the dean said. ❸ 482

"But you don't understand," Milly said. "It's very important. I 492
think I've found—" 495

"Oh, yes, I'll just bet it's important," the dean said sarcastically. 506
"Just like it was important last year when you had to buy three dozen 520
baby rabbits so you could plant them in Dr. Jenkins's lab and make 533
him think his two experimental rabbits had given birth to all those 545
babies." 546

"No, Dean," Milly objected. "This is different." 553

"I can see it's different," the dean said sharply. "Three dozen rabbits 565
cost less than fifty dollars. Your latest trick is going to cost 577
thousands." ❹ 578

Milly tried to convince the dean that she was not playing a joke, but 592
he wouldn't give her a chance to talk. At last, she became angry and 606

said, "All right. You can take the expenses out of my salary. Just 619
bill everything to me, but please approve the requests so I can leave 632
tomorrow." 633

The dean didn't agree at first. He asked who would take over Milly's 646
classes while she was gone. He argued that he wasn't sure how the 659
university would go about taking the money from Milly's salary. In 670
the end, however, he agreed and signed the requests. After signing the 682
last one, he said, "Milly, I personally have a great deal of respect for 696
you in most things, but if this is another one of your jokes, I'm going 711
to recommend they take your grant away from you." 720

Milly shrugged but didn't say anything. ❺ 726

INFORMATION PASSAGE

hearty   material   hurl   operation
maintained   depressed   historical

Terrible Tilly

The most costly lighthouse ever maintained is located in Oregon near the town of Tillamook. It is named the Tillamook Rock Lighthouse. As its name indicates, the lighthouse is on a rock about a mile and a half from the shore of the Pacific Ocean. The lighthouse is visible from the shore.

Before the lighthouse could be built, the top of the rock had to be blasted and made level. After the blasting, the top of the rock was 100 feet above the ocean. In 1881, engineers completed building a square lighthouse on top of the rock. The lighthouse was 35 feet tall. The first

floor of the lighthouse was home for the lighthouse keeper and his family. Above them was the tower and the Fresnel lens, which could be seen for a great distance. During the early years, the light was not run by electricity but by oil. The keeper's main job was to make sure that the light did not run out of fuel. ❶

During the time the Tillamook Rock Lighthouse was in operation, it got the nickname of Terrible Tilly. The main reason for this name was that the lighthouse is located in a place that has enormous waves when the weather is bad. These waves made it very dangerous for anybody in the ocean near the lighthouse and sometimes for people in the lighthouse.

During the construction of the lighthouse, several workers were killed trying to bring building material to the rock. Sometimes the waves were so dangerous that nobody was able to get on the rock or leave the rock for months. One keeper and his family were supposed to leave the rock for their vacation early in the fall. They were not able to leave the rock until after Thanksgiving. On Thanksgiving Day, they were almost out of food and felt depressed because they had looked forward to eating a hearty Thanksgiving dinner. Thanksgiving morning was so foggy that two geese flew into the lighthouse tower and were killed. The keeper and his family had a wonderful Thanksgiving dinner. ❷

The most serious problems occurred when gales of wind swept waves across the ocean. To imagine the size and power of these waves, think of the height of the lighthouse tower—135 feet above the ocean. That's as tall as a 13-story building. During bad storms, the waves would crash *over* the tower of the lighthouse and even hurl rocks that weighed 100 pounds into the lighthouse lens. The water would flow from the tower down into the keeper's home.

Because the lighthouse was more expensive to maintain than any other lighthouse in the world, it was officially closed in 1957. It's still standing and is listed as a place of historical interest. The lower parts of the rock now serve as a home for sea lions and the upper parts as a nesting place for sea gulls. ❸

Terrible Tilly is now a cemetery. It houses the ashes of hundreds of cremated people. Some call these people "The Keepers of the Lighthouse."

1 | sub   dis   un   re   tri   pre

2 | **less**   hopeless   fearless

pointless   regardless   hatless

3 | outsk<u>ir</u>ts   introdu<u>c</u>ed   <u>ex</u>cuse

thoughtful<u>ly</u>   inst<u>ea</u>d

4
1. hazy
2. arranged
3. scurried

5 | damaged   trousers   sprouted   entertain

noticed   actually   ain't   hesitation

recreational   device   landscape

indicated   vehicle   suspenders

washtub   glory   dynamite   special

6

Go for the Glory Hole

Milly was in Sacramento the following afternoon. The landscape ⁹
was flat and the sun was hot. She tried to see the mountains to the ²⁴
east. Her map indicated the mountains were not far away, but the ³⁶
hazy air over the city blocked her view of the mountains. Milly ⁴⁸
arranged for a driver to bring her four-wheel-drive pickup from the ⁵⁹
recreational vehicle place to the airport. With the help of three airport ⁷¹
maintenance men, she mounted the laser in the bed of the pickup. ⁸³
Then she checked the laser to make sure it hadn't been damaged ⁹⁵
during the trip. After loading her gear into the truck, she drove to the ¹⁰⁹
address of her guide, whose name was Gregory Hicks. He lived in a ¹²²
small white house on the outskirts of Sacramento. She parked the ¹³³
pickup in his driveway and knocked on his door. ❶ ¹⁴²

He looked exactly as she expected. Milly had discovered a long time ¹⁵⁴
before that people's voices usually don't indicate how people look. A ¹⁶⁵
man with a big husky voice could be small. A woman with an ¹⁷⁸
old-sounding voice could be young. But Milly figured Mr. Hicks would ¹⁸⁹
be an exception, and she was right. There he was, standing in the ²⁰²
doorway, dressed in baggy trousers and suspenders. A gray stubby ²¹²
beard sprouted from his chin; what hair he had on his head was white. ²²⁶
He was not wearing shoes, simply gray socks with red toes. "Howdy," ²³⁸
he said. "What can I do for you?" ❷ ²⁴⁶

Milly introduced herself, and Mr. Hicks invited her in. "You'll have ²⁵⁷
to excuse the mess," he said, waving his arm. "I live by myself and I ²⁷²
don't have much call to entertain people." The inside of the house was ²⁸⁵
indeed a mess. Dirty clothes were draped over the backs of two ²⁹⁷
well-worn easy chairs. A dog was sleeping on the matching couch, next ³⁰⁹

to an untidy pile of newspapers. There were dirty glasses and dishes   321
scattered around the room.   325

"As you can see, it ain't much of a watchdog," Mr. Hicks said,   338
pointing to the dog, who was now looking at Milly without moving its   351
head from the couch. Mr. Hicks then scurried to the couch, tossed the   364
pile of papers on the floor, slapped the dog gently on the rump, and   378
said, "Get on the floor where you belong, Doctor. Can't you see this   391
young woman wants to sit down?" ❸   397

"No, no," Milly said very sincerely. "I've been sitting for hours. I'd   409
much rather stand."   412

Mr. Hicks explained why he named the dog Doctor. "Thought it   423
would grow up to be something special if I gave it a high-class name,   437
but I guess that didn't work." Doctor was a large hound dog with   450
drooping eyes and ears. It walked over to Milly, sniffed her left shoe,   463
slowly looked up at her, and returned to its warm spot on the couch.   477

"Let's talk about tomorrow," Milly said. So that's what Milly and   488
Mr. Hicks did for the next few hours. Milly explained that she had   501
developed a gold-finding device. Mr. Hicks laughed. When he did,   511
Milly noticed that most of his teeth were missing. ❹   520

"Sure," Mr. Hicks continued thoughtfully, "I must have seen twenty   530
to thirty gold-finding devices in my day. I've seen divining rods. I've   542
seen dynamite devices. I've seen 'em all. And one thing you can say for   556
them: One works just about as good as the others. They don't work at   570
all—no how."   573

Milly didn't try to convince Mr. Hicks that her device actually did   585
work. Instead she went over the schedule for the next morning. She   597
took out her map and asked Mr. Hicks where he thought there would   610
be some gold. "Well," he said, rubbing his beard. "You can go after   623
bits and pieces, or you can go after a glory hole. Mind you, I don't   638

think you'll find a glory hole, but that don't mean you can't look for   652
one." Mr. Hicks explained that there are bits of gold in some of the   666
streams and that some people make a good living sifting through the   678
sand and gravel of the streambed for these bits. "With gold at about   691
six hundred dollars an ounce, you can make a pretty good living with   704
a few bits of gold. But gold don't come from streams; streams just   717
wash the gold from the rock in the mountains. That's where the real   730
gold is—up in them mountains—and if you're lucky, you'll find you a   744
pocket of gold chunks. Maybe that pocket is as big as a washtub. And   758
it ain't nothing but gold. That's what you call a glory hole. When you   772
find one of them glory holes, you never have to work another day in   786
your life."   788

"Let's go for the glory hole," Milly said without hesitation. ❺   798

1 | sub   dis   un   re   tri   pre

2 | **less**   groundless   meaningless
purposeless   motionless

3 | county   frequently   glancing   ahead   expect   replaced

4 |
1. impressive
2. rig
3. trough
4. speck
5. hailed
6. amusing
7. jostled

5 | bouncing   balance   ounce   suggested
convincing   occasionally   stared   equipment
continued   sluice   couple
shovelfuls   search   scraped

6

In Search of Gold

At seven the next morning, Mr. Hicks and Milly were turning off a   13
country road to follow a stream up into the foothills. The pickup   25
moved along slowly, bouncing over rocks alongside the stream and   35
sometimes going through parts of the shallow stream. Mr. Hicks was   46
driving, while Milly sat next to him, and Doctor rode in the bed,   59
sniffing the air. Milly looked out the back window frequently to make   71
sure that her laser was not being jostled too much. "Never have seen a   85
rig like that one before," Mr. Hicks said, glancing back at the laser.   98
"Thought I'd seen 'em all, but that one takes first prize. Sure looks   111
impressive."   112

"Is there gold in this stream we're following?" Milly asked.   122

"Oh, sure," Mr. Hicks said. "Might find half an ounce if you   134
panned. Might get three times that much with a sluice." ❶   144

Milly was about to ask what a sluice was when Hicks pointed ahead.   157
"Lookie there. There's some fellers with a sluice."   165

Two men were working in a place where the streambed was quite   177
narrow. They had built a long trough of wood. A pipe took water   190
from farther up the river and dumped it at one end of the trough. The   205
water flowed through the trough and spilled out the other end. The   217
men were dumping shovelfuls of sand from the bottom of the stream   229
into the trough. They were sifting through the sand as the water in the   243
trough flowed over it. After sifting through several shovelfuls of sand,   254
the men scraped the old sand from the trough and replaced it with   267
several fresh shovelfuls of sand from the streambed. ❷   275

Mr. Hicks said, "Those <u>boys</u> will get themselves a couple of specks   287
from that sluice."   290

High cliffs rose from each side of the narrow streambed, and the 302

sluice blocked the only place that the truck could pass. "We can't get 315

around them," Mr. Hicks said, stopping the truck. He stepped out of 327

the truck, and Doctor jumped from the pickup bed. "Hi, boys," he 339

hailed. "Looks like we got us a problem. Can't get by your sluice." 352

"That's your problem," one of the men replied. "We're not about to 364

take this rig down so you can get by." 373

"I can see your point," Mr. Hicks said. Milly was out of the truck 387

now. She asked, "Won't they move their sluice so we can pass?" 399

"Don't hardly think so," Mr. Hicks said as the men returned to 411

working their sluice. "Take them maybe an hour to set that sluice up 424

again after we pass. Can't hardly expect them to do that." ❸ 435

Milly walked up to the men. Neither looked up at her. One was 448

scraping sand that had already been sifted from the sluice bed. The 460

other man was standing ankle deep in the shallow stream, waiting to 472

shovel fresh sand into the sluice. 478

Milly said, "Would you move the sluice if I help you find enough 491

gold?" 492

The man standing in the water smiled sarcastically. "Sure," he said 503

flatly. "You help us find lots and lots of gold and we'll move the sluice 518

for you." 520

"How much is lots and lots of gold?" Milly asked. 530

"An ounce," the man said and shook his head. Then he scooped a 543

shovelful of sand into the sluice. 549

"Get ready to move that sluice then," Milly said. She climbed into 561

the bed of the pickup truck, uncovered the laser, and prepared the 573

metal detector and her other equipment. The two men, Mr. Hicks, 584

and Doctor stared at her. She pointed the laser at the riverbank next 597

to the truck and slowly began to swing it around. "Don't stand in 610

front of that beam," she said without looking at the men. She abruptly 623
stopped moving the beam. "There," she said. "Mr. Hicks, dig in that 635
spot where the beam is pointing, and you'll find a bit of gold that is 650
probably a fourth of an ounce." 656

Mr. Hicks didn't move. Then he and the other two men began to 669
laugh at the same time. Mr. Hicks slapped himself on the leg and said, 683
"If that don't beat all." He continued laughing. 691

"I'm serious," Milly said. "The gold is probably about a foot under 703
the sand." 705

"I'll just bet it is," Mr. Hicks said in an amused tone. But he didn't 720
move. ❹ 721

1

Mauna Kea   height   Whitney

impressive   frozen   compared

temperature   serious   Hawaii   world

ascend   Yosemite   conterminous

Anchorage   necessarily   ascend

2

1. sea level
2. peak
3. volcano
4. Himalayas
5. sheer
6. amazement

3

Many Mountains

The United States has many beautiful mountains, some of which tower more than 13,700 feet above sea level. Mount Whitney, in California, is the tallest mountain in the conterminous forty-eight states. (The forty-eight conterminous states have a common boundary, and they made up the United States before Alaska and Hawaii became states.) Mount Whitney climbs to a height of 14,494 feet. Mount Rainier, in the state of Washington, stands 14,410 feet above sea level and is the second-highest peak in the forty-eight conterminous states. The third-highest mountain in these states is Mount Shasta, in California. Mount Shasta stands 14,162 feet above sea level. Both Mount Rainier and Mount Shasta are volcanoes that were active thousands of years ago. ❶

The highest mountain in North America is Mount McKinley. It lies between the cities of Anchorage and Fairbanks, in Alaska. It rises to a height of 20,320 feet or almost four miles above sea level. Mount McKinley is very impressive, with massive ice flows and high cliffs. It is small, however, compared with the highest mountain on Earth, Mount Everest. Mount Everest is in the Himalaya range of Asia, on the border between the countries of Tibet and Nepal. It is 29,028 feet, or more than five and a half miles high. At the top of the mountain the temperature is very low and there is very little oxygen. A few groups of climbers have reached the top of Everest, but several members of these parties have paid for the climb with frozen toes, frozen fingers, and serious illnesses. ❷

Although Everest stands higher above sea level than any other mountain in the world, it is not the mountain that is highest from base to summit. Mauna Kea, a mountain in Hawaii, rises to 13,796 feet above sea level. However, measured from its true base under the water, Mauna Kea is 33,480 feet high, or more than six miles high. This measurement makes Mauna Kea 4,452 feet higher than Mount Everest.

The largest and tallest mountains are not necessarily the most beautiful. Some mountains that are famous for their beauty are less than 10,000 feet high. One face of Half Dome, a mountain in Yosemite National Park in California, is only 2,000 feet high. It is one of the most impressive mountains in the world, however, because it rises straight up from the floor of Yosemite Valley. From bottom to top, the sheer face of Half Dome is almost as straight as the walls of a building. Every year many experienced climbers scale Half Dome, and campers and tourists watch with amazement as the climbers ascend the sheer face. ❸

1 ly pre less dis

2 angri*ly* *pre*tended alr*ea*dy

motion*less* cl*ea*red

3
1. irritated
2. antics
3. expression
4. scan
5. dismantled
6. manner

4 daydreaming caught examining

invitation pleasure located

through trough touched fours

waved embarrassed scenery

supposed clowning jostled chili

5   Convincing the Miners

Milly was becoming irritated. She had located a piece of gold, but   12
Mr. Hicks didn't believe that she had.   19

"Mr. Hicks," Milly said angrily, "you're supposed to be working for   30
me. Now take your shovel and dig down in the spot where the beam   44
touched the ground."   47

"Yes, ma'am," Mr. Hicks said. He then pretended to move very fast   59
toward the spot, but he was simply clowning around. The two men   71
operating the sluice were laughing at his antics. Mr. Hicks began to   83
dig. He dug out three or four shovelfuls of sand. "Tell me when to stop   98
digging," he said, "unless, of course, that nugget is in China." ❶   109

"Stand back," Milly said. "I'll tell you if the piece is in the sand   123
you've already dug out." She turned the beam on the sand piled next   136
to the hole that Mr. Hicks had dug. "Yes," she said. "It's in that pile,   151
near the left side."   155

"Well, I'll sure find 'er," Mr. Hicks hollered in a comic manner. He   168
got down on all fours and made a great show of sifting through the   182
sand. Suddenly, his expression changed. ❷ Very slowly he held up a   193
very small stone. He spat on the stone and rubbed it. For a moment he   208
stared at it. Then he said, almost to himself, "I don't believe it." Then,   222
more loudly, "I don't believe it." He stood up and faced the men who   236
operated the sluice. "It's real," he shouted. "I don't know how she did   249
it, but it's real gold, and it's a good one."   259

The two men stood motionless for a moment. Then one of them ran   272
over to Hicks while the other one <u>walked</u>. "Wow," the first man said   285
after examining the nugget. "It's real."   291

The three men passed the nugget around, saying such things as "I   303
don't know how she did it" and "It's real."   312

Milly felt pretty proud. She stood there in the bed of the truck   325
looking at the men and feeling the clear morning breeze. The sun was   338
bright and hot, but the air was still quite cool. Beyond the sluice, the   352
streambed rose steeper and steeper into the mountain. For a moment,   363
Milly forgot about the gold and enjoyed the beautiful scenery. She   374
caught herself daydreaming and said, "Well, let's get on with it. We   386
still have about three-fourths of an ounce to find."   395

Milly turned on the laser beam and continued to scan the area near   408
the truck. Suddenly, she stopped scanning and said, "There's another   418
one, right there. It's bigger than the first one, but I think it's deeper." 432

Mr. Hicks began to run to the spot. ❸ One of the men from the   446
sluice beat him to the spot. "Take a break," he said to Mr. Hicks. "I'll 461
dig this one." He dug very fast. He stopped several times as Milly   474
trained the beam on the pile of sand he had dug to see whether he had   490
dug up the nugget.   494

After he had dug down about two feet, she told him that the nugget   508
was in the pile. "Near the very top of the pile," she said. And there it   524
was, a little bigger than the first nugget.   532

Milly helped the men locate two more nuggets. The last one was the   545
biggest. "There you are," Milly said to the men who operated the   557
sluice. "Now would you please move the sluice so that we can pass?"   570

"We sure will," one man said. "And thank you. I mean, thanks a lot.   584
And if you ever want to come back this way, we'll let you pass any   599
time. And if you want to come back for lunch, we're having some chili,   613
and we'd sure be pleased to share it with you." ❹   623

Milly felt a little embarrassed—not knowing what to say. "Thank   634
you for the invitation," she said politely. The men moved the water   646
pipe from the sluice and dismantled the sluice trough. Mr. Hicks   657
helped them. The men talked to Milly constantly as they worked.   668
They asked questions about the laser. They told her about places up   680

the bed that might have glory holes. They told her what a nice day it 695
would be. They told her about themselves. At last, a path was cleared 708
for the truck. ❺ 711

Each man shook hands with Milly. "We sure wish you all the luck 724
in the world," one man said as Milly got into the cab and Doctor 738
jumped into the bed. Then the men waved after the truck as it jostled 752
slowly alongside the streambed to the higher foothills. 760

Lesson 67

1

basical<u>ly</u>   ex<u>c</u>ited   adven<u>tu</u>re

<u>un</u>even   <u>dis</u>appeared   tr<u>ai</u>ned

2

1. adventurous
2. reliable
3. cascading
4. shimmering
5. grade
6. calculator
7. estimate

3

waterfalls   clouds   surface   beneath

brushed   repeated   blaster   procedure

interested   scientific   beautiful   dizzier

tried   terrific   dynamite   trailed

vertical   straight   series   deposit

4   Will They Strike It Rich?

Milly, half turned around in her seat so she could watch the laser in   14
the bed of the pickup, was becoming excited about the prospect of   26
finding a glory hole. She really wasn't too interested in becoming rich.   38
However, she was basically very adventurous, and this was a great   49
adventure. She was first—the first person to discover how to find gold   62
reliably with a scientific instrument. "This is really exciting," she   72
thought, as the truck bounced and jostled alongside the bed of the   84
stream. The grade was now becoming quite steep, and the stream,   95
which had moved slowly in the lower foothills, was now almost   106
cascading down the side of the mountain. The land alongside the   117
stream was becoming quite narrow and uneven, and the truck leaned   128
first to one side and then to the next as Mr. Hicks steered it alongside   143
the stream. At last he stopped and said, "Well, Dr. Jacobson, I think   156
we're at the end of the line." ❶   163

Milly looked out the front window. Ahead, the streambed rose   173
almost straight up, and the stream was a series of misty waterfalls.   185
When Milly looked back, she became a little dizzy. The truck had   197
been moving up a very steep grade, and now Milly could see how   210
steep it really was. Way, way below, she could see the place where the   224
two men had the sluice. The stream was a slim shimmering ribbon   236
that disappeared in a haze beyond the tiny speck that marked where   248
the sluice was. "What a beautiful sight," Milly said. She took a deep   261
breath and felt dizzier.   265

Mr. Hicks said, "The air's thin up here. Better take it easy at first <u>if</u>   280
you ain't used to it." ❷   285

"Good idea." Milly sat down next to the truck, which was leaning   297
to the right with the right wheels along the bank of the stream. Doctor   311

walked over to her and wagged its tail three times. Then Doctor   323
moved off to sniff for something to hunt.   331

"Do you think there are glory holes around here?" Milly asked.   342

"Sure there are," Mr. Hicks said. "Maybe not right in this spot, but   355
those specks of gold in the stream didn't come down from the clouds.   368
They came from up here someplace."   374

"Well, let's get on with it," Milly said, standing up. She brushed the   387
sand from the seat of her jeans. Then she climbed onto the bed of the   402
pickup and prepared the laser gun. She trained the gun on the rocks   415
that were on the right side of the truck. Nothing. The laser didn't read   429
a speck of gold. She turned the gun around and tried the rocks on the   444
other side of the truck. Again, not a speck.   453

"There's nothing here," she said.   458

"Well, then, we better start moving down because we ain't going to   470
move up." ❸   472

There wasn't enough space to turn the truck around, so Mr. Hicks   484
began to back down. He backed down about a hundred feet. Milly   496
tried the rock on either side of the truck. Nothing. Mr. Hicks backed   509
down another hundred feet and Milly tried again. This procedure was   520
repeated four more times, but the laser located only five bits of gold,   533
none of which was very big.   539

The seventh time Mr. Hicks backed down, things were different. ❹   549
The first spot where Milly pointed the laser gave a terrific reading. She   562
moved the laser to the right. Another terrific reading. She moved it to   575
the left and then up and down. Each time, the reading showed that   588
there was a great deposit of gold. "It's there," Milly said. "It's more   601
than a glory hole." She took more readings. She had Mr. Hicks drive   614
the truck forward. Then she pointed the laser to the same spots that   627
showed the great deposit of gold. She did this so that she could see   641
how big the deposit was and how far beneath the surface of the rock it   656

was. She took a pocket calculator from her pack and did some 668
calculations. At last she said, "That gold is six feet in the rock. I can't 683
estimate how much gold there is, but there is a lot—really a lot." ❺ 697

Mr. Hicks got out of the truck and walked toward the rock that 710
would have to be removed before the deposit was reached. "Hmmm," 721
he said, rubbing his hand over the almost vertical wall of rock. "The 734
only way to get through this rock is with dynamite. Hmmm." 745

"Can we do it?" Milly asked. 751

"I brung along some dynamite," Mr. Hicks replied, "but I ain't no 763
blaster. I've done some dynamiting, but . . ." His voice trailed off. 773
Then Mr. Hicks faced Milly and said, "Well, let's give it a try." ❻ 786

Lesson 68

1   **ness**   weakness   fitness   newness   boldness

2   interrupted   wound   explanation   motionless   reechoed

3
1. shorings
2. chisel
3. wick
4. impatient
5. initial
6. enlarged
7. assured

4   explained   examination   weakened

concealed   blaster   breathing   shaking

tumbling   closest   shrugged

layer   thunderous   reared   echo

scratched   chiseled   continued

struggled   attached   hazy

cube   cubic   downhill

5   Mr. Hicks, the Blaster

Mr. Hicks felt the cracks in the almost-vertical rock that concealed   11
the glory hole. He spat on the rock and rubbed that spot. He stood   25
back and looked at the wall of rock. Then he said, "Used to work with   40
an old boy named Elmer Tooley. That old boy was a blaster to end all   55
blasters. You'd tell old Elmer how much rock you wanted to drop, and   68
he'd set charges of dynamite. Boom. And if you told him to drop ten   82
cubic feet, you'd have ten cubic feet. If you told him to make a hole   97
five feet deep, you'd have a hole five feet deep." ❶   107

Milly was standing next to the truck. She said, "Well, that's   118
interesting, but—"   120

Mr. Hicks interrupted. "But I ain't no Elmer Tooley. Fact is, nobody   132
else is. That old boy could take on blasting jobs that nobody else   145
would touch. I remember one time when there was this mine. And the   158
shorings were weak. And old Elmer—"   164

"What are you trying to tell me?" Milly asked.   173

"I don't know if I can do 'er," Mr. Hicks said, shaking his head.   187
"That's hard rock, and it's steep. The wrong kind of blast might make   200
the whole side of the mountain come tumbling down." ❷   209

Milly didn't respond. She looked at the rock and then back at Mr.   222
Hicks. After a few moments, Mr. Hicks returned to his examination   233
of the cracks in the rocks. Then he scratched his head and went to the   248
truck. He returned with a chisel and a hammer. He chiseled four holes   261
in the rock. Each hole was about six feet from the hole closest to it,   276
and each hole <u>was</u> on a crack in the rock. Two of the holes were above   292
the glory hole, and two were below.   299

Then Mr. Hicks pulled three sticks of dynamite from his pack. He   311
said, "Now Elmer Tooley would set all four holes at the same time and   325

he could tell to the pound how much rock would fall. But I ain't no   340
Elmer Tooley, so I'm going to set them off one at a time. I just hope I   357
don't set too much in any hole." Mr. Hicks shrugged and stuffed the   370
three sticks of dynamite into the top hole on the right. He wound the   384
wicks of the dynamite sticks together. Then he connected a longer   395
wick to the wicks. As he worked, he explained to Milly why he wasn't   409
using blasting caps. Milly didn't follow his explanation, but Mr. Hicks   420
assured her four times, "This should work out OK." ❸   429

    Then he said, "We're ready. You'd better get uphill out of the way of   443
any falling rocks. I don't know what these rocks are going to do, so   457
we'd better get the truck out of the way, too." Mr. Hicks rubbed his   471
chin. He continued, "But if we have a slide and the truck is uphill,   485
we'll never get it back down. I'd better drive it way downhill where it's   499
out of the way."   503

    Mr. Hicks backed the truck downhill while Milly struggled uphill.   513
After she had gone about four hundred feet, she was breathing very   525
hard, and she felt dizzy. She sat on a rock and waited for Mr. Hicks to   541
return to the dynamite. She was becoming impatient as she watched   552
him get out of the truck and slowly start the climb to the dynamite.   566
Finally, he reached the blasting site. He waved to Milly, smiled, and lit   579
a match on the seat of his pants. He lit the wick that he had attached   595
to the shorter wicks, and then he began to run uphill, holding his hat   609
with one hand and calling, "Come on, Doctor, let's get out of here."   622
When he was still about fifty feet from Milly, the blast went off. It was   637
a very sharp sound that hurt Milly's ears. The initial sound was   649
followed by a deep, thunderous roar that echoed and reechoed from   660
the surrounding mountains. A large puff of light blue smoke spouted   671
from the rock and then fanned out, forming a hazy layer of smoke.   684
Milly then heard the sound of tiny bits of stone landing like raindrops   697
in the streambed.   700

Milly and Mr. Hicks ran down to the blasting spot. Nothing. The   712
blast had enlarged the hole that Mr. Hicks had made, but Milly could   725
see no new cracks in the rock or signs that the rock was weakened.   739

    "Maybe I should try four sticks in the next hole," Mr. Hicks said. ❹   752

Lesson 68

INFORMATION PASSAGE

fossil   pelvis   radioactive
elements   carbon

Why Did the Dinosaurs Vanish? Part 1

We know about dinosaurs from their
fossil remains. After some dinosaurs died,
their bones became buried under sand or
mud. Over millions of years, the material
on top of the bones became thicker and
thicker until the bones were buried far
below the surface of the earth. The
pressure was great, and over time the
bones turned into rock. They were still the
same shape and size they were when the
animal was living, but now they were
made of rock. They had turned into
fossils. ❶

There are different ways to determine
how long ago the dinosaurs lived. One
way is to look at the rock. You can see
layers of rock on the face of a cliff in
Wyoming or Arizona. The layers in which
dinosaur fossils are found are not near the
top of the cliff. The distance from the top
of the cliff indicates how old the fossils

are. Things close to the top of the cliff were put in the cliff recently. Things farther down were put in the cliff earlier.

The remains of dinosaurs are not near the top but are found only in layers that are far from the top. These rock layers show when the dinosaurs first appeared and when they vanished from Earth. ❷

When the remains of dinosaurs were first discovered in 1825, scientists thought they had found the remains of giant birds. That's because the pelvis of these dinosaurs looked like that of a bird. Much later, scientists accepted the idea that some dinosaurs had feathers and some of them were like the first birds.

Just because the rocks show us which dinosaurs lived first and which lived later, the rocks don't show how many years ago a particular dinosaur lived. Scientists have different ways of dating the age of rocks in which dinosaur remains are found. One of the more recent methods is called radioactive dating. Some elements are radioactive. The amount of radioactivity goes down over time. ❸

Scientists measure the amount of radioactivity in the rock where fossils are found and compare that to the amount of radioactivity in a rock that was recently buried. The less radioactivity in an older rock, the older that rock is. If the rock contains half of the amount of radioactive material found in a newly formed rock, the scientists know that the rock is about 5,800 years old. If the older rock contains only ¹⁄₆₄ the amount of the radioactive material found in the newly formed rock, the older rock is 5,800 times 6 years old. That's 34,800 years old. Only a very small amount of radioactive material is in rocks that contain dinosaur fossils. ❹

According to the current estimates, the earliest dinosaurs lived 230 million years ago. The last dinosaurs lived 65 million years ago.

All types of dinosaurs vanished at around the same time. This event seemed to have happened suddenly. Scientists came up with many theories about what could have caused so many animals and plants to vanish 65 million years ago. Some scientists thought the reason for the disappearance of the dinosaurs was that the climate changed. They found some evidence that there was a great climate change around the time the dinosaurs disappeared. But if the climate change occurred, what caused it, and how did it affect the plants and animals? ❺

1   **ness**   sickness   baldness   happiness   sadness

2   **tri**   **re**   **ly**   **un**   **sub**

3   triangular   reechoed   suddenly

heading   neither   revealed

4
1. glistening
2. scarcely
3. brilliance
4. flask

5   speechless   sparkling   crouched   sliding

scrambled   downward   downhill

stripped   jewelry   thickest   loose

whoopie   terrible   cough   deposit

aware   brilliant   golden

showcase   caught   visible

6

The Glory Hole

Mr. Hicks set four sticks of dynamite in the lower hole on the left. 14
Milly went uphill so that she would be out of the way if there was a 30
rock slide. This time she held Doctor as Mr. Hicks lit the wick. Mr. 44
Hicks scrambled up alongside the streambed, but before he reached 54
Milly, a terrible blast, much louder than the first, shook the ground. 66
But the rock looked almost as if nothing had happened. There was a 79
large triangular chunk of rock missing next to the hole formed by the 92
second blast, but the second blast apparently hadn't done much more. 103

Again Milly went uphill and waited with Doctor as Mr. Hicks set 115
the third blast, another four-stick blast. Again Mr. Hicks lit the wick 127
and scrambled up alongside the streambed. Again, the mountains 136
echoed and reechoed the sound of a great blast. When the smoke 148
cleared this time, however, Milly noticed that part of the mountain was 160
moving downward. It was sliding into the streambed. 168

"Oh, no," Mr. Hicks shouted above the crashing sound of the rock 180
as it peeled from the surface of the mountain and slid into the 193
streambed. "Shoot. There she goes." Mr. Hicks took off his hat and 205
threw it on the ground. He said how sorry he was that Elmer Tooley 219
wasn't around to do the blasting. ❶ 225

A great cloud of dust filled the streambed below. The rock had 237
stopped sliding, and the mountain was suddenly quiet. After the dust 248
had cleared some, Mr. Hicks and Milly went downhill to the blasting 260
site. The dust was still so thick near the blasting site that Milly 273
couldn't see where she was going. <u>She</u> began to cough. 283

"How much damage did that rock slide do?" Milly asked. 293

"I sure don't know," Mr. Hicks said. "That blast stripped off a lot of 307
rock, but it all depends on how it piled up. We may have to dig 322

through loose rock for a week before we reach the deposit." ❷ 333

A sudden breeze came up when Milly and Mr. Hicks reached the 345
pile of fresh rock in the streambed. As the breeze swept the dust away, 359
Milly and Mr. Hicks looked in the direction of the blasting site, 371
waiting for the dust to clear. Suddenly, Milly could see the spot. She 384
stood there for some time, but she wasn't sure how long. Everything 396
seemed to stand still. She wasn't aware of the breeze or the mountains 409
or Mr. Hicks, who was standing next to her with his mouth open. Her 423
eyes were fixed on a huge glistening mass of rock, sparkling with a 436
thousand sharp edges. Its color was gold, and it was so brilliant that 449
Milly could scarcely believe what she was seeing. It was glistening from 461
the side of the mountain like a giant golden eye, with more brilliance 474
than a jewel in a jewelry showcase. Still staring at the sight, Milly 487
moved her head to one side, and a thousand edges of gold caught the 501
sun and danced with sparkles. ❸ 506

Suddenly, Milly was aware that Mr. Hicks was talking. "Glory," he 517
said slowly. "Glory," he repeated. "Now I know why they call them 529
glory holes. I've never seen one before. Never seen nothin' like that in 542
all my born days. Never." 547

"Neither have I," Milly replied. She was almost speechless, still 557
staring at the huge gold deposit visible on the side of the cliff. The 571
deposit was shaped like a large flask turned on its side. It was at least 586
three feet wide in its thickest place. ❹ 593

"Here I am," Mr. Hicks was saying, "sixty-eight years old and 604
standing here looking at a glory hole. It's the most beautiful day there 617
ever was, in the most beautiful place in the whole world, and I'm 630
looking at the most beautiful sight that anyone could hope to look at." 643
He was talking faster now and starting to walk across the loose rock 656
toward the glory hole. "And who would think it? Me. Gregory 667
Hicks—who some folks think isn't worth his salt—would get to see 680

something like this. Would you believe it?" Now he was almost   691
shouting. "Well, dance me around the floor three times. This is my   703
day. Whoopie! My day," he shouted. ❺   709

He jumped up and down and began to talk and yell and sing. He   723
ran over to the glory hole and kissed the rock. Then he grabbed   736
Doctor and kissed the dog. Doctor ran uphill and crouched down   747
with its tail between its legs, as if to say, "Has my master lost his   762
mind?"   763

Milly began to laugh. Then she realized that there were tears in her   776
eyes. She was laughing and crying at the same time.   786

Lesson 70

1

amazing average full-grown

photographs Chamberlain Abdul-Jabbar

Kareem pituitary Iranian straight

doorway remember newborn

function greatest Delhi

2

1. coordinated
2. exaggerated
3. glands
4. abnormal

3

Human Height Records

People come in all sizes and shapes, but some of the record sizes and shapes are amazing. Professional basketball players sometimes stand a head taller than the average person. The average full-grown adult male in North America stands about 5 feet 9 inches tall. Wilt Chamberlain, who set more National Basketball Association records than any other basketball player, is 7 feet 1 inch tall. Another tall professional player was Kareem Abdul-Jabbar, who is 7 feet 2 inches tall. Although these men are referred to as giants, they are simply very tall people who are very well coordinated. ❶

Sometimes claims of height are exaggerated. The greatest exaggeration came from a professor who submitted photographs of an Iranian man 10 feet 5 inches tall. When the man was later measured at a hospital, he was only 7 feet 2 inches tall.

Lesson 70 **243**

Sometimes, when glands in the body do not function properly, a person will experience unusual growth patterns. An improper function of a gland in the brain called the pituitary gland can change an average-sized person into one who is abnormally small or abnormally large. The following people had pituitary gland problems. ❷

Zeng Jinlian of China is the tallest woman on record; she is 8 feet 1¾ inches tall. The tallest man on record was Robert Wadlow from Illinois. He continued to grow until his death at the age of twenty-two. By then he was 8 feet 11 inches tall. To get some idea of how tall that is, compare it to an average doorway. The top of this doorway would come to the middle of Robert's chest. The ceiling in most houses is 8 feet. Robert would not have been able to stand up straight in the average room. ❸

At the other extreme are people who are very small. The smallest full-grown adult was Gul Mohammad of Delhi, India, who was only 22½ inches tall. The most he ever weighed was 37½ pounds. To get an idea of how small Gul was, remember that is it not uncommon for newborn babies to be the same length as he was.

1   **ness**   **ly**   **less**   **pre**

2   foreh<u>ea</u>d   rev<u>ea</u>ling   m<u>ea</u>sured

<u>e</u>xpression   nu<u>dg</u>ing   sw<u>ea</u>ting

3
1. minerals
2. vein
3. greedy
4. stunted
5. nudge
6. area

4   cleared   description   throat   trailed

ain't   broadly   drained   realized

carefully   greatest   herd   trouble

aware   wagged   shimmering   stared

staked   terrific   guess   stunned

prospector   acres   public

5   Marking Off the Claim

The blast had been nearly perfect. It had peeled off a layer of rock $\quad$ 14
about thirty feet thick, revealing the glory hole. Mr. Hicks danced and $\quad$ 26
jumped and shouted for a few minutes. Then he said, "That's a terrific $\quad$ 39
blasting job. Fact is, I don't think Elmer Tooley could have done much $\quad$ 52
better—faster maybe, but not better." $\quad$ 58

Suddenly, Mr. Hicks slapped himself on the forehead and said, $\quad$ 68
"Oh, no. I never thought of that." $\quad$ 75

"What?" Milly asked. $\quad$ 78

"The claim," Mr. Hicks replied. "I never did seriously think that $\quad$ 89
you'd find any gold, so I just wasn't thinking about a claim. But . . ." $\quad$ 102
his voice trailed off and he stared at the vein of shimmering gold $\quad$ 115
visible on the side of the cliff. "But—," he continued slowly, "I guess $\quad$ 128
that we shouldn't have much trouble." $\quad$ 134

He explained to Milly how claims work. When people discover a $\quad$ 145
good find on public land, they can reserve twenty acres for their claim. $\quad$ 158
If they discover a vein, they can claim more than twenty acres. Mr. $\quad$ 171
Hicks said, "But I think we can get by with twenty acres. We just have $\quad$ 186
to be careful about marking it off so that we'll be sure to get all the $\quad$ 202
gold. Why be greedy?" He smiled. Doctor wagged its tail. ❶ $\quad$ 212

Marking off the claim took most of the day. The biggest problem, $\quad$ 224
Mr. Hicks explained, was to make sure the claim was well staked off $\quad$ 237
so he could mark it correctly on his map. "Many prospectors have lost $\quad$ 250
their claims because they didn't mark the map carefully," Mr. Hicks $\quad$ 261
explained. "Twenty acres is not a big area, and at the recording office, $\quad$ 274
they give you a claim according to your description of the claim. They $\quad$ 287
don't come out and look at your claim. They just record the $\quad$ 299

<u>information</u> you give them. If you don't mark the claim just right on 312
the map, you may have no claim at all." ❷ 321

Mr. Hicks took a large roll of string from the pickup. He measured 334
the distance from the stream to the cliff. Then he measured off about 347
three hundred yards along the cliff. The afternoon sun was hot. Milly 359
sat near the stream under a stunted tree. Doctor was resting next to 372
her, nudging her from time to time. Each time the dog nudged her, she 386
patted it on the head, and it wagged its tail two or three times. 400

At last Mr. Hicks said, "I think I've got it marked on the map." He 415
showed the map to Milly. Mr. Hicks explained that he marked the 427
claim so that the glory hole was right in the middle of the twenty 441
acres. "This claim ain't too hard to mark," Mr. Hicks said, "because 453
the cliff is easy to see on the map." 462

Before leaving the claim, Mr. Hicks and Milly made large piles of 474
stones at each corner of the claim. Mr. Hicks drove a stake into the 488
pile that was closest to the glory hole. He wrote a note that said, 502
"Twenty acres claimed by Milly Jacobson for gold and other minerals." 513
Then Mr. Hicks wrote the date and his address in Sacramento. He 525
stuffed the note into a tin can and placed it on top of the stake. ❸ 540

"Well, that does it," Mr. Hicks said, sweating freely. His shirt was 552
wet, and sweat was dripping down his face. "Yep, that does it." 564

Before leaving the claim, Milly and Mr. Hicks picked up the loose 576
chunks of gold and put them in a large cloth sack. "My, my," Mr. 590
Hicks said when the bag was almost filled. "I have never seen more 603
gold in one place before in my entire life." 612

As Milly and Mr. Hicks drove back down alongside the streambed, 623
past the place where the sluice had been, and back to the highway that 637
led to Sacramento, the sun was setting. Milly felt very tired—drained. 649
She had trouble keeping her eyes open as the hum of the truck engine 663
seemed to lull her to sleep. Suddenly, she became aware of Mr. Hicks 676

saying, "Well, here we are." Milly opened her eyes and realized that   688
the truck was parked in front of Mr. Hicks's house.   698

Milly took a piece of paper from her shoulder bag. As she wrote, she   712
said, "I want you to file the claim in the following way. I want one-third   727
of the claim to go to my university, one-third to go to the state of   742
California, and one-third to go to you." She handed Mr. Hicks the note.   755

Mr. Hicks stared at Milly with a stunned expression. ❹ "You   765
mean—" he said and stopped to clear his throat. "You mean you'd   777
give me part of your claim after I made fun of you—after I gave you   793
such a . . ."   795

Milly smiled and said, "I never would have found it without you."   807

"But," Mr. Hicks said, "there's nothing left for you. You gave your   819
whole claim away."   822

"Oh, there's plenty for me," Milly said, smiling very broadly. "I had   834
about the greatest time I ever had in my life." ❺   844

1

amazing<u>ly</u> villa<u>g</u>es popula<u>tion</u>

basical<u>ly</u> vegeta<u>tion</u> e<u>x</u>tremely

2

1. reduced
2. resident
3. capable
4. deceive
5. effective

3

rhinoceros elephant impala extinct

lion predators leopard antelope

wounded buffalo African favorite

designed series destroyed temple

heroes species welcomed equipped

thicket delicate frequently

4   # Dangerous African Animals—Part 1

Today many species of African animals are in danger of becoming   11
extinct. The lion, which used to hunt in many parts of Africa, is now found   26
in fewer places. Other African animals have followed the same pattern. The   38
African elephant, the African Cape buffalo, the rhinoceros, and the   48
leopard—all have been reduced in numbers. All could become extinct.   59

Not long ago there were so many wild animals in some parts of   72
Africa that the people living in those areas were in great danger. Big   85
game hunters were welcomed in villages where wild animals had been   96
killing the residents. Today we think of the big game hunter as one   109
who kills for the sport of it. But around 1900, when the population of   123
Africa was growing and the people were trying to build farms, some   135
big game hunters were heroes. They went to places where elephants   146
had destroyed crops that farmers had planted. They hunted down the   157
elephants and shot them. They went to places where lions were killing   169
people, and they hunted down the lions. ❶   176

When the sport of big game hunting in Africa was popular, there were   189
many arguments about which of the big game animals was the most   201
dangerous. The animals that were most frequently argued about were the   212
elephant, the lion, the rhinoceros, the Cape buffalo, and the leopard. ❷   223
Which animals do you think would be the most dangerous to hunt? After   236
reading the rest of the parts in this series, you may change your mind.   250

Before we look at some facts about which is the most dangerous   262
African animal, we should discuss some points about all African   272
animals. Basically there are two types of animals in Africa—grazing   283
animals and predators. ❸ The same two types lived millions of years   294
ago when triceratops and tyrannosaurs <u>roamed</u> the plain. Even the   304
most innocent-looking grazing animal in Africa is equipped to survive.   314

A delicate-looking antelope is quite capable of killing a person. The · 325
impala is a delicate-looking animal that survives by fast moves and · 336
high kicks. When a startled impala leaps, it gives two kicks. The first · 349
kick hurls the impala into the air. That kick has enough force to shoot · 363
the impala up about ten feet high, and the second kick has as much · 377
force as the first. The impala is capable of delivering a kick powerful · 390
enough to punch holes into any enemy chasing directly behind it. · 401

The fight for survival has made all African animals tough. Their looks · 413
may deceive you, but just remember that without effective defenses they · 424
wouldn't survive in a place filled with predators and other dangers. Some · 436
animals run very fast. Some are very strong and can fight off their enemies. · 450
Those that are designed to kill other animals are very good killers. ❹ · 462

Let's look at the big game animals one at a time and see just how · 477
dangerous each one would be to hunt. We'll begin with the biggest · 489
grazing animal, the African elephant. It stands ten feet tall and weighs · 501
as much as 12,000 pounds. It has huge tusks that may be six feet long. · 516
These tusks are very, very hard. It can run amazingly fast for its · 529
size—perhaps 30 miles an hour. And it is so strong that it could roll · 544
over a car as easily as you could overturn a chair. ❺ · 555

One more thing about the African elephant: It is extremely smart. A · 567
wounded elephant will use many tricks to trap its hunter. Perhaps its · 579
favorite trick is to leave a very clear trail into an area of dense bush, · 594
such as a thorn thicket. When the hunter enters the thicket, the · 606
elephant attacks. Because the vegetation is very dense, the hunter · 616
cannot see the elephant. With its head down, the elephant charges, · 627
knocking down the bush in front of it. This vegetation, which may be · 640
fifteen feet tall, hits and flattens the hunter. The hunter does not have · 653
a chance to take aim at the elephant. ❻ · 661

So the elephant can be very dangerous to hunt. But the elephant is not · 675
the most dangerous African animal. In the next part we will see why. · 688

INFORMATION PASSAGE

Cretaceous   atmosphere   meteor
devastation   iridium

Why Did the Dinosaurs Vanish? Part 2

Today, scientists agree about what happened to kill off the dinosaurs. The evidence that they found was a thin layer of dust that had a very rare element in it—iridium. They found iridium all around the world just above the rocks that had the last fossil remains of dinosaurs.

Some scientists believed that some kind of great disaster occurred and that billions of tons of iridium dust were hurled into the atmosphere. The dust blocked the sunlight, killing most of the plants and most of the animals that lived on Earth.

The problem with this explanation is that rocks on Earth do not contain iridium. Therefore, the dust must have come from outer space. Some scientists thought it could have been from a large meteor that struck Earth. Meteors contain iridium. The problem with this explanation was that such a meteor would have left a giant crater in the surface of Earth, miles and miles wide and hundreds of feet deep. Somewhere in that crater would be the remains of this huge meteor.

Scientists could find no such place. They knew of one place in Mexico that had a crater that is 112 miles wide, but there were no signs of a meteor; however, there were large deposits of nickel and iron particles in the crater. Nickel and iron are the basic elements found in meteors. ❶

At last the scientists figured out that the crater in Mexico was the one that caused the dinosaurs to vanish. At the end of the Cretaceous period, a meteor six miles wide streaked toward Earth at 40,000 miles per hour. It passed through the atmosphere so fast that it exploded just before it hit Earth. It had the impact of a million atomic bombs, and it blew millions of tons of particles into the atmosphere. There was so much dust in the air that the sky was totally dark for at least two years. Then a thin layer of iridium settled to the surface of the earth. Dinosaurs like Tekla starved because the plants they ate died. Other dinosaurs died from the cold that occurred after the great explosion. ❷

Among the survivors of this incredible climate change was a curious small animal, one of the earliest mammals. **During the Cretaceous period, mammals could not hunt during the day because they could not compete with dinosaurs for food. The small mammals were able to hunt in the dark because they had night vision. Dinosaurs could not hunt during the night because they had no form of night vision. The small mammals were warm-blooded so they could withstand the cold and survive the devastation at the end of the Cretaceous period. These animals were the remote ancestors of the mammals that live today. ❸**

Lesson 73

1 un pre ness less ly

2 extremely crouched weapons

situation claws raises

3
1. retreat
2. evolution
3. strides
4. bounding
5. hurtle
6. enormous

4 positions clever overhanging tusks

designed capable biting reports

thicket strength dense weight

actual incredibly tremendous keen

strangling growling effective pride

5 Dangerous African Animals—Part 2

The only animal that will make the African elephant retreat is the 12
ant. Indeed, any animal retreats when millions of biting and stinging 23
ants attack. An elephant can kill a lion or a Cape buffalo or step on a 39
leopard and crush it. But the elephant is not the most dangerous 51
animal for a person to hunt. Why? Because an elephant is big, and it 65
makes an easy target. The elephant is dangerous when a hunter tracks 77
it into a dense thicket, but then any animal can be dangerous in this 91
situation. All animals use clever tricks to kill their hunters, and the 103
elephant is no different. It has keen senses—good eyes, ears, and a 116
sense of smell—but it makes a very big target. An elephant cannot lie 130
down in the tall grass of the plain and hide from the hunter the way a 146
leopard can. ❶ 148

The hunter who cannot hit a target as big as an elephant should not 162
be a hunter. The hunter may have to use a very powerful rifle, but one 177
well-placed shot will kill an elephant. A bullet that hits the front of 190
the skull will not kill an elephant and probably won't hurt it, because 203
the front of an elephant's skull is very thick. But the side of its skull 218
(the temple) is very thin, so a bullet in the temple will kill it. Also, a 234
bullet hitting its neck or between its tusks will kill it. 245

Let's look at another dangerous animal, the lion. Through millions 255
of years of evolution the lion has developed into an expert predator. 267
The lion cannot run long distances, because after going a few hundred 279
yards it runs out of breath. But for short dashes it is extremely fast. 293
Starting from a crouched position, the lion can be running at a rate of 307
30 miles per hour after taking only a few strides. It can run a hundred 322
yards in about four seconds. A lion is incredibly strong. And it can lie 336
flat in tall grass or hide fairly well in a small thicket. ❷ 348

The lion can be very dangerous to hunt. Let's say that a hunter is walking across the plain and a four-hundred-pound lion is in the brush a hundred yards away. Suddenly the lion charges the hunter. It takes the hunter a second to realize what is happening. Soon the lion, moving at top speed, is only about two hundred feet away. The hunter raises a rifle and tries to aim at the form bounding toward the hunter through the shoulder-high grass. By now the lion is one hundred feet away. The hunter fires a shot and misses. Quickly the hunter takes aim again. The lion seems to be a bigger target than it actually is because its mane makes its head look twice its actual size. The lion is twenty feet away and is leaping toward the hunter. In panic the hunter shoots again. Even if the bullet hits its mark, the hunter might be killed. The lion, four hundred pounds of muscle and bone moving at 30 miles per hour, could hurtle into the hunter with enough force to kill the hunter. ❸

The lion has long claws that can cut like knives, and it has enormous teeth that can crush. Even more important than these weapons is the lion's tremendous strength. According to reports, a lion can leap over a ten-foot fence while carrying an animal of three hundred pounds in its jaws. The lion's neck muscles are so strong that it can toss a two-hundred-pound wart hog as if it were tossing a rag doll. ❹ Just one cuff from a lion's paw could break your neck or crush your ribs, but the lion is designed to kill animals that are far more powerful than humans. The lion can kill these animals in an instant. For instance, the lion can bring down a powerful antelope by grabbing the animal at the neck, biting its throat, and strangling it.

Yes, the lion is probably more dangerous to hunt than the elephant, but the lion is not the most dangerous African animal. The lion lives in a group of lions called a pride. A lion is very lazy and usually sleeps about twenty hours a day. A hunter can often find a lion snoozing with others in its pride. Although the lion can hide in the grass, it

gives away its position by roaring and growling. Even when the lion 747
retreats into the brush, the hunter can often locate its position by 759
throwing rocks into the brush. The lion's response—growling—will 769
give its position away. The lion is smart, it can kill, and it is dangerous 784
to the hunter; but the lion is not Africa's *most* dangerous animal. ❺ 796

1 **sub   dis   ness   re   tri**

2 l<u>ea</u>thery   harm<u>less</u>   p<u>ur</u>sue

dr<u>aw</u>   selec<u>tion</u>   actual<u>ly</u>

3
1. ill-tempered
2. matted
3. glance
4. confused
5. strategy
6. tick

4 ruled   cousin   weapons   ivory

suddenly   eyesight   neither   impossible

probably   dodging   frequently

remarkable   conclusion   ridge   instead

incredibly   fault   snout   discussed

pounding   bony   gored   trampled

5 Dangerous African Animals—Part 3

We have discussed the African elephant and the lion. Both can be   12
very dangerous to the hunter, but neither one is the most dangerous   24
African animal. Let's look at the rhinoceros. It is mean, ill-tempered,   35
and huge. An adult rhinoceros may weigh 3,500 pounds. Although it   46
cannot move as fast as the elephant, its top speed is about 20 miles per   61
hour. ❶ But it will attack anything—even an elephant. The rhinoceros   72
has two large horns on its snout. These are strange horns because they   85
are not made of ivory as the elephant's tusks are. They are made of   99
hair. The hair is matted together, forming horns so hard that a   111
rhinoceros could easily punch a hole in the side of a car.   123

The rhinoceros is probably the least dangerous of the African   133
animals—at least for the hunter. The rhinoceros has very poor eyesight   145
but a good sense of smell and of hearing. It uses tickbirds for its eyes.   160
These birds ride around on its back and sides, picking ticks from the   173
folds of its leathery hide. The tickbirds have very good eyes—when   185
something moves nearby, the tickbirds take off, giving an alarm call.   196
When the tickbirds fly away, the rhinoceros knows that danger is near. ❷   208

The rhinoceros has many other faults. It will charge at anything.   219
Once the rhinoceros puts its head down and begins to charge, it heads   232
straight forward. During such a charge, the hunter might be able to   244
step to one side, and the rhinoceros would go pounding right past the   257
hunter. The rhinoceros would then turn and again charge blindly with   268
its head down. The hunter could keep dodging the rhinoceros until   279
the rhinoceros got tired of the game.   286

Don't draw the conclusion, however, that the rhinoceros is a   296
harmless animal. If the hunter wounds the rhinoceros, it will trot off   308
into the bush and hide, waiting for the hunter. It may wait until the   322

hunter is in a place that makes it impossible to dodge the rhinoceros.   335

❸ The rhinoceros may wait until the hunter is only about fifteen feet   347
away—then charge. It doesn't make an easy target with its head down.   360
If a bullet hits the rhinoceros on its bony skull with its huge horns, the   375
bullet will glance off. But if a rhinoceros hits the hunter, that hunter   388
will be dead within seconds. The victim will be knocked down, gored   400
by the rhinoceros's horns, and trampled. Although the rhinoceros may   410
not be the most dangerous animal, it is still very dangerous.   421

We have ruled out the elephant, the lion, and the rhinoceros as the   434
most dangerous African animal. The two animals that remain are the   445
Cape buffalo and the leopard. At the beginning of this series you   457
probably didn't pick either of these animals, but they are very   468
dangerous to hunt. Consider the Cape buffalo. It is big and fast, and it   482
probably has the best senses of any African animal. Its eyesight and   494
sense of smell are incredibly keen, and its hearing is remarkable. With   506
these senses the Cape buffalo can keep far away from any hunter who   519
is trying to pursue it. It can spot a hunter at a remarkable distance   533
and avoid the hunter for days. The Cape buffalo can do a lot more   547
than stay away from the hunter; it can kill. ❹   556

People frequently confuse the African Cape buffalo with its cousin,   566
the Indian water buffalo. The African Cape buffalo looks quite a bit   578
like its Indian cousin, but the African Cape buffalo has larger horns   590
that form a ridge across its forehead and then arch back and out. Each   604
horn is about twenty inches long. The African Cape buffalo is also   616
bigger and more powerful than its Indian cousin. It can easily kill a   629
lion. The African Cape buffalo's usual strategy is to pretend it is   641
running from the lion. The lion will run after the buffalo. The buffalo   654
will allow the lion to catch up, so that the lion is running alongside   668
the buffalo. Just as the lion is ready to make its leap onto the buffalo's   683

back, the buffalo suddenly slows down and swings its head down and   695
toward the lion. The buffalo's horn goes into the lion's body. ❺   706

    The African Cape buffalo is a remarkable animal. We will examine   717
it further in part 4.   722

1
New Orleans   false   poisonous   cobra

deaf   mamba   wading   Australia

moccasin   heaviest   India   anaconda

squeezing   true   swamps   assortment   varieties

2
1. trance
2. venom
3. aggressive
4. coiling
5. comparison

3

Snakes

Some stories told about snakes are true, but many are false.

Take the question of speed. The black mamba of Africa is the fastest snake, but reports that it can move faster than a horse are untrue. Experts believe that this poisonous snake, which grows to 14 feet, can glide for a short distance at about 15 miles per hour, or about as fast as most people can run. Because of its size and speed, it is also capable of slithering over walls as high as 10 feet. ❶

The longest and heaviest snakes are not poisonous. They are constrictor snakes that kill their victims by coiling around them and crushing them.

One of the longest snakes ever found was a South American anaconda that was 37½ feet long, or the length of two full-sized cars parked end to end. The monster weighed about 1,100 pounds and was able to crush its prey with a force of more than 30 tons.

The most poisonous snakes of the ocean and the land are found near Australia.

The most poisonous ocean snake is the sea snake, which lives on reefs off Australia. When it strikes a victim, it spits out enough venom or poison to kill five hundred sheep. Sometimes it is very aggressive. Skin divers near the reefs must be very careful, because nothing can save the life of a diver bitten by a sea snake. ❷

The most poisonous land snake is the fierce tiger snake, which lives on islands near Australia. One bite from this snake contains enough venom to kill more than a thousand sheep.

Snakebite is a serious problem in India, where about twenty-five thousand people die from it each year. The most common poisonous snake in India is the cobra, which also happens to be the longest poisonous snake. One king cobra was 19 feet long.

The cobra is also the subject of a snake story that is false. A snake charmer's music is said to put the cobra into a trance. But, like other snakes, the cobra is almost deaf. When the snake's head sways to the music of a snake charmer's flute, it is not responding to the music but to the movement of the musical instrument. ❸

In comparison to the snakes of India, Australia, and Africa, the varieties found in North America are mostly harmless. Not many people die of snakebites in North America. There are swamps near New Orleans, however, where a visitor can find an assortment of poisonous snakes. Among these are the water moccasin and the copperhead, two snakes that nobody would want to meet on a Sunday picnic. Fortunately, not many people go wading in these swamps. ❹

1

able

curable

movable

believable

preventable

understandable

2

selec<u>tion</u>   inst<u>ea</u>d   exp<u>er</u>tly

h<u>ea</u>vier   experien<u>c</u>ed   n<u>ea</u>rly

3

1. in range
2. efficient
3. instantly
4. advantage
5. determined
6. rescue
7. in relation to
8. particularly

4

license   smarter   claws   extremely

nature   unusually   probably   decided

difference   effectively   wounded

well-designed   hooves   professional

heart   lose   impala   wrestling   incredible

5   Dangerous African Animals—Part 4

In part 3 of this story we discussed why the Cape buffalo is very   14
dangerous. The hunter will have great trouble getting within range of   25
the buffalo because of its very keen senses. Also, the Cape buffalo is an   39
efficient killer, far more efficient than the rhinoceros. The Cape buffalo   50
will charge, but unlike the rhinoceros, it will be careful about when it   63
charges. It will move much faster than the rhinoceros, so the hunter will   76
not be able to dodge it. The Cape buffalo can change direction very   89
quickly, and it uses its horns, its skull, and its hooves effectively. ❶   101

Another fact about the Cape buffalo is that it is hard to kill. Cape   115
buffalos have reportedly charged up to one hundred yards with a bullet   127
in the heart. Unless the shot is expertly placed, a bullet in the chest   141
usually will not kill the buffalo instantly. And if the bullet does not kill   155
the Cape buffalo instantly, the hunter may be the first one to die.   168

Experienced big game hunters agree that the Cape buffalo is a most   180
dangerous animal when wounded. Some professional big game hunters   189
have lost their licenses to hunt because they have failed to track   201
wounded buffalos into the brush. A professional hunter must kill an   212
animal—not wound it. If the animal is wounded, the professional   223
hunter must track it into the brush and kill it, but some hunters have   237
decided that they would rather lose their licenses than go into the   249
brush after a wounded Cape buffalo. The buffalo in the brush has a   262
great advantage. It can hide and wait, just like the rhinoceros. The   274
difference is that the buffalo is smarter and harder to kill than the   287
rhinoceros, and probably it is more determined to kill the hunter. The   299
<u>hunter</u> must be extremely careful when tracking a wounded buffalo,   309
because when the buffalo charges, it is probably too late for the hunter   322
to stop it. ❷   325

The Cape buffalo is dangerous indeed, but the smallest big game   336
animal, the leopard, is the *most* dangerous animal to hunt. How could   348
the leopard be more dangerous than an elephant, a lion, a rhinoceros,   360
or a Cape buffalo? A leopard may not weigh more than one hundred   373
fifty pounds. It is not much larger than a full-grown police dog, and it   387
certainly doesn't look very dangerous. Actually, it looks like an   397
overgrown house cat with spots and a long tail.   406

Look again, and you will see one of nature's best-designed predators.   417
Anybody who has ever tried to rescue a kitten from a tree knows how   431
much damage this small pet can do with its claws. If you took a house   446
cat and made it ten times heavier, you would have a powerful predator,   459
but it would not be as powerful as the leopard. The leopard has more   473
strength in relation to its size than nearly any other animal. ❸ With little   486
effort a leopard can carry a full-grown impala up the side of a tree to an   502
overhanging branch. The leopard moves up a tree with its prey as easily   515
as if it is carrying something that weighs no more than an overcoat.   528

Besides being almost as strong as a lion, a leopard can kill a hunter   542
nearly as quickly and as easily as a lion can. Although a leopard can't   556
crush someone with its charge, it can leap on the hunter and, holding   569
on with its teeth and front claws, tear into the hunter's body with its   583
rapidly moving back claws. The attack is quick and efficient. Even if   595
the hunter wards off the leopard's jaws, the leopard's claws—   605
particularly its back claws—can kill the hunter in a few seconds. ❹   617

There have been reports of a leopard killing two persons in less   629
than three seconds. The leopard moves with lightning speed and   639
incredible strength. Like the lion, the leopard is designed to kill   650
animals that are far more powerful than people. So don't believe those   662
old jungle movies that show people wrestling with leopards. A   672
wrestling match between a hunter and a leopard would be over quick   684
as a wink, and the winner would probably be the leopard.   695

1 **able** readable predictable

workable believable

2 brightly mentioned deadly lunge

3
1. downed
2. disadvantage
3. created
4. filtering

4
actually splattered clearly consider

frequently abruptly intelligence

crouched sailing bravery scarcely

instantly baboon favorite stray

warning invisible spotted listening

growls thrown stretched

straight appreciate designed

5   # Dangerous African Animals—Part 5

Like the lion, the leopard is a lazy animal. It spends most of the day   15
sleeping in its favorite spot—on the limb of a tree. It doesn't like the   30
open plain, and it doesn't often stray from the trees. The leopard will   43
move onto the plain to hunt, but after it has downed an antelope or a   58
baboon, it will return to the shade of the forest. And that brings up   72
another reason that the leopard is dangerous to hunt. The hunter who   84
goes after the leopard will have to go into the forest where the hunter is   99
at a great disadvantage. When the leopard stands out in the open, it   112
seems to be very brightly marked. When it is in the shade-splattered   124
forest, however, a leopard is almost invisible. Its tan-and-black-spotted   133
coat looks just like the spots of light and dark created by the sun's rays   148
filtering through the trees. The only thing that gives the leopard away is   161
its tail. It has a habit of letting its tail hang down from the limb of a   178
tree. Often its tail is the only part that is visible. ❶   189

When the leopard is on the ground in some brush, it is very difficult   203
for a hunter to find. A hunter can locate a lion in the brush by   218
throwing stones and listening for the lion's growls. However, the   228
leopard won't growl; silently it will lie there, flat against the ground.   240
Some of the stones thrown by the hunter may actually hit the leopard,   253
but it won't move, and it won't make a sound. With its ears back and   268
its eyes fixed straight ahead, the leopard will wait for the right   280
moment to leap out. ❷   284

A leopard in a tree usually will not bother a hunter unless the   297
leopard is <u>wounded</u>. The hunter may walk right under the tree, but the   310
leopard won't attack unless the hunter happens to look up. If the   322
hunter looks up, the leopard will attack instantly. The leopard, with   333
its very keen eyesight, watches the movement of anything that may be   345

dangerous. It considers people dangerous. As soon as a leopard feels it   357
has been seen, it will attack.   363

We mentioned how deadly the leopard can be. When a leopard   374
attacks, it is very difficult for the hunter to stop the leopard. Like the   388
lion, the leopard can move from a crouched position to full speed in   401
only a few steps. It easily can jump twenty feet from a crouched   414
position. Its legs are like springs, and with one powerful lunge it flies   427
at the hunter. ❸   430

Let's consider a hunter who is moving through the jungle. The   441
hunter looks around, knowing that leopards are near. Suddenly the   451
hunter spots a form in a tree that is twenty-five feet ahead. At that   465
instant, with no warning, the form leaps at the hunter. The hunter   477
scarcely has time to raise the rifle and take aim. The hunter must   490
shoot now—but consider the target. When a leopard is sailing through   502
the air, its body is stretched and its front legs are straight out on either   517
side of its head. The target, the leopard's head, is only about a foot   531
across. There will be no chance for a second shot before the leopard   544
reaches the hunter. ❹   547

So the leopard is clearly the most dangerous African animal to   558
hunt. The leopard is extremely powerful, very smart, and difficult to   569
find. It is quick, and it makes a difficult target. The hunter usually will   583
have less than two seconds to respond to an attack.   593

When you see leopards in a zoo pacing back and forth and panting,   606
it's hard to appreciate how dangerous they are. If you could see one in   620
its natural home, you would see what a well-designed predator it is.   632
Nature gave the leopard great bravery and a lot of intelligence.   643
Though a leopard will attack almost any animal, it will not attack at   656
any time, the way a rhinoceros will. It will choose the right time and   670
the right place for the attack. ❺   676

1   able   pre   ness   ly   re

2   pleasant   exhausted   creature   survival

3
1. magnificent
2. puny
3. required
4. concerned
5. apparent
6. intruder
7. referred

4

poison   outsmart   topics   usually

incredibly   protection   series

involves   through   defending   including

although   though   snooze   invade

listen   healthy   develop

efficient   fare   threaten

5   Dangerous African Animals—Part 6

Some of the things you've read in this series may have bothered you.   13
Killing and death are not pleasant topics. We don't like to think about   26
people being killed by wild animals or about people shooting wild   37
animals for sport. But the animals that we have discussed are   48
designed to survive, and their survival involves defending themselves   57
against other animals, including human beings. The magnificent   65
African elephant—that incredibly large and powerful animal—will   74
protect itself and the other elephants in its herd against any animals   86
that threaten it—including people. The lion and the leopard kill to   98
survive. If they don't kill, they don't eat, and if they don't eat, they   112
don't live. Every part of them has been designed to help them kill, but   126
they do it only to eat and to protect themselves. ❶   136

People, in contrast to the animals we have referred to, are rather   148
puny. If people were required to fight as the other animals are, they   161
wouldn't survive three seconds against a healthy leopard or lion. But   172
people don't fight the way other animals do. They hunt the leopard and   185
win, but they don't give the leopard a fair chance. Each hunter goes   198
into the forest with several dogs. Although a leopard could kill *any* dog   211
quick as a wink, the leopard usually runs if there is more than one dog.   226
Usually the leopard climbs a tree, and the howling of the dogs tells the   240
hunter where the leopard is. Now the hunter can stand sixty feet away,   253
take careful aim, and kill the leopard with no great danger. People   265
have chased the leopards and the lions from their homes by using   277
drums and fires and trucks and poison. With trucks the hunter has   289
chased the Cape buffalo—running it until it is exhausted <u>and</u> can run   302
no more. Then the hunter has shot that beautiful creature that was   314
doing nothing more than trying to escape. ❷   321

Ask yourself, do any of these African animals kill for the sake of   334
killing? Does the leopard mount the heads of the animals it kills so it can   349
show how brave it is? No, usually the leopard is concerned only with   362
eating or finding a cool spot high in a tree away from the bugs where it can   379
have a nice snooze. The only animal that attacks for no *apparent* reason is   393
the rhinoceros, which is only trying to keep intruders out of the area that   407
it considers its own. The rhinoceros attacks those who invade its home. ❸   419

Now look at what hunters have done over the past years. They have   432
shown they can outsmart even the smartest African animals. They have   443
shown they can develop weapons that are more effective killers than the   455
horns of the Cape buffalo or the teeth of the lion. The hunters have also   470
shown that often they may have killed just for the sake of killing. And   484
consider what they have killed. The African animals that we have   495
discussed are magnificent creatures that treat people as they would   505
treat any other intruders. Each has survived because it is the best at   518
what it does. The leopard is the most capable predator in the world.   531
The lion is the most effective killer on the plain. The Cape buffalo is   545
one of the most efficient grazing animals in the world. Each of these   558
animals has a place in nature. But people have changed all that. They   571
have taken away the places—with farms and fences and guns. And they   584
have killed these animals—in many cases with no good reason. ❹   595

When you consider that there are only about two thousand leopards   606
remaining in Africa, where once there were tens of thousands, it seems   618
a shame that this world may lose such a beautiful creature—brave,   630
smart, and efficient. The same is true of the elephant, the rhinoceros,   642
the lion, and the Cape buffalo. People have killed these animals by the   655
hundreds of thousands. Yet, in a fair contest with these animals, the   667
hunter would not fare well. Even with a gun, the hunter may not win   681
the contest, particularly if the contest is with the African Cape buffalo   693
or with the most dangerous of all African animals—the leopard. ❺   704

Giganotosaurus   Seismosaurus   Ornithomimus
carnivore   herbivore

Facts About Dinosaurs

The table on the next page presents interesting facts about a few dinosaurs. You've read about some of them in selections in this book. The others are huge dinosaurs.

The first huge dinosaur is Giganotosaurus. This dinosaur was about the same length as Tyrannosaurus, but it weighed 3,000 pounds more than Tyrannosaurus. Like Tyrannosaurus, Giganotosaurus was a carnivore. ❶

The largest dinosaur ever discovered was Seismosaurus, which lived millions of years before Triceratops. Like Triceratops, Seismosaurus was a herbivore; however, it was about ten times heavier than Triceratops and four times longer. It weighed over 200,000 pounds, which is several times the weight of Triceratops.

The table on the next page shows that Ornithomimus was an omnivore. Omnivores are animals that eat both meat and plants. Ornithomimus was shorter than any of the other dinosaurs and weighed less.

	Dinosaur	Length	Weight	Diet
	Giganotosaurus	40 feet	18,000 pounds	carnivore
	Ornithomimus	11 feet	385 pounds	omnivore
	Seismosaurus	120 feet	215,000 pounds	herbivore
	Triceratops	30 feet	22,000 pounds	herbivore
	Tyrannosaurus	40 feet	15,000 pounds	carnivore

How many dinosaurs listed in the table have you already read about in the reading selections? ❷

What are the names of dinosaurs you have not read about in the passages? ❸

The table on page 274 indicates that Tyrannosaurus weighed 3,000 pounds less than Giganotosaurus. How much did Tyrannosaurus weigh? ❹

How much did Giganotosaurus weigh? ❺

How many dinosaurs listed in the table ate both meat and plants? ❻
Name that dinosaur. ❼

What do we call animals that eat both meat and plants? ❽

The table above indicates that Seismosaurus weighed over 100 tons. A more exact weight is shown in the table. What is that weight? ❾

How many dinosaurs were larger or weighed more than Seismosaurus? ❿

How long was the shortest dinosaur listed in the table? ⓫
How long was the longest dinosaur listed in the table? ⓬
How much heavier was Seismosaurus than Tyrannosaurus? ⓭

1

less   ness   dis   ly   re   un

2

mana<u>g</u>ed   direct<u>ly</u>   physi<u>c</u>ists   p<u>au</u>sed

experien<u>c</u>e   <u>re</u>vising   <u>disbelie</u>f   w<u>ea</u>kness

3

1. reaction
2. presentation
3. duplicated
4. coincidence
5. nagged
6. bombardment

4

permission   experimental   occasionally

delivered   Chicago   slumped   computer

memorized   procedures   awakened

stretched   pizza   scheduled   wearing

laboratory   various   data   amazement

5

Milly Prepares Her Paper

Milly Jacobson returned to State University still wearing the dusty   10
jeans and other clothes she had worn in the mountains. She had gone   23
directly to the airport from Mr. Hicks's home and had managed to get   36
on a late-night flight. The plane landed at four in the morning, and   49
Milly went directly to her laboratory in the physics building. She   60
noticed, on her way into the building, that the piles had been removed   73
from the lawn. She turned on the desk lamp in her lab, sat down,   87
stacked her records on one side of the desk, turned on her computer,   100
and typed the title of her paper: "The Reaction of Gold to Laser   113
Bombardment."   114

She paused for a moment before beginning to type the paper. She   126
thought about how the other physicists would react when she   136
presented her paper at the International Convention of Physicists.   145
That was Milly's plan, but she had to work fast, for the convention in   159
Chicago was only three weeks away. ❶ Milly had to complete the   170
paper and then get permission to present it. The program for the   182
convention had already been set for months. Milly would have to talk   194
somebody into letting her make her presentation at one of the   205
sessions. But first, she had to complete the paper.   214

She typed for about two hours. Occasionally, she referred to her   225
notes, but she had memorized most of the data. The first part of her   239
paper described the experimental procedures. She told how she tested   249
the various metals and how they reacted to the short laser blasts.   261
Before Milly could begin the second part of her paper—which was to   274
tell about her field experience with the laser gear—she fell asleep in   287
the lab, sitting at her computer. Waking up in the middle of the   300
morning, she noticed that several people were working in the lab. She   312

greeted them, slumped over her computer, and went to sleep again.   323

Around noon Fred Frankle awakened her by gently shaking her   333
shoulder. "Come on, Milly. If you want to sleep, you should go home   346
and go to bed."   350

"I don't want to sleep," Milly said. "I want to write. But I'm so   364
tired." She stretched and yawned, stood up, and stretched again. "I'm   375
awake now. I'll just have a cup of coffee and I'll be fine."   388

Milly typed all afternoon. She called a pizza place and had a small   401
pizza delivered to the lab. Eating and typing at the same time, she   414
completed the first draft of the paper before she finished the pizza.   426
Then she began revising the paper; she crossed out sentences; she   437
rewrote parts; she read the paper over carefully; and just to be sure,   450
she reread it once more.   455

At nine at night, the paper was completed. By nine the next   467
morning, the paper had been retyped and duplicated by a typist that   479
Milly hired. Milly had offered the typist three hundred dollars if he   491
typed the paper before noon of the following day. ❷   500

Next Milly called the program chairperson for the International   509
Convention of Physicists and explained that she had a very important   520
paper to present.   523

"That's a nice coincidence," the chairperson said. "We find that one   534
of our scheduled presenters can't be with us for the convention. His   546
wife is going to have a baby, and he wants to stay home."   559

"That's great," Milly said.   563

Now Milly waited. She was dying to tell somebody about her   574
discovery, but she wanted to surprise everybody when she presented   584
her paper at the convention. She realized that she was sort of a   597
show-off, but she also realized that she had made an important   608
discovery and that she deserved the chance to show off. ❸   618

There were several times during the next three weeks that she   629

almost told Fred about her experiments. For three days after she   640
returned he nagged her, trying to find out what she did in California.   653
Each time, Milly responded, "I was doing a field study." But each   665
time, she wanted to tell him. She wanted to see his eyes become large   679
with amazement and his mouth fall open with disbelief. But she made   691
herself keep the secret. To keep it was getting more difficult each day. ❹ 704

1

parents   inherited   skeleton   millions

vitamins   proteins   minerals   possibility

nutrients   stunned   enormous

potential   generation   influences

2

1. ancient
2. nutrition
3. genetic
4. starvation
5. plentiful
6. diet

3

Are People Getting Taller?

Some people think that the human race is taller than it used to be. Is it?

No. Even though some groups of people today are taller than their parents and grandparents were, the whole human race is not growing taller.

Height is a genetic, or inherited, characteristic. ❶ That means that the possibility of being a tall person or a short one is something that you are born with. This possibility is passed on to you from your parents, grandparents, great-grandparents, and so on. Each person's genetic inheritance goes back many, many generations.

Inheritance sets a limit on growth. If you come from many generations of tall people, you may grow to be very tall too. But if you come from many generations of short people, you will probably be short.

Inheritance is only part of what determines how tall you will become. One of the things that most influences how you grow and develop is nutrition: the amount, kind, and quality of food you eat. ❷ If two people have the same growth potential, the person who always has enough good food to eat will grow taller and stronger than the person who hasn't. Although genetics might permit you to be tall, a starvation diet would not give your body the proteins, vitamins, minerals, and other nutrients it needs to grow tall.

Good food is not always easy, or even possible, to get. At many times and in many places during the history of the human race, there have been long periods of starvation. People who lived during those periods were smaller than they would have been if they had lived when food was plentiful. ❸

Some ancient skeletons of adults are very small, and at one time people thought that all ancient people were small. Not all of them were. Some skeletons have shown that many ancient people were as tall as tall people of today.

Today there are still many places in the world where people don't get enough good food to eat. These people are a lot shorter than they would have been if they had always had enough to eat.

1

weather   persuaded   audience   angrily

2

1. hassle
2. peeved
3. acoustics
4. moderator
5. podium

3

discussion   interrupted   exploding

seriously   performance   entertaining

conference   laughter   thought

originally   curtain   wandering   delayed

introducing   apparently   trouble

stumbling   quieted   scheduled   entire

equipment   phony   embarrassed

scene   irritated   bombardment

4 Milly's Arrival

The weather in Chicago was rainy when Milly's plane arrived two 11
hours late. She was a little irritated because it seemed that the entire 24
trip had become a hassle. The dean didn't want her to go. He had told 39
her that she was scheduled to go to only one conference that year, not 53
two. After some discussion, Milly persuaded the dean to allow her to 65
go. Then Fred became angry with Milly. He had told her, "Sometimes 77
you're too much! First you go into the mountains for days, and then 90
you take off for another convention." She had tried to explain to him 103
that it was important for her to go to the convention, but he had still 118
seemed peeved with her. Then Milly had a great deal of trouble trying 131
to ship her laser equipment to the meeting. She wanted to put it on 145
display for the physicists. And on top of everything, bad weather 156
delayed the plane. 159

But now Milly was in a cab on her way to the convention hall, and she 175
was beginning to feel better. She loved conventions. She hadn't prepared 186
any jokes for this convention—no exploding cigars or exploding cue 197
sticks, no red-and-white pins. She had a handshake buzzer in her 208
suitcase, but she wasn't seriously thinking about using it. ❶ 217

When she walked into the hotel lobby, one physicist said, "Oh, no, 229
there she is. Watch your step around Dr. Jacobson." 238

Four physicists came over and began to joke around with Milly. 249
One said, "We all heard about your last performance. Are you going 261
to put on a better show at this convention?" 270

Milly smiled and answered, "It will be different. I plan to give a 283
very important paper." 286

"It's a joke, right?" one of the physicists asked. "I can see that 299

<u>phony-serious</u> expression on your face. A very important paper," he 309

said sarcastically. "I'll just bet it's important." 316

"No, really," she said. "This is serious." 323

"Listen, we've heard about how serious you are. Like setting off 334

smoke bombs and—" 337

Another physicist interrupted. "And what about that paper you 346

passed out at the last convention? That was pretty serious." 356

"Believe me," she said. "This time I'm really serious." 365

"Listen," one of them said and patted her on the shoulder. "We'll be 378

there. I wouldn't miss your paper for anything." ❷ 386

Milly met other physicists before the meeting, and most of them 398

reacted the same way the first group had reacted. It seemed that 410

everybody expected her to play a superjoke on the group. As one 422

physicist said, "We need you, Milly. We take ourselves so seriously 433

that we sometimes forget we're just a bunch of people stumbling 444

around trying to find out new things. We need you to remind us about 458

what we are. Give a good talk." ❸ 464

The meeting room where Milly had originally been scheduled to talk 475

held about fifty people. But apparently the word got out that she was 488

going to put on an entertaining show, because more than two hundred 500

physicists showed up and the meeting room had to be changed. The 512

new room, a large conference hall that had more than four hundred 524

seats, was on the first floor of the convention center. By the time 537

everybody got settled in the new room and Milly set up her laser 550

behind the curtain, it was already fifteen minutes after the meeting had 562

been scheduled to begin. 566

Milly waited another half hour as a physicist from Michigan gave a 578

talk on acoustics. Milly tried to become interested in the speech, but 590

her mind kept wandering back to the glory hole. She remembered that 602

scene when the smoke cleared and she stared at the glory hole for the 616
first time. Milly's thoughts were in the middle of that scene when she 629
realized that the audience was applauding. The paper was completed, 639
and it was now Milly's turn to present hers. ❹ 648

The woman who moderated the panel stood before the podium 658
introducing Milly. "The title of Dr. Jacobson's paper is 'The Reaction 669
of Gold to Laser Bombardment.' " Several people in the audience 679
began to laugh. 682

Someone yelled, "Get ready for the put-on of your life." Then 693
everybody began to laugh. 697

The moderator looked embarrassed. She said, "Well, without 705
further delay, I give you Dr. Milly Jacobson." 713

Great cheers went up from the group. It sounded more like a 725
football game than a physics convention. "Go, Milly," some of the 736
physicists yelled. 738

At last the audience quieted. Milly held her hands out and said, 750
"Some of you are expecting a joke, but the paper I'm about to deliver 764
is no joke. It is very serious." 771

At that, the audience again broke into waves of laughter. ❺ 781

Lesson 82

1 participants imagined expression announced demonstration

2
1. summary
2. modified
3. formulas
4. confirm
5. interruption
6. routine

3 audience disbelief substance explained

applause snickers decided indicated

calculations identify equipment apparently

serious concrete nugget moment

exit mathematical data aisle

volunteer dozen scan guy

4   The Presentation Begins

The audience wouldn't let Milly talk. Every time she tried to say   12
something, the people began to laugh and shout. At last the   23
moderator for the meeting stood up and said, "Ladies and gentlemen,   34
let's try to give Dr. Jacobson a chance to present her paper."   46

"Yes, be quiet," somebody yelled from the audience.   54

Milly said, "Well, let me try to give you a quick summary of what I   69
discovered. I discovered that I can identify gold—even when it is   81
underground—by using a modified metal detector and short bursts of   92
laser light."   94

There were a few snickers from the audience, but most of the   106
participants were quiet and smiling. Their expressions indicated that   115
they were waiting for the big joke. Milly presented the details of her   128
experiments, showing slides of the different metal-detector readings   136
and presenting mathematical formulas and calculations that explained   144
the difference in the readings between gold and other metals.   154

Then Milly said, "And to confirm these findings, I took the laser   166
equipment to the mountains near Sacramento, California." She showed   175
the slide of herself with Mr. Hicks standing next to the pickup truck.   188

"That's great," somebody from the back of the audience yelled, and   199
everybody began to laugh. ❶   203

A young woman near the back of the audience said, "I've got a   216
question."   217

"Yes," Milly responded.   220

"Where did you find that guy in the picture? He looks like he's right   234
out of some old movie."   239

Everybody laughed. Milly explained how she had located Mr.   248
Hicks. Again, everybody laughed. Some people were laughing so hard   258
they had tears in their eyes.   264

Milly was beginning to realize that her entire paper sounded like a   276
big joke. For a moment she imagined how she would react to the   289
paper if she were in the audience. What would she <u>think</u> if she saw   303
that picture of Milly and Hicks next to a dirty pickup truck with a   317
laser gun mounted in the bed? What would she think if somebody told   330
her that gold could be identified with a laser gun? She decided she'd   343
probably laugh, too. ❷   346

"Please, let me go through the rest of my paper, and then I'll answer   360
questions." The audience remained quiet until Milly told about the   370
glory hole.   372

Then somebody from the third row yelled, "Come on, Milly. This is   384
too much."   386

"Everything I have told you is the truth," Milly said, but not many   399
people heard her above the laughter of the group. Three interruptions   410
later, Milly finished her talk. Apparently nobody in the audience took   421
it seriously. Even the moderator was laughing.   428

Milly opened the curtain, showing her laser gun. Everybody   437
clapped and cheered, but the audience's response was not serious. One   448
physicist yelled, "Don't shoot, Milly—we'll be good."   456

Milly walked to the side of the stage where she had a large shoulder   470
bag. She reached into the bag and pulled out a large nugget, bigger   483
than an orange. People in the audience cheered and whistled. ❸   493

Milly said, "I'd like to put on a demonstration to show you that the   507
data I have reported is real." She pointed to the wall to her left. "That   522
wall is concrete," Milly said. "If somebody in the audience would   533
volunteer to take this gold nugget and—"   540

"I'll take it," somebody yelled, and everybody laughed again.   549

Milly repeated, "If somebody will take it and hold it in different   561
spots on the other side of this wall, I'll demonstrate that I can locate it."   576

"I'll volunteer," the moderator said. Milly handed the nugget to her.   587
As the moderator headed down the aisle, she was met with applause   599
and laughter. She smiled and nodded to the members of the audience   611
as she walked down the side aisle to the back of the room and out one   627
of the exits.   630

Then Milly said, "Will somebody near the rear of the hall tell me   643
when she's got the nugget in place?"   650

About six physicists walked out of the meeting room. After a   661
moment or two, they returned. "She's ready," one of them announced.   672

Milly adjusted her laser gun and pointed it at the left wall. She said,   686
"I'll start in the rear and move forward."   694

She aimed the gun at the far end of the wall and began to scan it   710
with short laser bursts. Each burst left a small dark mark on the   723
painted wall. Soon the smell of burning paint filled the room.   734

"Oh, no!" somebody yelled. "It's the old smoke bomb routine."   744

About a dozen physicists stood up and left the room. ❹   754

INFORMATION PASSAGE

exaggerated   abandoned   merchants   immigrants   journeyed
desperately   thriving   trend   realization

The California Gold Rush

In 1848, James Marshall found a
gold nugget not far from Sacramento,
California. The news traveled fast and
became more exaggerated the farther
it went. It reached farmers, salesmen,
factory workers, and
businessmen. Thousands of
them quit what they were doing
and moved to California. By 1849, hundreds
of thousands of people had moved to California
to search for gold and get rich. Shiploads of Chinese
immigrants were among the first to reach the gold
fields. Even sailors, who heard about great gold nuggets
the size of rocks, abandoned their ships and joined the army
of others in the California Gold Rush. San Francisco was a
thriving city before the gold rush began. By 1849, the city had been
reduced to a ghost town with abandoned buildings, abandoned ships
in the harbor, and most businesses closed. ❶

Only a few of those who sought their fortunes finding gold were
successful. Most of the rest lost what money they had trying to buy
supplies that were 50 times the regular price. Many of them who could
afford it went home. Others, including thousands of Chinese

immigrants, journeyed 120 miles to San Francisco, where they desperately looked for any job they could find. During this time, San Francisco was a booming city, larger than it had ever been. Labor was cheap, and prices remained high. The crime rate in San Francisco soared. For many people, crime provided the only opportunity they had to feed themselves or their families. By 1860, twelve years after the discovery of gold, the people who had benefited most from the gold rush were the merchants, the landowners, and the farmers. ❷

There were other gold rushes in states close to California, but none were as gigantic as the one in California. Gold was also discovered in Oregon, Arizona, Idaho, and New Mexico.

The same trend that had occurred in California took place in these other states. In Oregon, a community near the John Day gold field swelled from less than 1,000 people to over 20,000, including over 10,000 Chinese immigrants.

Following the rush, however, most of those who had sought their fortunes had the sad realization that there were no fortunes for them. In fact, there weren't even jobs, so cities that had sprung up were abandoned. The picture below shows a ghost town in Gilmore, Idaho. During the gold rush, Gilmore had been a thriving community. ❸

Lesson

83

1   **ly   ness   re   less**

2   ceiling   steady   rear   precisely

3
1. typical
2. adequate
3. reinforced
4. ducts
5. distinguish
6. proceed

4   piece   hurried   collection   foolish

lengths   detection   reappeared

excitedly   exactly   demonstration

treated   damaged   zinc   ignore

touched   entire   electrical   scanned

moderator   system   iron   smokey

identify   agreement   spray

5 Demonstrations

Milly tried to ignore the comments from the audience as she
scanned the left wall with the laser gun. The wall near the rear of the
room looked as if somebody had used a can of black spray paint to
paint zigzag lines over it. More people were leaving the room, which
was now becoming quite smokey. ❶

Milly began to scan the middle of the wall. Suddenly the needle on
the metal detector gave its typical gold reading. "There," Milly said,
holding the laser beam steady. It was pointing to a spot near the
bottom of the wall, about halfway between the front and the back of
the meeting hall. "Would somebody mark that spot?" Somebody did.
Then the moderator was called back into the room. "Where did you
place the nugget?" Milly asked.

"I'll show you exactly," she said through the smoke. She stood with
her back against the rear wall of the hall. Then she began to walk
forward, placing the heel of her foot against the toe of her other foot.
She marked off fifty foot-lengths. She bent down and touched the
exact spot marked on the wall.

"Put-on," somebody yelled. "She's part of the gag."

"No," Milly said. "She's not, and it is not a gag."

One physicist stood up and said, "I feel a little foolish asking a
serious question, but how do we know you couldn't do that with any
metal, given that you have adequate detection equipment?" ❷

"Let's do it again," Milly said. "This time, I'll give somebody four
smaller bits of metal—one gold and three zinc."

"Why not some other metals, too?" somebody asked.

"Because the wall is made of reinforced concrete," Milly said. "It
has iron reinforcing bars in it, copper wires for the electrical system,

and steel heating <u>ducts</u>. If you wish, I can locate these metals. 308

However, I can't identify them precisely. I can only distinguish 318

between gold and not gold." Milly walked to her shoulder bag and 330

brought out four bits, each smaller than a dime. She handed the bits 343

to the moderator and said, "Please place them somewhere near the 354

back or middle of the wall. I don't want to mess up the entire wall." ❸ 369

A few moments passed as the moderator left the room with three 381

other physicists who went with her to place the metal pieces. When 393

they reappeared at the rear exit door, the moderator said, "They're set." 405

Milly turned on the gun and began scanning the wall. She stopped 417

near the back ceiling. "There," she said. "That's a bit of zinc." 429

"Exactly right!" the moderator said. 434

A man who had helped the moderator set the pieces said, "That's 446

right. I set it there." 451

Milly moved the laser gun and stopped again. The audience was 462

quiet now. "There's another bit of zinc," Milly announced. 471

"Wrong," a woman said. "It's a dime. I taped it there." 482

"As I told you," Milly explained, "I can only distinguish between 493

gold and not gold." ❹ 497

Milly moved the gun again. She scanned for about thirty seconds. 508

By now she was almost to the middle of the room. Suddenly she 521

stopped. "And there is the gold." 527

"Right," the moderator said. The others nodded their heads in 537

agreement. 538

"This is fantastic," one of them said. 545

"Hey, wait a minute," somebody in the audience said. "Do you 556

mean this demonstration is on the level?" 563

"As far as I know it is," the moderator said. "We placed those pieces." 577

"Hey," a man from the audience said. "I want to place that gold 590

piece myself. OK?" 593

"Sure," Milly said. The man hurried out of the room. Fifty or sixty 606
people from the audience followed. After he returned to the 616
conference hall and announced that the piece was placed on the other 628
side of the wall, Milly scanned the wall with her gun. She stopped 641
near the ceiling in the back. "There," she said. "It's about six inches 654
from the ceiling." 657

"I can't believe it!" the physicist who placed the piece said. "It's not 670
a put-on." 672

Members of the audience began to talk excitedly among themselves. 682
"Do it again," somebody from the audience said. "This time with 693
more than one piece." 697

"All right," Milly said. "And I'll be able to tell you the size of 711
each piece." 713

"Not that I don't trust you," the physicist said, "but that gold you 726
used may be treated. I have a gold ring, and I'm sure other people in 741
the audience have things made of gold. Let's use those. They won't be 754
damaged, will they?" 757

"No," Milly answered, and the man proceeded to collect several 767
things made of gold from members of the audience. ❺ 776

1 dis   sub   pre   ly   less   ness

2 gath<u>e</u>red   ment<u>io</u>ned   alre<u>a</u>dy   comfortabl<u>y</u>

3
1. rectangle
2. technical
3. subsided
4. refused
5. encounter

4
articles   seriously   importance

disbelief   prepared   necklace

probably   applauding   thundering

scanned   distinguish   trained

scheduled   deposit   special   platinum

fault   group   worth   million   aisles

heard   earlier   brilliance

5   Milly's Reward

A large group from the audience left the conference hall to see   12
where the different gold articles were placed on the other side of the   25
concrete wall. A crowd gathered around the rear exits. "OK,"   35
somebody yelled from the rear of the hall, and Milly trained the laser   48
beam on the rear part of the wall.   56

Suddenly she stopped the beam and said, "At that spot on the other   69
side of the wall is a gold object that is fairly large. It is probably a   85
pocket watch."   87

"Correct," a woman from the rear of the hall shouted. Some   98
members of the audience applauded, this time seriously.   106

Again Milly moved the beam, and again she stopped. "Right there   117
is a small gold object that is quite long. Could it be a gold necklace?" ❶   132

"Yes," said the voices from the rear of the conference hall. More   144
applause followed. Milly bowed and smiled.   150

She scanned the wall for another moment, stopping near the floor   161
about two-thirds of the way toward the rear wall. "That," she said,   173
"must be a gold ring."   178

"Yes," a chorus of voices shouted, followed by thundering applause.   188
Then members of the audience crowded down the aisles with their   199
hands raised, shouting out questions.   204

"Hey," Milly shouted back, "why don't you sit down, and I'll try to   217
answer your questions."   220

The questions came for the next hour. Another meeting had been   231
scheduled in the conference hall, but Milly's group refused to leave.   242
When people who were going to the next meeting heard what was   254
happening in Milly's meeting, they stayed to listen and ask questions.   265

Soon the hall was packed, with people standing in the aisles and   277

crowding around the rear exit doors.   283

After members of the audience had asked a number of technical   294

questions about the laser equipment <u>and</u> how it worked, a woman   305

said, "Earlier you mentioned that, using the laser, you had discovered   316

a glory hole. How much was the gold worth that you found?"   328

Milly said, "I would estimate that the deposit was worth close to   340

one hundred million dollars." ❷   344

The audience was silent for a moment. Then a voice asked, "What   356

do you plan to do with all that money?"   365

Milly explained that part of the claim would go to her university,   377

part would go to the state of California, and part would go to Mr.   391

Hicks. "What about you?" somebody asked. "Don't you get anything   401

from the gold find?"   405

Milly smiled and didn't say anything for a moment. Then she   416

replied, "I already got my share. Ever since I was a little girl, I wanted   431

to do something special, something that would be really important   441

and would help other people. I'll never be able to explain the feeling to   455

you, but when the dust cleared and we saw the glory hole for the first   470

time, reflecting its brilliance in the sunlight, I got a large part of my   484

reward. And I got the rest of it today, when I presented my paper to   499

you. I live comfortably, and I have a very good job. I'm not hungry for   514

gold or for the things that gold can buy. The real gold for me is the   530

discovery I made, and it's all the reward I need." ❸   540

The audience applauded. "I think you've lost your mind,"   549

somebody from the back of the hall shouted after the applause had   561

subsided.   562

"Maybe I have," Milly said. "But I'll tell you one thing: I'm very   575

happy. And if I ever happen to change my mind, I can always go back   590

to Sacramento with my laser and find another glory hole. I'll bet 602
there are quite a few others that haven't been found yet." 613

Somebody from the audience said, "That may be, Milly, but now 624
that the secret of the laser is out, other people will be able to use lasers 640
to search for gold. If you don't act fast, those glory holes will be found 655
before you can return." 659

Milly said, "You're probably right, but there are so many things 670
about our world that we don't understand. Who knows, maybe I'll 681
discover some way to find silver or platinum." 689

That day at the International Convention of Physicists was probably 699
the biggest day in Milly's life, but it didn't change her very much. 712
Today she is still working in her lab at State University and playing 725
jokes on the other physicists. 730

1

calm unbelievably fought Philippine

encountered completely undersea earthquakes

position observe Canadian

2

1. plunge
2. hurl
3. plumes
4. gale
5. tides
6. exceed

3

Ocean Waves and Tides

When you observe the ocean on a calm day, you can't really imagine what it looks like when it is angry. Even when the wind blows and the waves plunge against rocks and hurl plumes of spray into the air, you may think that you're looking at the sea when it is at its worst. But, occasionally, the sea can become even more wild. For example, in 1933, a ship on its way from the Philippine Islands to California encountered a gale with winds of more than 75 miles per hour. As the ship fought the gale, the waves rose higher. One soared 112 feet. That's as high as an eleven-story building.

Undersea earthquakes sometimes cause waves that exceed the height of those caused by high winds. The reason that waves caused by earthquakes become higher is that they move faster. ❶ Suddenly, part of the ocean floor drops. The wave that results moves out from the earthquake, forming a ring on the surface of the water. This ring is a wave. As this wave starts to move, it is not very high, perhaps only a foot or so. Unlike wind-pushed waves, however, this kind of wave moves very fast. Some of these waves have traveled at a speed of about 500 miles per hour.

When this kind of wave comes near the shore, it begins to grow in height. The bottom part of the wave begins to drag along the ocean floor. The top part of the wave then begins to fall forward. More water keeps moving and climbing over the water that has slowed down. The result of this pileup is a great wave. ❷ Sometimes the wave will grow to a height of about 96 feet. The Alaska earthquake in 1964 caused a wave that measured 220 feet. That is the height of a twenty-two-story building.

One of the most unusual things that happens in the ocean—the tides—occurs every day. Tides are caused by the pull of the sun and the moon. The part of the Earth that is closest to the sun or moon is pulled the most. When both the sun and moon are in the same part of the sky, the tides are the strongest. ❸

A bay between the state of Maine in the United States and the Canadian provinces of New Brunswick and Nova Scotia has the strongest tide in the world. The greatest difference between the high and low tides for a twenty-four-hour period is about 52 feet. The tide is not this great on every day of the year—only when the sun and moon are in the right positions.

1

A	B
tial	spe<u>cial</u>
cial	par<u>tial</u>
	fa<u>cial</u>
	so<u>cial</u>
	poten<u>tial</u>

2

able   less   ly   re   un

3

garage   compl<u>ai</u>ning   <u>re</u>ferred   <u>un</u>tang<u>led</u>   succe<u>ed</u>ed

4

1. inhabitants
2. insist
3. invent
4. unconvincing

5

refrigerator   kitchen   respond

outskirts   occasional   houseful

routine   rarely   accident   putter

Einstein   break   Edison   defend

salesperson   Lark   admitted   shove

gloves   solar   exactly   machine

redden   draped   pour   mumble

persist   Agnes   scraped

6 A Houseful of Inventions

Agnes Lark was an elderly woman. And while she wasn't exactly   11
poor, she didn't have much money. Agnes lived in a small house on the   25
outskirts of Redmond with her cat, Einstein, and her dog, Edison.   36
Although the house had four rooms, the three inhabitants had to eat   48
and sleep in the kitchen. The rest of the house and the garage were   62
filled with junk. If anybody referred to the junk as "junk," Agnes would   75
become angry. Her eyes would seem to pop out, and her face would   88
redden. "Junk?" she would say. "Don't refer to my inventions as junk!"   100

Actually, Agnes didn't have many occasions to defend her junk, because   111
she rarely had visitors. In fact, aside from an occasional door-to-door   122
salesperson or youngster selling candy, nobody came to Agnes's house. ❶   132

The daily routine in Agnes's house started at six in the morning.   144
Einstein was the first to wake up. The cat would then wake up Agnes   158
by standing on her back as she snored on a couch in the corner of the   174
kitchen.   175

"Go away," Agnes would mumble, giving the cat an unconvincing   185
shove.   186

Einstein would respond with a half-purr, half-meow, and the cat   196
would jump down to the floor. The cat would continue to meow while   209
Agnes untangled herself from her blanket, stumbled to the   218
refrigerator, and poured a bowl of milk. ❷   225

Edison slept (usually with his paws on either side of his nose and his   239
long ears draped over his paws) until the refrigerator opened. Then   250
the old hound opened his red-rimmed eyes, stood up, and walked   261
slowly to Agnes.   264

"I suppose you want something to eat, too," Agnes would complain,   275
and Edison would respond with a few tired wags of his tail.   287

After the animals were fed and put outside, Agnes began to work 299
on one of her inventions. She usually worked on it until long after the 313
sun had set and the animals were asleep. Now and then Agnes took a 327
break during the day to walk to the store or putter in her garden, but 342
she always returned to her work. The only problem with Agnes's 353
inventions was that they weren't really inventions. It's true that she put 365
together new things, but none of them did what they were supposed to 378
do. Over the past forty years, she had invented three hundred new 390
gadgets, and not one worked as it should have. Her high-speed corn 402
picker didn't work, and it now stood in the hall as a coatrack. (It didn't 417
even make a very good coatrack.) ❸ 423

Her automatic shoe-tying machine didn't tie shoes. It scraped skin 433
from your ankle if you tried to use it, and it didn't even do a good job of 451
that. (Agnes had thought of using it as a toast scraper, but the machine 465
tore toast into small bits.) Agnes's egg cracker didn't simply crack eggs, 477
it splattered them all over the room. Her shoe-shiner was a pretty good 490
shoe-cutter. Her electric fork gave some hair-raising shocks. Her cell 500
phone was so heavy that two strong men could barely lift it, and her 514
solar furnace didn't make enough heat to melt ice cubes. 524

But Agnes went on. Forty years ago, she had told herself that she 537
would be an inventor, and now it was too late to admit that she hadn't 552
succeeded. If she admitted that her inventions didn't work, then she 563
had wasted forty years of her life. That's probably why she insisted on 576
referring to all her junk as "inventions." ❹ 583

It's a good thing that Agnes had persisted in trying to become an 596
inventor. If she had given up years ago, she would never have invented 609
the dop machine. Of course, Agnes invented the dop machine by 620
accident, but it was a *real* invention because it worked. And it worked 633
so well that it could have changed the history of the world. ❺ 645

1

A	B
tial	offic<u>ial</u>
cial	confiden<u>tial</u>
	spe<u>cial</u>
	ini<u>tial</u>
	so<u>cial</u>

2

r<u>ai</u>nbow   arran<u>g</u>ed   c<u>au</u>sed   rem<u>ai</u>n

3

1. crest
2. penetrate
3. electromagnetic

4

sunburn   suffering   dangerous   machines

shooting   produces   actually   waves

visible   materials   radio   violet   Biv

indigo   ultraviolet   X rays   travel

although   plate   billions   microwave

5 **From Radio Waves to X Rays**

To understand how Agnes invented the dop machine, you have to   11
understand something about waves. These waves aren't the kind you   21
see at the beach but the type that make up the light of a rainbow or an 38
X-ray picture. These are electromagnetic waves. The waves that you   48
see at the beach measure more than three feet from the crest of one   62
wave to the crest of the next. Electromagnetic waves have the same   74
shape as waves at the beach, but they are much smaller. Some   86
electromagnetic waves are only a millimeter from crest to crest.   96
Electromagnetic waves travel through space at the speed of light.   106

Each type of electromagnetic wave is a particular size. When you   117
change the length of the wave, you create another type of   128
electromagnetic wave. Let's see what happens when we start with the   139
longest electromagnetic wave and shorten the distance from the crest   149
of one wave to the crest of the next. The longest waves are radio   163
waves. Let's say that a radio wave measures four inches from the crest   176
of one wave to the crest of the next. When we shorten the distance so   191
that there is less than half an inch from crest to crest, the radio wave 206
turns into a heat wave. It no longer produces a radio signal. It now   220
produces heat. This is the kind of wave that is used in microwave   233
ovens to cook things very fast.   239

When we make the heat wave shorter, the wave turns into a light   252
wave. ❶ And as we change the length of the light wave, the color   265
changes. The longest light wave is red. The shortest light wave is   277
violet. When you look at a rainbow, you're actually looking at the   289
different wave lengths of light, arranged from the longest to <u>the</u>   300
shortest waves. Red is always at the outside of the rainbow, and violet 313
is always at the inside. ❷ If you want to remember the order of the   327

colors in the rainbow, think of the name Roy G. Biv. Each letter
stands for a color:

> R stands for red.
>
> O stands for orange.
>
> Y stands for yellow.
>
> G stands for green.
>
> B stands for blue.
>
> I stands for indigo (which is purple-blue).
>
> V stands for violet (which is purple).

The most important point to remember about the rainbow is that
the color with the longest wave is red and that if the wave is made
longer than red, it turns into a heat wave. Violet light has the shortest
wave. If we take a violet light wave and make it a little shorter, it turns
into an ultraviolet wave. The waves in ultraviolet light are so small
that one thousand of them stacked together would be as thin as a
sheet of paper. ❸

Sunburn is caused by ultraviolet waves. People may not feel burned
when they leave the sun; however, later that day their body will feel
hot and very tender because it is suffering from a burn caused by
ultraviolet waves.

When we make an ultraviolet wave very small, it becomes an X ray.
Now it is an extremely dangerous wave. If we are continually hit by
X-ray waves, we will die. People who work around X-ray machines
must stand behind a lead plate when the machine is shooting out
X-ray waves. ❹ X rays cannot go through lead, but the waves are so
short that they can penetrate most other materials.

An X ray is a hundred times shorter than a wave of violet light and
billions of times shorter than a radio wave. The X ray is not the
shortest wave there is. Agnes Lark invented a machine that picked up
waves much shorter than X rays. ❺

Lesson 88

1

special produce paused

frightened partial burr

2

1. failure
2. indeed
3. whir
4. tug
5. panic
6. prickly

3

noise screwdriver overpowering

noticed screen hairs aloud calmly

experienced hooked gadget visible

electromagnetic television particular

ultraviolet gamma microwave smokey

apparatus kitchen plastic-handled

flattened glued desired

4   Agnes's First Dop

Last time you learned that the longest electromagnetic waves are   10
radio waves. And you learned that as radio waves become shorter,   21
they change into heat waves. As heat waves become shorter, they   32
become light waves. Each color of visible light has a particular wave   44
length. Red light has the longest wave length. Violet light has the   56
shortest wave length. (The name Roy G. Biv helps us remember the   68
order of colors from longest to shortest wave lengths.)   77

Waves that are shorter than light waves are ultraviolet waves. And   88
waves still shorter than these are X rays.   96

The shortest waves known are gamma waves—or at least this was   108
true before Agnes Lark invented the dop machine. Gamma waves are   119
so small that a pile of one million of them would not be as thick as a   136
sheet of paper. ❶ Agnes didn't know much about these waves. In fact,   148
Agnes didn't exactly know what she was trying to invent. She started   160
out trying to make a device that would turn on the microwave oven   173
when the garage door opened. Such a gadget had already been   184
invented, so Agnes decided to make a garage door that could be   196
opened with a CB radio. This invention didn't work out too well   208
because any CB radio within ten miles could open Agnes's garage.   219
Every time somebody said, "Ten-four, good buddy," or, "Have you   229
seen Smokey today?" the garage door would pop open. ❷   238

Agnes tried to fix the garage door so that it would work only for   252
one special sound. To make this sound, she hooked up a small electric   265
motor with some parts from a microwave oven.   273

She then connected this apparatus to her CB radio and turned on   285
the motor. To her surprise, however, no special noise came over the   297
CB set. <u>Agnes</u> didn't become upset, because she'd learned to expect   308

failure. Instead, she went calmly to her tool kit to find a screwdriver.   321
She thought that she might be able to produce the desired noise if she   335
made the electric motor turn faster. ❸   341

Agnes selected a long, plastic-handled screwdriver from her tool   350
box and was carrying it back to the kitchen where the apparatus was   363
hooked up. As she walked past her television set, she felt a small tug   377
on the hand holding the screwdriver. Something was pulling her arm   388
toward the television set. It was not an overpowering pull, but it was   401
strong enough for Agnes to notice it. She paused for a moment,   413
listening to the quiet whir of the electric motor in the kitchen and   426
feeling the gentle tug on her arm.   433

"What have we here?" she asked herself, allowing her hand to move   445
closer and closer to the television set. The force became stronger until,   457
like a magnet, it pulled the screwdriver to the screen with a loud   470
clunk! ❹ For a moment, Agnes was frightened. Her hand, still holding   481
the screwdriver, was stuck to the television screen. Her skirt was   492
flattened against the screen, and she could feel the small hairs on her   505
arm leaning toward the set. Agnes tried to pull her hand away, but all   519
she did was move the entire television set. "This is indeed strange," she   532
said aloud.   534

And then, quite suddenly, Agnes experienced her first dop. It came   545
to her like a message, but not in words. It was more like a very strong   561
feeling. The feeling was, "I have a burr in my fur and it hurts." For an   577
instant, Agnes felt as if she were not herself, but someone or   589
something else. That instant was followed by a feeling of panic. Agnes   601
felt trapped, glued to the television while strange things were   611
happening to her. ❺ She dragged the television set over to the kitchen   623
table and turned off the electric motor. As the motor turned more and   636
more slowly, the tug of the television set died away. Agnes pulled her   649
hand from the set and dropped the screwdriver. She opened and   660

closed her hand several times to see if it had been injured. She rubbed
her arm. But there was no pain and no sign of injury.

    "That was strange," Agnes said, glancing down at the screwdriver.
Next to the screwdriver was the cat, Einstein, trying to bite something
in its fur. In a flash, Agnes knew what was in the cat's fur, and she
knew where it was. It was a burr, a prickly burr, just below the cat's
right shoulder. Even before she picked the cat up, she knew. **❻**

INFORMATION PASSAGE

combined	treacherous	considering
bonanza		trek

The Klondike Gold Rush

The California Gold Rush of 1849 and those that followed in the states near California were gigantic; however, the Klondike Gold Rush was larger than all the others combined.

The map to the right shows where the Klondike is. It is close to Alaska in northern Canada. The route that led to the Klondike was both long and treacherous. Prospectors first landed in southern Alaska and then went to the Chilkoot Trail, which led over steep mountain passes. There they built boats that would take them 500 miles down the Yukon River to the gold fields. The only other route involved traveling 1,600 miles up the Yukon River from the west coast of Alaska into Canada. ❶

The Klondike gold discovery occurred in 1896. Skookum Jim Mason, his sister Kate, and her husband, George Carmack, discovered rich gold deposits near a remote part of Rabbit Creek called Bonanza. Skookum Jim was a Native American. George Carmack was not. The group thought that it would be better to put the claim in Carmack's name. They were afraid that the claim would be rejected if it were in the name of a Native American. ❷

The news about the gold find spread quite quickly, considering how long it took people to travel from Bonanza Creek to the nearest town.

The news did not reach the United States until 1897. Prospectors arrived in Seattle, Washington, with large

amounts of gold. Within weeks, thousands of miners and prospectors made their way to Alaska, where they started the long trek to the gold fields. ❸

The photo above shows how many prospectors took this difficult journey. You can see a solid line of hundreds of prospectors on the Chilkoot Trail, climbing over a mountain in the late winter. The prospectors in the picture did not have pack animals (horses or mules) with them because earlier prospectors had discovered that pack animals could not make it up the last steep slope of the Chilkoot Trail. Prospectors carved 1,500 steps from the solid ice of the trail. Neither horses nor mules could make it up the slope, and more than 3,000 horses died along the trail, which had the nickname of Dead Horse Trail. An amazing number of prospectors took this journey to Bonanza Creek—over 100,000 of them. ❹

Dawson was a small summer fish camp for Native Americans. It was close to the gold fields. Within two years of the discovery of gold at Bonanza Creek, Dawson had become a thriving community with a population of 40,000. After the Klondike Gold Rush was over, the population dropped to less than 1,000. Today, Dawson's population is about 2,000.

During the winter, the average low temperature in Dawson was about zero degrees. Frequently, however, the low would be 15 degrees below zero or colder. The cold, combined with the lack of food, meant that many prospectors died during the five years of the Klondike Gold Rush. Tens of thousands, those who did not die, had to work their way back to the United States, without riches, and some without much hope. ⑤

1   **pre**   **re**   **less**   **able**

2   predicting   diseases   reliving   radiation

3
1. slanting
2. risk
3. palm
4. conscious
5. indifferently
6. scold
7. anxiety

4

frightening   worthless   apparatus

pleading   twice   perspire   tulip

glanced   inventions   during   severe

experienced   adventure   argued   famous

combination   diagnosing   electromagnetic

solo   invaded   scratching   succeeded

downward   antenna   mushy   rectangle

5

Cats, Dogs—and People, Too

On the day that Agnes experienced her first dop, she had a lot to   14
think about. During most of the afternoon, she argued with herself   25
about whether she should try the dop experiment again. There were   36
two sides to the argument.   41

One side insisted that the machine might allow Agnes to read the   53
thoughts of animals. She could become very rich with such an   64
invention. She might become famous by joining a circus as an animal   76
trainer or by diagnosing diseases in animals.   83

The other side of the argument warned her that the electromagnetic   94
waves created by the machine could be dangerous. Perhaps they   104
would cause severe radiation burns or make one go mad. ❶ She really   116
didn't know anything about these new waves.   123

Shortly before supper, when the light was slanting though the   133
kitchen window, casting a bright rectangle on the wall, Agnes picked   144
up the screwdriver. She had decided to try the experiment. After all,   156
she had lived a good, long life, and she wasn't going to live forever. It   171
was worth the risk. Nevertheless, as she picked up the screwdriver, her   183
hand was shaking. Her palms were sweating, and a voice inside was   195
pleading, "I don't want to die. I'm afraid." ❷   203

Agnes tried to ignore her anxiety. She put down the screwdriver,   214
took several deep breaths, and looked down at Einstein. "Well," she   225
said, in a voice that sounded stiff, "it won't get any easier by waiting."   239

In her mind, she kept reliving that moment in which she had   251
received the message about the burr. It hadn't been a thought, and it   264
hadn't been words. It was as if she had become Einstein for a moment   278
and was able to experience what the cat was feeling. It was as if some   293

other being had invaded her mind. <u>It</u> was like becoming two beings at
the same time: Agnes/Einstein.

As Agnes turned on the apparatus, she stood staring first at
Einstein and then at Edison. The dog was in the corner, scratching
behind his ear. "This is it," Agnes said. The television set was on; the
apparatus was running. All that remained was to pick up the
screwdriver.

"You worthless old thing," Agnes scolded herself. "Don't you have
any spirit of adventure left? Pick up that screwdriver and get on with
it." She did. She stood about three feet from the television set and
closed her eyes. Slowly she allowed her hand to be pulled to the
screen. Her heart was pounding wildly. She began having second
thoughts about her decision. (Maybe twice a day is too much.
Tomorrow might be better.) Clunk! Her hand was stuck to the screen.
But there were no thoughts, no other beings invading Agnes's
consciousness. ❸

She opened her eyes and glanced around the room. Edison was
biting a flea on his back, but Agnes received no messages. The cat was
staring somewhat indifferently at Agnes, but there were still no
messages. "Perhaps the field isn't working," Agnes thought. To test the
strength of the field, she tried to pull her hand from the set. All she
succeeded in doing, however, was to rotate the screwdriver so that the
handle was directed downward. ❹

What Agnes didn't know was that the screwdriver acted something
like a radio or TV antenna. As it turned, it picked up messages from
different directions. Suddenly, Agnes received a message. It was a very
strong feeling—an urge—a great hunger to eat dog food. Agnes felt
her mouth watering as her mind pictured a nice big bowl of mushy
dog food. "Yum," she said to herself.

Without realizing it, Agnes rotated the screwdriver a bit and   608
received a new message: "But where is three sixty-one Tulip Lane? The   620
way these streets zig and zag, they ought to pay a taxi driver double   634
just to come out here." Agnes felt very angry and had an urge to drive   649
faster.   650

Again she rotated the screwdriver. Suddenly, she experienced great   659
anxiety. She was on her first solo flight, and she was preparing to land 673
the plane. She was talking to herself. "First trim the plane and then   686
glide slowly, no more than ten degrees down. Keep the wings level."   698
Agnes began to perspire.   702

She reached over and turned off the apparatus. Slowly, the thoughts   713
of Dottie Collins, an eighteen-year-old pilot flying directly over   722
Agnes's house, began to fade away. ❺   728

1
San Diego   gorillas   chimpanzees   evidence

orangutans   century   language   institute

captivity   cords   investigators   occasions

mirror   incredibly   recognized

2
1. intriguing
2. image
3. capacity
4. personality
5. accurate
6. focused

3

Great Apes

The great apes are the gorillas, the chimpanzees, and the orangutans. They are the three animals that are most like human beings. Both the likenesses and differences between people and the apes are very interesting.

A full-grown chimpanzee may weigh 180 pounds, or a little more than the average adult male. Chimpanzees have a very powerful grip and can exert tremendous force when they pull. ❶ A male chimpanzee at the Bronx Zoo that weighed 165 pounds set a record with a right-handed pull of 847 pounds. A human male of the same weight has the capacity to pull about 210 pounds. A female chimpanzee at the Bronx Zoo once achieved a right-handed pull of 1,260 pounds when she was very angry. Her pull was almost six times the pull of an average human male.

People live longer than the great apes. The average person in the United States lives about seventy years. In captivity, some chimpanzees have lived forty years. The oldest great ape whose age is accurately known was an orangutan. It lived for 59 years. ❷

People may outlive the great apes, but in a contest of weight a great ape would be the winner—the gorilla. The heaviest gorilla ever in captivity was at the San Diego Zoo. This huge male stood 5 feet 7¾ inches tall, measured 78 inches around the chest, and weighed more than 683 pounds.

People would clearly win an intelligence contest with the great apes, but the question of ape intelligence has intrigued scientists for more than a century. One question that is particularly fascinating is whether or not any of the great apes have the ability to learn language. At the Institute for Primate Studies at the University of Oklahoma, scientists work with chimpanzees to see if they can learn to speak and understand language. Their prize subject was Washoe. Because chimpanzees do not have the kind of vocal cords that would allow them to produce the sounds people can produce, the investigators taught Washoe to use sign language. ❸ She learned the signs for many, many words. Investigators then observed Washoe to see if she would put signs together to express ideas that they had not taught her. The first time Washoe was presented with a mirror, she looked at the image and made the sign for her own name, showing that she recognized herself in the mirror. On many other occasions, Washoe used signs to express new ideas.

Not all scientists agree that chimpanzees are intelligent enough to use language, but those who have worked with Washoe think that she provides strong evidence that they are capable of using language.

1

porch   uncertainties   social

apparently   ceremonies

2

received   possibilities   roam   message

limitless   demonstrate   usually   attached

experimented   displayed   focused   conducted

immediately   imaginative   accurate   millionaire

crazy   summarized   effective   rocker

personality   diagram   schemes   aimed

penetrating   necessary   filing

3

1. incurred
2. associated
3. productive
4. transmit
5. screens
6. patent
7. assuming

4   # Display of Personalities

Agnes usually went to sleep early. But on the night that she first   13
experimented with her dop machine, she sat on her front-porch   23
rocker, drinking root beer until long after midnight. She finally   33
summarized her experiences by saying, "That crazy machine displays   42
personalities." And that's how it got the name, dop: *display of*   53
personalities. It displayed more than thoughts. It transmitted the   62
feelings that were associated with thoughts. "Dop," Agnes said over   72
and over to herself. "I have invented a dop machine." ❶   82

She realized, of course, that the machine was important; however,   92
she wasn't certain how important it was or how it could be used   105
productively. "I don't mind being unsuccessful at inventing," she   114
concluded. "But I never wanted to invent something that could be   125
harmful."   126

In keeping with her uncertainties about the dop machine, Agnes   136
told no one about it for three months. During that period, she   148
conducted a number of experiments. ❷ This is what she discovered: 158

1. When the dop machine was attached to a second TV screen, it was   172
   capable of transmitting feelings of people on TV.   180
2. The machine could also be hooked up to a telephone.   191
3. Two coat hangers wired together at right angles provided the best   203
   antenna—much more powerful than the screwdriver, and more   212
   accurate in locating different targets.   217
4. The dop rays were not dangerous to one's health. (During some   229
   days, Agnes spent as many as five hours on the machine.)   240
5. The dop rays were capable of penetrating any substance that Agnes   252
   had tried, including lead. (Lead screens out most other rays,   262
   including gamma and X rays.)   267

6. If there were a great many people in the area where the dop was   282
   aimed, no dops would be transmitted. (When Agnes focused on the   293
   audience of a TV show, no <u>dops</u> were received. When she focused   305
   on the guest star, however, she received strong dops.) ❸   314

   Inventors must be imaginative. They must be able to look at all sorts   327
of untried possibilities and let their imaginations roam. Agnes   336
frequently found her imagination turning to the idea of fame and   347
fortune. When the master of ceremonies of a quiz show presented   358
questions, Agnes always knew the answer because the master of   368
ceremonies knew the answer. And the dop machine transmitted the   378
answer to Agnes. Agnes's imagination saw fantastic possibilities of   387
entering quiz shows and winning thousands—*millions* of dollars! She   397
might become the most famous quiz-show participant in the history of   408
television. ❹   409

   In the end, however, Agnes rejected this scheme. It seemed a shame   421
to let this foolproof, money-making possibility go by, but Agnes   431
wanted to be recognized as an inventor, not as a famous quiz-show   443
winner or a millionaire. Therefore, it was only a question of time   455
before Agnes contacted a patent attorney to see about getting a patent   467
for her machine. Yet, when Agnes took her invention to the attorney,   479
she began to have second thoughts. ❺   485

   The attorney spoke in a very businesslike manner as she asked,   496
"What, exactly, is this machine designed to do?"   504

   "It's a personality display machine," Agnes explained. "I can   513
demonstrate how it works, and that should tell you more than I could   526
with words."   528

   "I don't really think that will be necessary," the attorney said. "I   540
think that a diagram of the machine and a simple explanation of what   553
it does will be quite adequate for our purposes."   562

"I don't have a diagram," Agnes answered, "but I *can* explain how it works."

Agnes began to explain, but before long she realized how crazy she sounded. Here she was, a little old lady who had never invented anything successful before, talking about displaying personalities through waves that she couldn't describe. "I can appreciate how this must sound to you," she said, smiling and shrugging. "But it really does do what I say." ❻

"I'm sure it does," the attorney replied sharply. "But, Miss Lark, let's discuss practical matters for a moment. My initial fee, after adequate diagrams of the machine are provided, will be two thousand dollars. This amount will pay for a patent search to find out if someone else has already patented such a machine. And, if yours is the first such machine, the two thousand dollars will pay for filing a patent in your name. Assuming that we don't hit any great snags, no additional fee will be incurred. However, the two thousand dollars must be paid in advance. I'll be blunt. Do you have the money?" ❼

"No, not right now, but I think—"

The attorney held up her hand. "I think that you should either look for another attorney or contact me when you have the money. Good day." The woman's smile faded, and Agnes felt very embarrassed.

1

experie<u>n</u>ce <u>r</u>ewarded ni<u>gh</u>tmares obvious<u>l</u>y

2

weeping calmed chuckled hallway

guard laughter microphone dismal

shuffled fantastic suspect detective

guilty address inspector drawer

court cabinets museum

subjects security Cypress

society doughnuts district

3

1. superb
2. attentive
3. humiliating
4. approach
5. lingered
6. process

4   Agnes Gets a Superb Idea

Agnes was quite upset about her visit to the patent attorney. "That   12
was the most humiliating experience," she said to herself. "I'll show   23
them. I'll go to Las Vegas and play blackjack. I'll win more money   36
than anyone ever has in the history of Las Vegas." ❶   46

By the next day, Agnes had calmed down and decided on another   58
approach. She would demonstrate her invention to a local science   68
society that met at a nearby museum each Wednesday. Agnes didn't   79
realize that this plan would lead to an experience even more   90
humiliating than her meeting with the patent attorney. She took her   101
apparatus to the meeting, but she wasn't allowed in.   110

"I'm sorry," a young man at the door of the museum said. "This   123
meeting is for members only." ❷   128

Agnes wasn't going to take no for an answer, so as the first two   142
members arrived, she tried to interest them in a demonstration of her   154
machine. She quickly explained the apparatus and then pleaded,   163
"Would you try it out? It really works."   171

"Is it safe?" the younger of the two members asked. The other   183
chuckled and said, "We're not very good subjects. Why don't you try   195
someone on the fourth floor? They have much better subjects up there."   207

Both of the members began to laugh, and Agnes felt herself   218
becoming embarrassed and angry. "It works! Why won't you listen?"   228
she found herself saying in a loud voice as they turned away.   240

The next club member to come to the meeting listened attentively as   252
Agnes explained to her how the machine worked. "If you will just   264
allow me to demonstrate it, you'll be *well rewarded*."   273

"I'm sorry. I don't have time," the woman said, and walked into the   286

meeting. Agnes heard her ask someone inside, "Who is that strange   297
person in the hallway?"   301

"I don't know," someone replied. "But maybe we ought to get a   313
security guard and have her thrown out." ❸   320

"You don't have to have me thrown out," Agnes shouted into the   332
room. "I'm leaving!"   335

"She must have read our thoughts with that machine of hers,"   346
someone said, and everyone laughed. The sound of that laughter   356
lingered in Agnes's mind for hours. She felt like weeping. They   367
wouldn't listen; they didn't understand. What's worse, they didn't want   377
to understand. ❹   379

That night Agnes had a nightmare in which she was running on a   392
wheel much like those found in hamster cages. In one hand, she held a   406
microphone through which she kept yelling, "But if you'll let me stop,   418
I'll show that the machine works." The problem was that the   429
microphone wasn't attached to anything. And there was no one   439
around to hear her pleas.   444

When Agnes awoke in the morning, she had a splitting headache. She   456
tried to shake the dismal thoughts and the pain from her head, but she   470
couldn't. She shuffled to the door in her slippers, picked up the   482
newspaper, and looked at the headline on the first page. "Suspect in   494
Jewelry Robbery Questioned," it read. Suddenly she felt everything stop.   504

Almost before the idea was formed in her head, Agnes knew that it   517
was a good one—a superb one, a *fantastic one.* "I'll be a detective,"   531
Agnes said out loud. "Nobody can stop me from doing that. I can do   545
something that is good, and . . ."   550

It was a nice day—the nicest morning that Agnes had seen in a long   565
time. There would be no more trying to talk to attorneys or anyone   578
else. Agnes was going to do great things. ❺   586

Agnes was getting ideas faster than she could process them. At the 598
same time, she was trying to pour milk for Einstein, get dressed, call 611
the police station, and look at the newspaper to see if the robbery 624
suspect was going to be on television. "Hello," Agnes said as the 636
phone at the police station was picked up. "This is Miss Lark, and if 650
you would let me talk to your jewel robbery suspect, I could tell you 664
whether he's guilty." 667

"We have enough trouble around here as it is," the police officer 679
said, "so stop joking around, lady." 685

Agnes said, "All right. Just tell me the address of the jail at which 699
they're holding the suspect." 703

"Fifteenth and Cypress. Now get off the phone and don't call back." 715

"Thank you," Agnes said. She dashed to the wall in back of her TV 729
set, where she'd hung a large map of the city. She stuck a pin on the 745
corner of Fifteenth and Cypress and then rotated the hangers. She 756
turned on the dop machine and tried to make contact with the suspect. 769
The first message came immediately: 774

"Hurry up and pick the doughnut you want. I don't have all day. 787
You're not the only police inspector on coffee break." **❻** 796

Agnes turned the antenna slightly. "Where are we supposed to store 807
this stuff? These district attorneys fill half a file drawer every time 819
they go to court, but we ran out of file cabinets three months ago, and 834
the cases keep on coming in. The district attorney expects us . . ." 845

Agnes moved the antenna again. This time the message was: "I 856
better watch my step. I'm supposed to be polite to cranks that call in, 870
but I can take only so much." **❼** 877

Agnes was getting close. That was the officer who answered her 888
phone call. Now all she had to do was find the suspect and read 902
his thoughts. 904

trudged	agitation	undulations	lure
desperate	flung	imperceptible	

A Story about the Klondike

The Klondike Gold Rush sparked a great number of stories and poems. The most famous stories were written by Jack London, who was one of the prospectors who trudged up the Chilkoot Trail and staked out a claim in the Yukon. London wrote about the lure of the north country. Below is part of one of his most famous short stories, "To Build a Fire." The first part of the story gives a chilling description of the hero's adventure on the Yukon Trail. This story takes place during the winter when the sun is not visible along the south horizon. ❶

The man flung a look back along the way he had come. The Yukon River lay a mile wide and hidden under three feet of ice. On top of this ice were as many feet of snow. It was all pure white, rolling in gentle undulations where the ice jams of the freeze-up had formed. North and south, as far as the eye could see, it was unbroken white, save for a dark hairline that curved and twisted from around the spruce-covered island to the south, and that curved and twisted into the north, where it disappeared behind another spruce-covered island. This dark hairline was the trail—the main trail—that led south five hundred miles to the Chilkoot Pass, Dyea, and salt water; and that led north seventy miles

to Dawson, and still on to the north a thousand miles to
Nulato, and finally to St. Michael on Bering Sea, a thousand
miles and half a thousand more. ❷

Later, the man in the story becomes desperate. His fingers are
freezing. He manages to gather some twigs and builds a fire under a
spruce tree, where there was a supply of twigs. The story continues:

It was his own fault or, rather, his mistake. He should not
have built the fire under the spruce tree. He should have built
it in the open. But it had been easier to pull the twigs from
the brush and drop them directly on the fire. Now the tree
under which he had done this carried a weight of snow on its
boughs. No wind had blown for weeks, and each bough was
fully freighted. Each time he had pulled a twig he had
communicated a slight agitation to the tree—an
imperceptible agitation, so far as he was concerned, but an
agitation sufficient to bring about the disaster. High up in
the tree one bough capsized its load of snow. This fell on the
boughs beneath, capsizing them. This process continued,
spreading out and involving the whole tree. It grew like an
avalanche, and it descended without warning upon the man
and the fire, and the fire was blotted out! ❸

1

convince   perfumed   concerned   special

2

bracelets   innocent   scent   unusual

descriptions   urge   approximately

suspect   skillful   focused   janitors

lying   jewels   velvet   spangled

extension   obviously   assured

Rialto   district   populated

3

1. fidget
2. momentary
3. acquainted with
4. adjustment

4

Contacting the Suspect

It was almost eight o'clock in the evening before Agnes made   11
contact with the suspect in the jail. At the time, she was holding a cold   26
chicken leg in one hand and fidgeting with the coat-hanger antenna in   38
the other. (She had become quite skillful with the dop machine.) She   50
had been making small adjustments in the antenna for several hours   61
but still couldn't locate the suspect. Agnes could tell from the dops she   74
was picking up that the machine was still focused on the police   86
station, but she seemed to make contact with everyone except the   97
suspect. Agnes had become acquainted with four police officers, two   107
people in the crime lab, five secretaries, two janitors, and a young   119
woman who sold sandwiches and doughnuts.   125

As Agnes was about to take a bite from the cold chicken leg, she   139
made contact with something unusual. Apparently, the dop machine   148
was focused on a phone line in the police station. "Eddie," one voice   161
said, "don't say anything. Do you get my message?" The message that   173
came through the dop machine was that Eddie was guilty.   183

"It's a bum rap," Eddie replied. "I didn't do a thing. They're just   196
giving me trouble!" ❶   199

Agnes could feel that Eddie was lying and that he didn't trust the   212
other man. Eddie was also hoping that the police were listening in on   225
the call, because he wanted to convince them that he didn't know   237
about the jewels. *The jewels!* Agnes had made contact.   246

"Sure, Eddie," the other man said. "Of course it's a bum rap. But   259
don't talk to anybody. Don't say anything. I'll get you out before   271
tomorrow morning."   273

The man Eddie called had been involved in some of Eddie's other   285
jobs, and he was afraid that Eddie would tell the police about him.   298

That's <u>all</u> he was concerned about—Eddie talking. And all Eddie was 310
concerned about was trying to convince the police that he didn't know 322
anything about the stolen jewels. ❷ 327

Suddenly Agnes picked up the image of a large velvet box that had 340
a perfumed scent. Inside were rings and bracelets, all spangled with 351
diamonds. Agnes had a momentary urge to possess those jewels. But 362
then Eddie pushed the thought of the jewels from his and Agnes's minds. 375

"They're just out to lay a bum rap on me, and I'm innocent," Eddie 389
repeated to the man he had called. Then the conversation was over. Agnes 402
quickly marked the position of the antenna and then began to move it 415
slightly, trying to follow Eddie. For some reason, however, she couldn't. 426

Before Agnes went to bed that night, she attached a wire from the 439
antenna to her big toe. After she'd been asleep for an hour or so, a 454
phone conversation awakened her. Agnes shared the anger of a young 465
woman who'd been picked up for speeding. The woman was asking a 477
friend to come and get her out of jail. ❸ 486

The next phone call was at six in the morning. Agnes awoke sharing 499
the anger of a man who was trying to reach his lawyer but kept getting 514
a wrong number. 517

At 9:15, Agnes experienced another call between Eddie and the man 528
he had phoned the evening before. The man assured Eddie, "I'll have 540
you out before dinner tonight." 545

This time, when Eddie talked to the man, Agnes got a strong feeling 558
of where the jewels were hidden. They were in a dry cleaning place not 572
far from the Rialto Movie Theater. The jewels were in a red velvet 585
box, which was in a large bag of clothes that had been sent to the 600
cleaners. The bag was checked under the name of Ruth Costello. ❹ 611

"I've got it!" Agnes said, jumping up. Einstein had been sitting in 623
her lap and leaped clear as Agnes came out of the chair. "I'll go to the 639
dry cleaning place and pick up the jewels." 647

Then Agnes realized that she wasn't sure of the cleaner's exact   658
location. It was near the Rialto Theater, but so were dozens of shops. 671
The Rialto was just west of the downtown district in a heavily   683
populated area, and the streets were lined with businesses of all   694
descriptions. Probably several of them were dry cleaning   702
establishments.   703

1

un   re   ly   able   ness

2

sw<u>ee</u>ping   dire<u>ction</u>   plast<u>e</u>red   ben<u>ea</u>th

3

importance   approached   sternly

convincingly   arranged   search   assure

railroad   addition   striking   clothes

half-price   bargain-hunting   hey

stuff   ticket   background

carrying   uniforms   indicated

4

1. abruptly
2. rehearse
3. scrawl
4. bulge
5. mission

5   Finding the Cleaners

Agnes took a cab to the Rialto Theater. When she got there, the   13
clock in front of the savings and loan building down the street was   26
striking eleven. An usher was sweeping the area in front of the Rialto's   39
ticket window. "Excuse me," Agnes said to the usher. "Is there a dry   52
cleaning place near here?"   56

The usher stopped sweeping, leaned against his broom, and shrugged.   66
"I don't know," he said, smiling, "I don't get my clothes cleaned." ❶   78

"Well, thanks anyway," Agnes said, and began to walk away.   88

The usher began sweeping again but abruptly stopped and said,   98
"Hey, I just remembered. The theater has our uniforms cleaned at one   110
of those two places on the next block. There are two shops there almost   124
next door to each other." He pointed to show Agnes the direction. ❷   136

Agnes thanked him and walked in the direction he'd indicated. As   147
she moved along the street, she began to rehearse what she'd say when   160
she went into the first shop. To get the bag, Agnes would have to tell a   176
lie, and she wasn't very good at lying.   184

The first cleaning place was a small shop with a large window. Signs   197
were plastered all over it. The largest read, "Dresses half-price,   207
through June 1."   210

The words "June 1" had been crossed out, and "July 4" was   222
scrawled beneath them. Agnes found herself reading with interest and   232
then sternly reminded herself that she wasn't bargain-hunting. Her   241
mission was of much greater importance. ❸   247

She took a deep breath, rehearsed her lie once more, and walked   259
inside. A young woman was behind the counter. Agnes approached   269
her and said, "I have a problem. I'm supposed to pick up Ruth   282
Costello's clothes, but I seem to have lost the ticket."   292

"You do have a problem," the young <u>woman</u> said. "No ticket, no clothes." ❹

"Please," Agnes said. "I've got to have those clothes. It's really important. Can't I pay you a little extra and maybe—"

"I meant what I said," the young woman answered. "You can't just walk in off the street and tell me you're supposed to pick up someone else's clothes. How do I know that you're for real?"

"Oh, I assure you that I wouldn't do that," Agnes said, trying to lie convincingly.

"Besides," the young woman went on, "we don't check things by names. We have them arranged by number. I'd have to know the number, or else I'd have to sift through a big stack of stuff." ❺

"The number," Agnes said to herself. She began to search her memory of the dops with Eddie. Had there been a number?

Agnes called up a mental picture of the box. There it was—in a bag checked under the name Ruth Costello. The bag was white with a red tag around its neck. The tag looked something like a railroad ticket with black numbers on a red background. There was a big letter and then some smaller numbers. The letter was *A*. The first numbers were 135, and then there were others. ❻

Agnes looked at the young woman. "I believe that the bag began with the letter *A* and then 135."

"Really?" the woman asked. "And what was the rest of it?"

"I can't remember," Agnes said.

"I can't find it from that number. You'd have to tell me the last part."

"The last part," Agnes said to herself, and again searched her memory. She could now see a small *t*. And the numbers immediately before it were 56.

"The rest was 56 followed by a *T*," Agnes said. 593

"All right," the young woman said, smiling. "Maybe I *can* help you 605 out." She went into the back room and came out carrying a large bag. 619 "You know I can't turn it over unless you can tell me what's in it." 634

Agnes knew that in addition to the jewel box there were clothes 646 inside, but she couldn't describe those clothes because Eddie hadn't 656 thought about them while Agnes was sharing his thoughts. 665

"Well?" the young woman asked. "What's inside the bag?" 674

Agnes pressed her lips together and tried to think of an answer. She 687 could see the bulge of the jewel box at the bottom of the bag. ❼ 701

1

earthquakes   volcanoes   liable

Indonesia   period   nuclear

explosion   hydrogen   destructive

unstable   tremors   damage

2

1. erupted
2. lava
3. coastal
4. dwellings

3

Volcanoes and Earthquakes

The earth appears to be solid and lasting, but powerful forces are at work beneath it. These forces sometimes result in volcanoes and earthquakes. A volcano is an outpouring of hot molten rock called lava through a weak point in the earth's surface. A volcano's first stage is called an eruption and is usually a great explosion. Following the explosion comes the river of lava. ❶

In 1815 a volcanic eruption in Indonesia continued for two days. During that time, the opening at the top of the volcano spread until it measured 7 miles from one side to the other.

In 1883 another eruption occurred in Indonesia. It began with an explosion estimated to be twenty-six times as powerful as the most destructive hydrogen bomb ever tested. It threw rocks 33 miles into the air and caused a giant wave to roll over 163 villages, killing more than 36,000 people. The sound of the eruption was so powerful that four hours later it was heard almost 3,000 miles away. ❷

Earthquakes are caused by sudden shifts in parts of the earth. Earthquakes frequently occur in coastal areas where mountains rise next to deep seas. The great difference between the depth of the sea and the height of the mountains makes such an area unstable. For this reason California is the part of the United States most liable to experience serious earthquakes. ❸

Earthquakes can cause immense loss of life and property. In China in 1556 an earthquake killed an estimated 830,000 persons. In Japan in 1923 another earthquake resulted in the death of more than 140,000 people and the destruction of 500,000 dwellings.

The most powerful earthquake in recent years was the Alaskan earthquake of 1964. However, the Lisbon earthquake of 1755 may have been the most powerful, but there were no instruments then to measure its strength. Scientists believe it was one hundred times stronger than the largest nuclear device ever exploded. It was so powerful that it disturbed lakes in far-off Norway.

About 500,000 earthquakes occur every year, but of these only some 100,000 can be felt by people living in the area where they occur, and of these only about 1,000 do any damage. ❹

1

st<u>all</u>   <u>ai</u>n't   par<u>tial</u>

chan<u>g</u>e   <u>a</u>wkward   brisk<u>ly</u>

2

patience   managed   glanced

swerve   vision   imitation

blur   laugh   lousy   establishment

counter   doorway   dared

scurried   bumped   intersection

attempted   revolving   proof

3

1. confidential
2. surge
3. sensed
4. hulk
5. determination
6. skirt around
7. convey
8. disguise

4   **Agnes Gets the Jewels**

The young woman asked Agnes again, "What's in the bag? I can't 12
wait all day." 15

"You see," Agnes said, trying to stall for time, "I'm not sure about 28
the things that are in the bag because my friend didn't tell me." 41

"Look," the young woman said. "I can't turn this bag over to you 54
unless you can give me proof that you're supposed to have it." ❶ 66

"All right," Agnes said, and leaned over the counter. "I can tell you 79
one thing that's in the bag, but this is highly confidential. There is a 93
jewel box in the bottom of the bag. Inside that box are some of the 108
finest imitation jewels in the world." 114

"Imitation jewels in a cleaning bag?" The young woman shook her 125
head. She began to laugh. She reached down in the bag and pulled out 139
the box. "Well, I'll be," she said, staring at the box. "There *is* a jewel 154
box in here." She opened the box and looked at the jewels. "But you're 168
wrong about one thing," she continued. "These aren't the finest 178
imitation jewels in the world." 183

Agnes felt her heart pound faster. The young woman continued, 193
"These are lousy imitations. They're too showy. Nobody would think 203
that these things are real. Some of those stones are as big as ice cubes." ❷ 218

The young woman laughed and closed the jewel box. "OK, I'm 229
convinced. The bill for this cleaning is $9.83." 237

Agnes gave the young woman ten dollars, told her to keep the 249
change, and walked briskly from the dry cleaning establishment. As 259
she was walking through the door, she almost ran into a man, and 272
Agnes experienced a surge of panic. She instantly sensed that this 283
man was connected with Eddie. Suddenly she realized who the man 294
was—the man on the <u>phone</u>. And she realized why he was here—to 308

get the jewels. Agnes tried not to look at him, because there was $\quad$ 321
something about him that conveyed meanness—the kind of meanness $\quad$ 331
that was disguised with patience and cunning. For an instant their $\quad$ 342
eyes met. "Excuse me," Agnes said, stepping to one side. $\quad$ 352

The man walked through the doorway past Agnes as if she didn't $\quad$ 364
exist. Once outside, Agnes began to walk as fast as she dared. ❸ $\quad$ 376

"Where's a taxi?" she said to herself. The streets were becoming $\quad$ 387
crowded with people. It was nearing noon. As Agnes scurried down $\quad$ 398
the street, she glanced back after every eight or ten steps to make sure $\quad$ 412
that nobody was chasing her. "Where's a taxi?" she said aloud. She $\quad$ 424
was almost a full block from the store now. $\quad$ 433

"Hey, watch where you're going," somebody shouted. Agnes had $\quad$ 442
walked into a woman. $\quad$ 446

"I'm sorry," Agnes said, and she tried to dodge through the growing $\quad$ 458
crowds. She glanced back and saw a large form running down the $\quad$ 470
street—a huge hulk that moved without much grace but with great $\quad$ 482
power and determination. "Oh, no," Agnes said, and she began to $\quad$ 493
run. She bumped into people who were knotted at an intersection. She $\quad$ 505
managed to skirt around them, but she was forced into the street. ❹ $\quad$ 517

Screech—crash. $\quad$ 519

Agnes had stepped right in front of a car that attempted to swerve $\quad$ 532
out of her way. Unfortunately, the car hit another car in the oncoming $\quad$ 545
lane. "This is terrible," Agnes said, and then she began to run again. $\quad$ 558
There were so many people on the sidewalk that Agnes, almost $\quad$ 569
without thinking, began to run down the middle of the street. People $\quad$ 582
were laughing and pointing at her. Drivers were yelling, but Agnes $\quad$ 592
barely heard them. $\quad$ 595

She was becoming tired. She wasn't a very fast runner at best—not $\quad$ 608
at her age. And now she was out of breath. It felt as if her arms and $\quad$ 625
legs were filled with heavy sand. They seemed to be moving in slow $\quad$ 638

motion, and her lungs felt as if they would burst. Agnes couldn't catch 651
her breath, and her vision was starting to blur. The hulk was catching 664
up. There he was behind Agnes, running down the middle of the 676
street, now less than half a block behind. ❺ 684

"I'll never make it," Agnes realized. She slowed to an awkward 695
stumble. "If you can't run, hide," some part of her mind said above 708
the roar of her burning breathing. Agnes stumbled between two 718
parked cars and again tried to hide in the stream of people on the 732
sidewalk. But the hulk was getting closer. 739

Almost without thinking, Agnes ducked into a doorway and then 749
through a revolving door. She was inside the lobby of a large office 762
building. ❻ 763

1   **less   re   ly   able   ness   dis**

2   countless   surrounded   revolving

frightened   forehead

3   disapprovingly   realized   hound   frozen

lobby   flooded   pictured   restaurant

public   jogged   library   terrible   trotted

silent   earth   sciences   shelves   lapidary

aisle   cough   neighborhoods

MacCarthy   elevators   recognized

4
1. familiar
2. echo
3. illegal
4. descended
5. trace
6. volume
7. precious

5 | **A Rock Hound's Hiding Place**

Agnes stood frozen in the lobby of the office building. Where   11
could she hide? The lobby was large and almost empty, except for   23
some elevators.   25

Suddenly the doors to the elevators opened and a seemingly   35
countless crowd of people filled the lobby. Agnes found herself moving   46
with them toward the door. As she was leaving the building, she saw   59
the hulk coming through a revolving door and pushing his way   70
through the crowd. ❶   73

"Move," Agnes said to herself. "Just keep moving." She was now   84
outside the building, and the hulk was inside. Agnes pictured what   95
would happen if the hulk caught up with her. He would crush her like   109
a child's toy; then he would take back the jewels.   119

Agnes realized that it might be a good idea to hide the bag   132
somewhere, but she couldn't think of a likely spot. There was a   144
restaurant to her left. Could she hide the bag in there? What about the   158
bookstore next to the restaurant? But how would she hide the bag? ❷   170

Across the street was a large building—the public library. Agnes   181
hadn't been quite sure where she was up to now, because she hadn't   194
been trying to reach a particular place, merely trying to get away.   206

Agnes knew that people often return to safe, familiar places when   217
they are frightened. And the library was just such a place, one in   230
which Agnes had spent many pleasant hours. She already felt better as   242
she jogged across the street and up the front steps of the library. She   256
trotted through the large lobby, and her feet seemed to make a terrible   269
echoing sound in the silent halls. Several people looked   278
disapprovingly at her. ❸   281

Agnes went into one of the smaller rooms to the right of the main   295

reading room. The sign <u>over</u> the door said, "Earth Sciences." Inside, 306
twenty long tables were arranged in two rows. On all sides of the 319
tables were shelves of books. Only two people were in the room, one 332
studying a huge volume, the other apparently asleep. Agnes quickly 342
walked down one of the aisles of bookshelves. The sign on the end of 356
the aisle said, "Lapidary." Lapidary is the art of cutting precious 367
stones. What better place to hide the bag? 375

At the end of the aisle Agnes stopped. The sound of her breathing 388
seemed to echo through the room. "Stop puffing like that," she told 400
herself. She rubbed her hand over her sweating brow and then pulled 412
about ten books from one of the shelves above eye level. She piled the 426
books on the floor and stood on them to look inside the hole she'd 440
made. Yes, indeed, there was room for the bag inside the hole. ❹ 452

Agnes stuffed the bag into the hole, shoved the books back in place, 465
and then walked slowly along the rows of shelves into the open area of 479
the Earth Sciences library. The same two people were at the tables. 491
Outside the door two young people who looked like students were talking. 503

Agnes walked through the hall and down the wide front steps of the 516
library. She felt as if she were on display as she descended the steps, so 531
she put her hands in front of her face and pretended to cough. When 545
she reached the bottom of the steps, she realized that somebody was 557
looking at her. Quickly, she looked up. 564

"Taxi?" the driver said. 568

"Yes, thanks," Agnes said, walking toward the dirty green cab 578
parked illegally in front of the library. "Yes," she repeated under her 590
breath four or five more times. 596

As the cab moved through the downtown traffic and then through 607
less crowded neighborhoods, Agnes kept looking out of the back 617
window of the car. It wasn't until she stood on her own front porch 631
that she felt safe. She sat down with Edison on one side and Einstein 645

on her lap. ❺ "Oh, it's good to be home," Agnes said to her pets. 659

"Yes," she said over and over again. 666

Later, after rinsing her face with cold water and drinking a glass of 679
root beer, Agnes called the police station. She recognized the voice of 691
the officer who answered the phone. It belonged to Ray MacCarthy, 702
the officer who had talked to her earlier. 710

"Officer MacCarthy," Agnes said, "I can help you prove that Eddie 721
is guilty of that jewel robbery." 727

There was a brief pause during which Agnes could hear MacCarthy 738
say to somebody, "Trace this call." 744

Agnes didn't want the call to be traced, so she hung up. ❻ 756

1 instruc<u>tio</u>ns spe<u>cia</u>l slight<u>ly</u> inno<u>c</u>ent

2 attached   exactly   evidence

outskirts   convince   imprisonment

trace   impossible   thoughts

dismantled   sore   banana   aisle

unusual   cooperative   focused

activity   Ramsey   confessed   buzzing

touch   solve   robbery   detective

crazy   possibility   impatient   ached

3
1. rigged
2. futile
3. respected
4. retrieve
5. guaranteed
6. responsible

4   The Police Cooperate

Agnes was impatient. She wanted to tell the police about the jewels, 12
but she didn't want her calls traced. So during the night she rigged up 26
another phone line from her house to the main cable that ran nearby. 39
Now, when she telephoned, it would be impossible for anybody to 50
trace the call. 53

As Agnes dialed the police station again, she realized how tired she 65
was. She'd had very little sleep lately, and her legs ached from 77
yesterday's chase. 79

"Hello, Officer MacCarthy," Agnes said, moving the antenna of her 89
dop machine slightly so that she could talk to MacCarthy on the 101
phone and at the same time read his thoughts from the dop machine. 114
Now the dop contact was strong. ❶ 120

Agnes said, "Attempting to trace this call will be futile. This phone 132
is attached to a main cable. Furthermore, if you even think of tracing 145
it, I'll hang up. Please understand that I can read your thoughts at any 159
moment." 160

"I'm very glad for you," MacCarthy said. "Now tell me what I can 173
do for you." 176

"Just listen," Agnes said. "I'll help you prove that Eddie is guilty." 188
"So prove it," MacCarthy said flatly. 194

"First," Agnes said, "let me convince you that I can read your every 207
thought. Think of something unusual, and I'll tell you what you're 218
thinking." 219

At the time MacCarthy was thinking that he was hungry, even 230
though he'd already eaten breakfast and that the banana in his lunch 242
bag didn't look very good—it had big brown spots on it. 254

Agnes told MacCarthy what he'd been thinking, and MacCarthy 263
responded, "Well, I'll be." ❷ 267

Then Agnes said, "Do exactly as I say, and you'll have all the 280
evidence against Eddie that you need. Go to the Earth Sciences room 292
of the main library, third aisle on <u>the</u> left. At the end of the aisle, on 308
the sixth shelf from the bottom, is the book *Lapidary for Fun*. Pull out 322
the book and you'll see a dry cleaning bag. The jewels are inside that 336
bag." 337

Agnes repeated the instructions as MacCarthy wrote them down. 346
Agnes then said, "I'll be in touch with you after you retrieve the 359
jewels. Hurry." 361

"OK," MacCarthy said. ❸ 364

Later that afternoon Agnes focused the dop machine on the police 375
station and discovered that the place was buzzing with activity. The 386
jewels had been found. Agnes called MacCarthy. 393

"I see that you have the jewels," she said. "Now find out the name of 408
the huge man who was at the Speedy Dry Cleaning place on State 421
Street, one block north of the Rialto." 428

"I don't have to look that up. That's Ramsey the Crusher; he owns 441
part of that cleaning business. What's he got to do with this?" ❹ 453

"Pick him up," Agnes said. "He's in on this with Eddie. Then tell 466
Eddie that Ramsey confessed. Eddie will tell you everything you want 477
to know." 479

"How do you know all this stuff?" MacCarthy asked. 488

For a moment Agnes didn't know how to respond. At last she said, 501
"I have unusual powers. I call them dop powers." Agnes went on to 514
explain what *dop* stood for. Then she said, "In the future I hope you'll 528
be more cooperative when working with me. Also, my fee is one 540
hundred dollars per day. If I don't solve the case, I'll return the money. 554
My work is fully guaranteed." ❺ 559

"We'll be glad to cooperate. Just tell us what to do, uh, uh . . ." 572
MacCarthy's voice trailed off. 576

"Just call me Dop," Agnes said. "Dr. Dop." 584

"OK, Dr. Dop." 587

Agnes Lark still lives on the outskirts of Redmond with her cat, 599
Einstein, and her dog, Edison. She still works at inventing different 610
things. And she still has a house full of junk. But her life changed 624
somewhat after she broke the big jewel robbery. Now Agnes has 635
plenty of money, and she is a respected detective who operates from 647
her home. She focuses the dop machine on suspects, and before long 659
she knows who is guilty and who is innocent. Agnes feels very good 672
about what she does. During her first six months as a detective, she 685
was responsible for five innocent prisoners being set free and for the 697
imprisonment of more than a dozen guilty criminals. "Not bad for an 709
old lady who people thought was crazy," she tells herself. ❻ 719

Agnes considered the possibility of telling the truth about her 729
invention and perhaps giving it to the police. But after thinking about 741
it, she decided that the machine could be far too dangerous in the 754
wrong hands. According to Agnes's will, all her inventions will be 765
dismantled and sold as junk when she dies. But the way she has it 779
figured, all those dop waves may have given her other powers. She 791
says to herself once in a while, "I may just live forever." ❼ 803

INFORMATION PASSAGE

| dread | cremation | 'tain't | ghastly | sleigh |
| burrowed | grisly | ere | dwell | |

A Poem About the Klondike

Many writers told stories of the Yukon during the gold rush. You read part of one of those stories. Some poems about the Yukon were also popular. The man who wrote the most famous poems was Robert Service, who worked as a banker in Whitehorse in the Yukon Territory. The most colorful poem he wrote is titled, "The Cremation of Sam McGee."

The poem is very long, but the main parts of it appear below. ❶

The Cremation of Sam McGee

• • •

Now Sam McGee was from Tennessee, where the cotton
   blooms and blows.
Why he left his home in the South to roam 'round the Pole,
   nobody knows. ❷
He was always cold, but the land of gold seemed to hold him
   like a spell;
Though he'd often say in his homely way that "this is no
   place to dwell".

• • •

Well, he seemed so low that I couldn't say no; then he says
   with a sort of moan:
"It's the cursèd cold, and it's got right hold, till I'm chilled
   clean through to the bone.
Yet 'tain't being dead—it's my awful dread of the icy grave
   that pains;

So I want you to swear that, foul or fair, you'll cremate my
   last remains." ❸
A pal's last need is a thing to heed, so I swore I would not fail:
And we started on at the streak of dawn; but Oh! He looked
   ghastly pale.
He crouched on a sleigh, and he raved all day of his home in
   Tennessee; ❹
And before nightfall a corpse was all that was left of Sam McGee. ❺

⋅ ⋅ ⋅

Some planks I tore from the cabin floor, and I lit the boiler fire;
Some coal I found that was lying around, and I heaped the
   fuel higher;
The flames just soared, and the furnace roared—such a
   blaze you seldom see; ❻
And I burrowed a hole in the glowing coal, and I stuffed in
   Sam McGee.

⋅ ⋅ ⋅

I do not know how long in the snow I wrestled with grisly fear;
But the stars came out and they danced about ere again I
   ventured near; ❼
I was sick with dread, but I bravely said: "I'll just take a peep inside.
I guess he's cooked, and it's time I looked"; . . . then the door
   I opened wide.

And there sat Sam, looking cool and calm, in the heart of
   the furnace roar;
And he wore a smile you could see a mile, and he said:
   "Please close that door.
It's fine in here, but I greatly fear, you'll let in the cold
   and storm—
Since I left Plumtree, down in Tennessee, it's the first time
   I've been warm." ❽

1

noctu<u>r</u>nal intelli<u>g</u>ent ni<u>gh</u>ttime disapp<u>ea</u>red

2

chimpanzees lizards nerves replaced

messages existence keener

information mammals reptile cranial

tongue rotating similarities

demonstrate Mesozoic tyrannosaur

triceratops meant developing concluded

dinosaurs wired acquired theory

3

1. adjust
2. modeled
3. combine
4. impression
5. conclusion
6. complicated

4

Mammals and Reptiles

Mammals such as chimpanzees, horses, cows, dogs, and mice are   10
capable of learning much more than reptiles and other cold-blooded   20
animals like fish and frogs. One theory of why mammals acquired   31
more powerful brains is quite interesting. Before beginning the story,   41
however, we have to understand some things about the reptile brain.   52
In some ways a reptile brain is the same as that of a bird or a horse or   70
even a human being. For one thing there are twelve nerves leading   82
from the brain to the body. These are called cranial nerves. Each nerve   95
has a role. Particular cranial nerves, for example, move the tongue in   107
a lizard or a chimpanzee. Other specific nerves move the eyes. ❶   118

Although there are some similarities between the brains of reptiles   128
and the brains of mammals, there are important differences. A reptile   139
brain is small and doesn't weigh as much as the brain of a mammal of   154
the same body size. Also, the eye is actually an important part of the   168
reptile's brain. This theory can be modeled by rotating the eyes of a   181
lizard—up is now down and left is now right. When the lizard tries to   196
strike at an insect that is high on his left side, the lizard will strike   211
down and to its right. What's more, the lizard will never learn to   224
adjust. The reason is that the reptile is wired in a fixed way. The eye is   240
part of the wiring. ❷   244

Many people think that mammals first appeared in the Mesozoic   254
era when great reptiles like the tyrannosaur and the triceratops ruled.   265
Early mammals had the reptile eye. However, they could not compete   276
with the reptiles during the daytime. So these mammals became   286
nocturnal, or nighttime, animals. At night they could not use their   297
reptile eye <u>because</u> it was a daylight eye. Finally, mammals no longer   309
had the reptile eye. ❸   313

Some scientists believe that the early mammals adjusted to the 323
darkness by developing senses other than sight. They developed ears, 333
which are body parts that are not well developed in reptiles. Reptiles 345
are nearly deaf. Mammals also developed a sense of smell much 356
keener than that of reptiles. The brain of the early mammal had to 369
change so that it could use the information that came to it from its 383
nose and ears. ❹ The nose and the ears were not part of the mammal's 397
brain, which meant that the mammal's brain had to have a new kind 410
of wiring system. While the reptile's brain responds directly to 420
impressions on its eye, the mammal's brain had to combine 430
impressions from the ear with impressions from the nose. Perhaps the 441
mammal's ear told the mammal that a heavy form was moving in 453
front of it. The mammal's nose indicated that the form was a bird. 466
The mammal's brain combined the information about where the 475
animal was with how the animal smelled, and concluded: "There is a 487
bird ahead of me." This conclusion could never be drawn by a reptile. ❺ 500

Some people think that after millions of years passed and the great 512
dinosaurs disappeared from the earth, some mammals began to 521
change into daytime animals. For the mammals to operate in the 532
daytime, however, they needed daytime eyes again. And somehow, 541
these eyes developed. But they were not like reptile eyes; instead, they 553
became wired into the brain the way the ears and nose were wired 566
into the brain. Messages from the eye went to the brain. There they 579
were combined with messages from the ears and from the nose. The 591
brain that performed this job was far, far more complicated than the 603
brain of the reptile. ❻ 607

It is interesting to think that the night existence of the early   619
mammals may have set the stage for them to develop brains capable of   632
learning a great deal. They could no longer use the reptile eye. What's   645
more, they needed other senses to locate objects in the dark—smell   657
and hearing. Since the mammal had to use information from more   668
than one sense organ, the mammal needed a brain that could combine   680
the information from the various sense organs. That kind of brain is   692
far more complicated than the brain of a reptile. **7**   701

Lesson 100

1

Egyptians experience ancient

succeed various meant

future rapidly aggressive

foretold expression

unpleasant emotionally

2

1. theory
2. rejected
3. interpretation
4. symbol
5. nonsense
6. represent

3

Dreams

Dreams are thought pictures, or stories, that pass through the mind during sleep. Very little was known about dreams until the late 1950s. There is still much about dreams that scientists do not understand.

There have been theories and beliefs about dreams since very ancient times. One belief was that a dream predicted what was going to happen. The ancient Egyptians believed that dreams foretold the future. Dreams that predict are also mentioned in the Bible. Another very old belief was that the soul left the body during sleep and that dreams were things that happened to the soul while it was wandering in another world. ❶

In the 1800s, people who studied dreams made up lists of dream symbols. Everything that happened in a dream was supposed to be a symbol that stood for something else. For example, falling in a dream represented failure. Climbing meant an attempt to succeed. Dream books that give the supposed meanings of dreams are still sold. They tell of dreams that mean good or bad luck, and foretell certain events. Scientists have rejected such interpretations as nonsense. ❷

Today, many scientists think that dreams in some way reflect real experiences. Although dreams are still not clearly understood, they probably have something to do with how people feel about themselves and their lives. Some scientists think that people express feelings in dreams that they cannot express while they are awake. Such feelings might be fear or love or hate.

There have been some interesting discoveries recently about dreams. Scientists can now tell when a person is dreaming. They also know what changes take place in the body during a dream.

REM, or rapid eye movement, was first observed and studied in the late 1950s. When you dream, your eyes begin to move rapidly from side to side. Your heart begins to beat faster, and other signs of body activity increase. ❸

Dreaming seems to be necessary for people. If a person is awakened every time rapid eye movement shows that a dream is beginning, that person will become upset, restless, and angry. By letting us express and get rid of strong or unpleasant feelings in a harmless way while we are asleep, dreams may help keep us emotionally healthy.

1

p<u>er</u>fectly cho<u>i</u>ce situ<u>ation</u>

<u>re</u>sponded f<u>ea</u>ture incredib<u>ly</u>

2

Baluchitherium powerful interesting

positions creatures thousands full-size

strange-looking grazing survived opossum

predators developed attempted porpoises

weighing tongue kingdom horsepower

lizards adequate whales complicated

3

1. occupied
2. avoid
3. marvelous
4. beneficial

4   The Spread of Mammals

Some scientists tell us that when the great reptiles ruled the earth, they were in the sky, in the sea, and on the land. They came in all forms, from tiny lizards to animals that could easily look into third-story windows of today's buildings. ❶

For reasons that are not perfectly clear, the great reptiles of the Mesozoic era died off, leaving the sky, the sea, and the land open to new animals. Thousands of new birds and mammals appeared. We would consider many of the early mammals strange-looking. They were as different from each other as the reptiles they replaced. Some were huge, much larger than the African elephant, which is the largest living land animal. *Baluchitherium,* the largest land mammal that ever lived, stood more than twenty feet tall at the shoulder and weighed almost 40,000 pounds. That's more than three full-sized elephants weigh. ❷

Like the great reptiles, not all mammals survived. Some types died off. Some changed. And some live today in much the same way they lived during the Mesozoic era. The opossum, for example, lives at night, does not use its eyes very much, and has a fairly small brain. The reason it has a small brain is that the opossum doesn't need a larger brain. The brain that it had in the Mesozoic era was adequate.

The brains changed most in animals that changed the way they lived. The horse became a daytime animal, changing in size from an animal no bigger than a fox to the full-sized horse of today. ❸ Its brain also changed so that it could survive in the open among predators that hunted it. As grazing animals like the horse developed larger brains, they learned more tricks to avoid their hunters.

One theory is that predators or hunters needed even <u>bigger</u> and $\qquad$ 301
more complicated brains than the hunted. Unless predators were $\qquad$ 310
smarter than grazing animals, they would not be able to catch their $\qquad$ 322
prey, and they would starve to death. Therefore, predators developed $\qquad$ 332
larger and more powerful brains, even larger than those of grazing $\qquad$ 343
animals. ❹ $\qquad$ 344

Among the most interesting predators are those land mammals $\qquad$ 353
that became sea animals. Many of them live today as whales and $\qquad$ 365
porpoises. Their legs became flippers and tails. Their bodies took $\qquad$ 375
the shape of fish. Although they changed in many ways, they kept $\qquad$ 387
the mammal brain. $\qquad$ 390

A killer whale's brain weighs more than the brain of a human being. $\qquad$ 403
This does not mean that the killer whale is smarter than a person. The $\qquad$ 417
killer whale is a very large animal, weighing as much as an elephant. $\qquad$ 430
To handle messages in a body this large, the killer whale's brain must $\qquad$ 443
be quite large. ❺ $\qquad$ 446

Whales are among the most amazing creatures in the animal $\qquad$ 456
kingdom. In addition to being smart, some are incredibly large. The $\qquad$ 467
largest animal that is alive today is the blue whale. To get an idea of its $\qquad$ 483
size, let's compare the blue whale to an African elephant. A blue whale $\qquad$ 496
is about as large at birth as a full-grown African elephant! A $\qquad$ 508
full-grown whale may be over one hundred feet long and may weigh $\qquad$ 520
200,000 pounds. Its heart weighs more than one thousand pounds, and $\qquad$ 531
its tongue weighs almost nine thousand pounds. When it travels at top $\qquad$ 543
speed, which is over twenty miles an hour, it develops 520 horsepower. $\qquad$ 555
Indeed, the blue whale is one of the most marvelous creatures in the $\qquad$ 568
animal kingdom. ❻ $\qquad$ 570

Lesson
102

1 un   less   re   pre   sub   dis

2 conference   advertised   beneficial

displayed   marvelous

3 motionless   supermarkets   convince

occasionally   college   consumers

approached   particularly   appliance

refrigerator   self-defrosting   problem

demonstrated   practically   wasting

supplying   continued   graduated   choosy

loosens   fret   special   product

4
1. tantrums
2. valves
3. favor
4. campaign
5. commission
6. manufacturer

5 Super Salesperson

This is a story about Joe Kappas, a salesperson who had remarkable   12
success in the 1970s. Joe Kappas had a special talent, which was that he   26
could talk anybody into anything. When he was still a child, he could   39
talk his parents into letting him do just about anything he wanted to   52
do. He wouldn't fret and cry and throw tantrums the way some kids   65
do. Instead he would sell his parents on the idea that he wanted them   79
to buy. By the time he was a teenager, he had become a marvelous   93
salesperson. For example, one time when he was in high school, he   105
wanted to use the family car, but his dad had told him that he couldn't.   120
Joe waited a few moments and then approached his father. "Dad," Joe   132
said, "my friend Pete really knows car engines, and he says that the   145
valves in your engine are starting to stick. He says that if they get   159
really stuck, it will cost over a hundred dollars to fix them." Joe then   173
held up a can of valve oil. He continued, "Pete says that if you put this   189
valve oil in your engine, you can prevent the valves from sticking." ❶   201

"Well, let's put it in," his dad remarked.   209

"OK," Joe said, smiling. "There's just one thing, Dad. You should   220
only put the oil in when the engine is warmed up. You should drive   234
the car for at least one hour after you put the oil in. That way you can   251
make sure that the oil loosens up the valves."   260

"That's a problem," his dad said. "I'm going to be at home for the   274
rest of the day. But I guess I can do it tomorrow."   286

"Good idea," Joe said and started to leave the room. He stopped   298
abruptly <u>and</u> turned around. "I've got an idea," he said. "If you want   311
me to, I could put that oil in today. I don't have anything really   325
important to do, and I'd be willing to do it, particularly if it will save   340
you over a hundred dollars."   345

"Well, thanks a lot, Joe," his dad said. Joe used the car all ₃₅₈ afternoon, and his father thought that Joe was doing him a great ₃₇₀ favor. ❷ ₃₇₁

Joe demonstrated his talent for fast thinking and fast talking ₃₈₁ throughout high school and college. He had more friends than ₃₉₁ anybody else in his town. Occasionally people would get mad at him, ₄₀₃ but they didn't stay mad very long. In college Joe didn't work very ₄₁₆ hard, but he studied enough to learn about advertising and about ₄₂₇ managing a business. In his last year of college he got the top grade ₄₄₁ for putting together an advertising campaign. ❸ ₄₄₇

After Joe graduated, he decided to get some sales experience by ₄₅₈ working in a store. He chose a big store that paid good commissions, ₄₇₁ and he got a job selling appliances. "Why don't you take a management ₄₈₄ job?" some of his friends asked. "Why do you want to sell?" ₄₉₆

Joe replied, "As a salesperson, I'll make a commission on every ₅₀₇ appliance I sell. I believe that I can sell enough appliances to make a ₅₂₁ lot of money." ❹ ₅₂₄

And Joe did make money selling appliances. Everyone who stopped ₅₃₄ to look at the stoves or refrigerators or toasters ended up buying ₅₄₆ something. Joe convinced one woman that a toaster with a special ₅₅₇ electric eye would always produce perfect toast. One couple, who had ₅₆₈ a practically new stove at home, bought a model with a self-cleaning ₅₈₀ oven after Joe reminded them that oven cleaning is a nasty job and ₅₉₃ pointed out how much time they'd save. He also sold a lot of ₆₀₆ self-defrosting refrigerators—usually the most expensive models. ❺ ₆₁₃

Joe made more money in commissions than any other salesperson ₆₂₃ in the store. But Joe felt that he was wasting his talent selling ₆₃₆ appliances. He thought that he could sell bigger things to more ₆₄₇ people. So in less than a year he moved to another job, selling soap. ₆₆₁ He didn't sell to the consumers—the people who use the soap. He sold ₆₇₅

to supermarkets, which is not an easy job. All soap manufacturers   686
want to get their brands into the supermarkets. And each   696
manufacturer finds it beneficial to have its soap displayed on as many   708
shelves as possible. There is only so much shelf space in a   720
supermarket, however. So the buyers for the supermarkets are very   730
choosy about which manufacturers they deal with. If you go into the   742
buying office for a supermarket chain, you will usually see several   753
salespeople waiting to see the buyer, all ready to convince the buyer   765
that their product is the best. All will tell the buyer that there is a   780
great demand for their brand, that their brand is advertised, and that   792
the customers will be mad if they don't find that brand in the   805
supermarket. Then the salesperson will offer the buyer a deal. If the   817
buyer orders so many carloads of the brand, the price will be reduced   830
by quite a bit.   834

    That's how most other salespeople worked, but Joe Kappas was   844
smart enough to know that he had to think of a new approach. ❻   857

INFORMATION PASSAGE

astronomy   magnifying   telescope   atmosphere
particles   incoming   circular

The Hubble Space Telescope—Part 1

Scientists have learned a lot about astronomy, which is the study of stars, planets, moons, and other objects in the universe. The main tool that astronomers use to study the universe is the telescope. A telescope works like magnifying glasses and binoculars. Telescopes, magnifying glasses, and binoculars enlarge the image that you see. The stronger they are, the farther you can see. The first telescope was invented in 1610. This telescope did not enlarge the image of things very much. ❶

A good pair of binoculars that you could buy today makes things look ten times their actual size. Below are two rectangles. The one on the right is ten times larger than the one on the left. So if the small rectangle on the left shows the size of the image seen with the naked eye, the larger rectangle on the right shows the image through binoculars.

Some telescopes enlarge the image of things over a thousand times. These telescopes are so powerful that they show details of the moon and other planets that would not be seen with the naked eye. ❷

The most serious problem facing powerful telescopes is the atmosphere. The atmosphere carries particles of gas and dust. These particles make it difficult to see distant stars. The reason some stars seem to twinkle is that you are looking at them through the atmosphere.

As you go higher, there is less atmosphere above you, so the less stars seem to twinkle. To get as high as possible, astronomers have constructed the most powerful telescopes on mountaintops. One of the more famous telescopes, Gemini, is over two miles above sea level, on top of an inactive volcano in Hawaii. ❸

For years, scientists have tried to figure out ways of getting a telescope above the atmosphere, in outer space, where no dust and gas block the view. In 1990 they succeeded in putting such a telescope in orbit. It is called the Hubble Space Telescope. This telescope magnifies things 1,152 times larger than they appear with the naked eye. That means if you looked through the telescope at a dime that was 200 miles away, you could read the date on it.

The Hubble Space Telescope uses a large curved mirror that is almost eight feet across. The diagram on the next page shows how the telescope works. The incoming light strikes the mirror. The mirror directs all the light to one tiny point. That point has the image that is sent back to Earth.

The illustration shows light from a distant object in blue.

The light strikes the mirror. The reflected light is shown in green.

The red point shows the location of the image that is sent back to Earth.

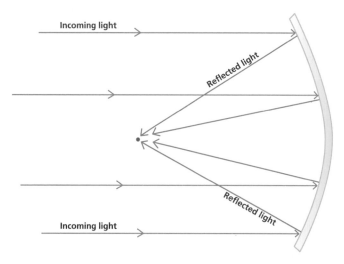

Below is a picture of the Hubble Space Telescope. The mirror is inside the circular tube. This tube also contains the instruments that permit astronomers on Earth to focus the mirror on different parts of the sky. ❹

1

announcement   discussions

puncture   arrangement

2

shrugged   wholesale   attention

submarine   invitations   opportunity

statement   professional   badminton

possibilities   reliable   promotion

3

1. motive
2. auction
3. gimmick
4. invoice
5. receipt
6. bill of lading

4   Soap Auction

Joe Kappas had an idea for selling soap to supermarket buyers.   11
First he made arrangements for a great party. He sent out invitations   23
to the buyers for all the major supermarket chains. He hired some   35
professional football players to come to the party, because he knew   46
that the buyers would like to meet professional football players. ❶   56

As it turned out, over half of the buyers he invited attended the   69
party, which began shortly before noon with a light lunch. It was an   82
outdoor party at an expensive country club. Joe made sure that the   94
buyers had a good time. They played tennis or badminton, or went   106
swimming in the pool. They told jokes, talked to each other, and   118
laughed a lot.   121

At about two o'clock Joe climbed up on the diving board at the   134
swimming pool to make an announcement. "May I have your   144
attention?" he shouted. Slowly the talk and laughter died down.   154
"Ladies and gentlemen," Joe said, "I brought you here to sell you   166
soap. It's that simple. I hope you're having a good time, and I don't   180
want you to feel that you have to buy soap. But my major motive in   195
bringing you here was to sell to you." ❷   203

Somebody yelled, "I'm here to party, not to buy." Everybody laughed.   214

"So don't buy," Joe said. "But if you don't, somebody is going to get   228
one whale of a deal. There is a railroad siding less than three miles   242
from here, and on that siding are seventeen railroad cars, each loaded   254
with Senso soap. Right now Senso Soap Company owns that soap, but   266
by tonight *every bit of that soap will be auctioned off.* I don't care how   281
much each carload goes for—all the soap will be sold." ❸   292

"What kind of gimmick is this?" one <u>buyer</u> asked.   301

"There's no gimmick," Joe said. "We're going to have an auction— 312
one carload at a time. Those who bid may get the bargain of a 326
lifetime. They may save their companies thousands of dollars. And 336
your bosses are always glad when that happens, isn't that right?" 347

Buyers shouted comments, but Joe ignored them. He held up his 358
hands and said, "Carload one is now up for auction. I'm not going to 372
try to sell you on the product because you know that Senso is a good, 387
reliable soap. So what am I bid for carload one?" 397

"One dollar," one of the buyers shouted. 404

"Good," Joe said above the laughter. "We have a bid of one dollar. 417
Will anybody bid two dollars?" 422

"I'll give you five," a tall woman buyer shouted, holding up a five 435
dollar bill. 437

Joe said, "We have five dollars for a full carload of Senso soap. As 451
you know, that carload is worth $84,000 on the wholesale market. Do 463
I hear any more bids?" 468

The buyers looked at each other and looked at Joe, but nobody else 481
bid. "Going once . . . going twice . . . sold to the woman with the five 493
dollar bill." Joe shrugged and smiled. As the buyer walked up to the 506
diving board, the other buyers clapped and laughed. Joe took the five 518
dollar bill and handed the buyer some papers. "Here's the bill of 530
lading, here's the invoice, and here's the receipt. You just purchased 541
one carload of Senso soap." ❹ 546

"Hey, is this for real?" one of the other buyers asked. 557

The buyer who had purchased the carload of soap was looking over 569
the papers that Joe had handed her. At last she said, "I can't believe it. 584
This is a real bill of lading." 591

"As I told you at the beginning," Joe said, "all seventeen carloads 603
will be sold this afternoon. They can go for five dollars or for two 617
dollars. It makes no difference to me. But they're all going to be sold 631

today. The next carload is carload two. Does anybody want to start the bidding?" ₆₄₃ ₆₄₅

People were shouting out numbers so rapidly that the bidding, which started at five dollars, was up to over $2,000 within a few seconds. Carload two sold for $40,000, less than half of its value on the wholesale market. ❺ ₆₅₅ ₆₆₈ ₆₈₁ ₆₈₄

When Joe turned over the bill of lading and the invoice to the buyer who purchased that carload, he said, "Well, you didn't buy it for five dollars, but you saved your company more than forty thousand dollars with your wise purchase." ₆₉₈ ₇₁₁ ₇₂₁ ₇₂₆

Buyers were running to the telephones, calling their offices to get permission to bid on carloads. But Joe didn't wait for them. "Carload three is now up for auction," he announced. Carload three sold for $62,000. Joe shrugged. "Ladies and gentlemen, I see that some of you are not bidding. I hope that all of you have understanding bosses, because some of them may be curious about why you passed up the opportunity to save your firm thousands of dollars. Maybe you're not thinking of the promotion possibilities. Consider this fact: Your stores could price Senso soap at a great savings, which means that you could attract customers to your stores. And you know that once those customers come into the market, they'll buy more than soap. But that's up to you." ❻ ₇₃₇ ₇₄₉ ₇₆₁ ₇₇₃ ₇₈₅ ₇₉₈ ₈₀₉ ₈₁₉ ₈₃₂ ₈₄₃ ₈₅₄ ₈₅₈

The auction went on. ₈₆₂

1

reception   commercials   agency

conversation   embarked

2

billboards   realized   pleasant

inexpensive   advertising   conference

tremendous   embarrassed   commission

occupying   Niota   economy   representing

ability   intriguing   bawled   mileage

3

1. average
2. conclude
3. bid
4. challenge
5. executive
6. reputation
7. proposition
8. skyscraper

4

From Senso to Niotas

By four thirty in the afternoon, Joe had auctioned off all seventeen   12
carloads of Senso soap. They brought an average price of $68,000. All   24
the buyers who purchased a carload felt that they had made very good   37
deals, and they had. But Joe also made a very good deal. He didn't   51
make any money on the sales, but he didn't lose any money either.   64
And he achieved three very important goals. First, he forced nine   75
major supermarket chains to sell Senso soap. Second, he made sure   86
that the buyers would never forget the name Joe Kappas. Now he   98
would have an edge on all the other salespeople because the buyers   110
would remember the auction and the fun they had. ❶ Finally, Joe   121
succeeded in making some of the buyers look good to their bosses.   133
When a buyer goes to the boss and says that she purchased $84,000   146
worth of soap for $68,000, the boss is going to conclude that the buyer   160
is a pretty smart person.   165

During the next year, Joe did not have to sit in reception rooms   178
waiting to see buyers. Even the buyers who didn't bid at the auction   191
welcomed him. Some of them were embarrassed after their bosses had   202
bawled them out for passing up the opportunity to purchase Senso   213
soap at the auction. Within a year Senso soap went from the   225
fifth-best-selling brand to the number one brand in the area that Joe   237
serviced. ❷   238

However, Joe didn't want to sell soap for the rest of his life. He   252
wanted a new challenge. He thought that he was probably the best   264
salesperson in the world, and he wanted to prove it by doing bigger   277
and better things. And as it happened, he became involved in one of   290
the biggest deals a salesperson could hope to find. <u>One</u> day, Joe   302
received a call from an executive of a large advertising agency. (An   314

advertising agency works for different companies. The agency makes 323
up magazine ads, television commercials, billboards, and other 331
display pieces that help sell products.) The advertising executive who 341
called Joe said, "You have quite a reputation in sales, and I think we 355
have a proposition that will interest you." ❸ 362

A meeting was set up for Joe at the advertising agency. The agency 375
was very large, occupying two full floors in a downtown skyscraper. 386
The offices were very plush. A secretary with a pleasant smile met Joe 399
and led him into a large conference room. On the walls were pictures 412
of a small economy car. Three people were seated at the conference 424
table, while two others stood near the door, carrying on a lively 436
conversation. One man shook hands with Joe and introduced himself 446
as the person Joe had talked to on the phone. After everyone was 459
introduced, the man said, "Sit down, Joe, and I'll explain the deal." 471

The deal seemed very intriguing to Joe. The advertising agency was 482
representing a Japanese manufacturer that built an automobile called 491
the Niota. "Here's our problem," the executive explained. "We can't 501
seem to come up with a hot idea for promoting this product. It's a 515
good car, just like a lot of other imports. It's well built, it gets good 530
gas mileage, and it's inexpensive. But we don't have a big advertising 542
budget. And there are only six dealers in the country who handle this 555
car. We've got to figure out a way to increase the number of 568
distributors, and somehow we've got to reach the people with a small 580
advertising budget. Frankly, we're fresh out of ideas. That's why we 591
brought you in. We figured that a guy with your sales ability may be 605
able to give us some ideas." ❹ 611

"And what do I get out of it?" Joe inquired. 621

"I want to give you a chance to make a lot of money," the executive 636
replied. "But I don't have much money to work with. So here's what 649
I'll do. Last year, three thousand Niotas were sold in this country. If 662

we use your ideas, we'll give you a commission of one hundred dollars on every Niota over three thousand that is sold during the year. In other words, you don't receive any commission for the first three thousand, but for every car sold after that, you will make one hundred dollars—if we use your ideas."

"You have made a deal," Joe announced. "Draw up the papers, and I'll have my lawyer look them over. Give me all the information you have on the Niota, and give me one to drive. I'm not going to sell a product before I know that product."

And that's how Joe embarked on the biggest deal of his life. ❺

675
688
699
712
718
730
743
759
765
777

1

hypnosis hypnotist mesmerism wailing

investigator Hamelin entertainment

flinch Sigmund trance Freud

predictable Vienna fascinating knowledge

conscious psychiatrist technique

2

1. feat
2. rigid
3. expectations
4. anesthetic
5. extracted
6. considering

3

Hypnosis

Hypnosis is a condition in which a person goes into a trance. People who are hypnotized are often not conscious of what is happening. However, they do things that are suggested by others. They may also see things that are not actually present.

The power of ancient "witches" and "magicians" over others may be explained by hypnosis. The Pied Piper of Hamelin may have used hypnosis to lure that town's children into following him. ❶

People didn't study hypnosis until the eighteenth century, when Franz Mesmer developed a technique now called "mesmerism," which could put people into a trance. Early investigators thought that hypnosis was some kind of "magnetism." They believed that the trances were caused by a magnetic force present in certain trees and rocks. People who were mesmerized would cling to "magnetized" rocks and trees for hours, wailing and weeping. After coming out of the trance, they would report that they were cured of serious illnesses. ❷

In the 1800s, hypnosis became a popular form of entertainment. Traveling hypnotists could hypnotize members of an audience and cause them to do strange things. "You can feel nothing in your hand," the stage hypnotist would suggest to a subject. Then, to the amazement of the crowd, the hypnotist would stick a needle in the subject's hand, apparently without causing pain.

In another popular feat the hypnotist would tell the subject, "Your body is as stiff as a board." The subject's body would become rigid. The hypnotist would then suspend the person between two chairs, leaving the subject supported only by the neck and heels.

In addition to being used as entertainment, hypnosis was used as an anesthetic on people who were having teeth extracted. Hypnosis was also used to bring back memories of painful events that a patient couldn't consciously recall. The famous psychiatrist Sigmund Freud used hypnosis in this way during his early years of work in Vienna. ❸

Research into hypnosis continues today. It is now known that the behavior of a hypnotized person depends both on the situation in which the hypnosis takes place and on the expectations of the subject. Someone who is hypnotized in a quiet office, for instance, will behave quite differently from a person hypnotized on a stage before an audience.

It is also known that a subject can experience different degrees of hypnosis. One investigator had listed over twenty such degrees. A person who is only slightly hypnotized may be more willing to do or to think whatever the hypnotist suggests. A person in a deep state of hypnosis will see and hear things that do not exist and will ignore things that do exist. That person may see pink elephants, or put on a coat that doesn't exist. ❹

In spite of our increased knowledge of hypnosis, we are still unable to understand it entirely. And hypnosis continues to be a fascinating subject.

1 | **dis   ly   less   re**

able   un   ness

2 | commercials   research

exclaimed   mileage   process

3 | departments   features   information

unfortunately   insulted   business

adequate   agreement   insisted

creative   patents

4 |
1. contract
2. mechanic
3. disassembled
4. clients
5. media
6. inexpensive
7. convince
8. grumble
9. bellow

5   Preparing for the Campaign

Joe signed a contract with the advertising agency. According to the 11
contract, he would receive one hundred dollars for each car sold over 23
three thousand that was sold during the year. Joe spent the next week 36
studying all about the Niota model of car. He took the car to a garage 51
and had a mechanic take it apart and put it back together. The 64
process took over two days. When the car was disassembled, the 75
garage was covered with parts—pistons from the engine, door 85
handles, bumpers, nuts, bolts—thousands of parts. And Joe studied 95
most of them. He asked the mechanic at least a thousand questions. ❶ 107

Eight days after Joe had signed the contract, he was again sitting at 120
the advertising agency conference table. Also sitting at the table were 131
people from different departments of the agency. There was the man 142
who headed the creative department. (That department makes up ads 152
and commercials.) There was the woman who headed the marketing 162
department. (That department does research for clients and studies 171
marketing problems.) And there were the heads of the art department, 182
the media department, and the new-business department. 189

"What have you come up with?" the president of the agency asked Joe. 202

"Let's start with what we can't do," Joe said. "Then I'll tell you my 216
plan." 217

"Sounds fair," the president said, and everybody else nodded in 227
agreement. 228

"Here's what we can't do," Joe said. "We can't compete with the more 241
popular Japanese imports because the Niota is not as good a product." 253

"It most certainly is!" the president insisted, standing up. "It's a fine 265
product. I drive one myself." 270

"Look," Joe said, "you can either kid yourself or face the facts. You say it's a fine product. Sure, it's OK. It gets fair mileage, but look at the <u>big-selling</u> Japanese imports. They get better mileage. The Niota handles well, but the other imports handle better. It has a pretty good engine, but that engine can't hold a candle to the Rondo. The Niota is fairly inexpensive, but it costs more than the Rondo. ❷ So what do we have to sell? Should we tell people that we have a good second-place car that's almost as good as some of the others?"

"It's got features that other cars don't have," the president responded.

"Sure it does," Joe replied. "And it's a nice little car, but it wouldn't do us any good to try to convince people that it's better than other cars. So let's not try." ❸

The head of the creative department was on his feet. "Listen, I'm a busy man. I don't have time to sit in here and be insulted like this. You're telling us that we should throw up our hands and not even try to sell the product. You're crazy. What do you think we're here for?"

"I didn't say we're not going to sell the product. I said that we shouldn't try to convince people that it's a better car."

"What's the difference?" the president bellowed.

"Why don't you settle down and listen to my plan? Then if you don't like it, I'll go my way and you can go yours."

"All right," the president said in a grumbling voice. "But try to make it quick. I have the distinct feeling that we're not going to like it."

"Here's the plan. We'll rename the car. We'll give it the kind of name that will force every other car manufacturer to advertise our car."

"What kind of name did you have in mind?" the head of the marketing department asked.

"Car," Joe replied. "We'll call the Niota 'Car.' " ❹

The room became very silent. At last the president said, "I don't get it."

The head of the creative department said, "I think I do. If the 628 product is called Car, all other manufacturers will say the name of our 641 product when they talk about their products. Another manufacturer 650 who says, 'This is the finest car on the road,' will be saying the name 665 of our product." 668

"I get it," the head of the media department exclaimed. "Every time 680 they say 'Car,' they're saying the name of our product." 690

"We can't get away with that," the president said. "The word *car* 702 refers to any car. We can't use that word just to refer to one brand of car." 719

"I think we can," Joe said. ❺ 725

Lesson 107

1 authentic specialize nation displeasure exclusive

2 purchased designers original exhausted

probably releases dealer displayed

billboard explaining imitations broadcast

campaign models middle-priced worth

advertising patent developed according

3
1. copyright
2. century
3. agency
4. commercial
5. import
6. frantic
7. budget
8. franchise

4

Car

Joe was explaining his idea to the executives of the advertising   11
agency. He had proposed naming the Niota "Car."   19

He was saying, "I've been in touch with three lawyers who   30
specialize in patents and copyrights. According to them, we can   40
probably use the name 'Car.' And even if a lawsuit is brought against   53
us, we'll probably be able to use the name for three or four years." ❶   67

"Car?" the president said. "You mean we'll just call the Niota 'Car'?   79
That just doesn't sound right."   84

"Oh, no," Joe said, smiling. "It sounds beautiful. It's different. It's   95
something you'll remember. It's something you'll think about. The   104
Car won't be just another import; it will be the talk of everybody.   117
We'll get ten million dollars' worth of free advertising. Everybody will   128
know about Car, and if enough people know about it, we'll sell a lot of   143
cars and get a lot of new dealers." The marketing director was   155
standing up. "It's great," she said. "If we can pull it off, it's the   169
greatest idea of the century." ❷ The president was frowning and   179
shaking his head. He said, "But it just doesn't sound right—Car."   191

At last the president agreed to the plan, and the work began. Joe   204
spent the next three months working with the people at the agency. He   217
developed names for the different models of Car. He named the   228
cheapest line of Cars "Biggest Selling." He worked out commercials   238
and billboards with the creative director. One billboard showed a very   249
small picture of the Car. The message on the billboard said, "Now the   262
Biggest Selling Car is in this country." (The word *is* was very small to   276
make the message look as if it said, "Now the Biggest Selling Car in   290
this country.") At the bottom of the billboard was <u>another</u> message: 301
"See it at your Car dealer." ❸   307

Joe named the middle-priced line of Cars "The Number One in the 319
Nation." One billboard showed a picture of "The Number One in the 331
Nation." The message said, "This Car is The Number One in the 343
Nation. See it at your Car dealer." 350

Joe named the highest-priced line of Cars "The Original Imported." 360
One billboard displayed the car and had the message, "See The 371
Original Imported Car at your Car dealer." 378

Activity at the advertising agency was frantic for three months. 388
Lawyers argued with each other. Designers and artists argued with 398
each other, as did the heads of different departments. And the 409
president of the agency walked around shaking his head and saying, 420
"It still doesn't sound right to me." ❹ 427

The agency planned to spend the entire advertising budget to put 438
on a big show for one week. After that week, there would be no more 453
money in the budget. Television time had been purchased. Ads had 464
been placed in newspapers across the country. News releases were 474
sent to newspapers and broadcasting stations. Billboards had been 483
prepared. ❺ 484

At last the advertising campaign began. The first commercial came 494
on the morning news as the announcer said, "There's only one Car. 506
There are lots of imitations. If you want to see the only car that is 521
named 'Car,' where can you go? To your Car dealer. Don't be fooled, 534
however. There are a lot of dealers who call themselves car dealers. 546
Remember, there's only one Car, but a lot of imitations." 556

That commercial ran twenty times on national news broadcasts. 565
On every television channel, there were also quick commercials 574
throughout the day. All were the same—opening with pictures of 585
more popular automobiles. As each automobile was shown, the voice 595
said, "Is this a Car? No." Then a picture of a Car flashed on the 610
screen. "There's only one Car in this country. See it at your authorized 623

Car dealer. Don't settle for imitations. The car you see in the picture `636`

happens to be the Biggest Selling Car. See it and other authentic `648`

Cars—The Original Imported Car and the Car that is The Number `660`

One in the Nation. Call the toll-free number for the location of the real `674`

Car dealers." `676`

Things went wild; a flood of calls came into the advertising agency `688` before the campaign had been going three hours. ❻ Everybody from a `699` senator to a group of local car dealers called, and most were furious. `712` "What are you trying to pull?" one dealer demanded. "I'm a car `724` dealer, but I don't sell that thing you're calling Car. People are calling `737` me and asking about Car." `742`

Joe told the dealer, "The solution is simple. Keep your name and `754` keep the cars you're selling. But add Car to your line. Then anybody `767` who is interested in a Car will think of you first. We can give you an `783` exclusive franchise in the city if you act immediately." The dealer `794` acted immediately and became a Car dealer. ❼ `801`

Lesson

108

1

commercial   reputation   glanced

undermining   dealership

2

1. hectic
2. exhaust
3. brochure
4. dealership
5. legal
6. vast
7. assess
8. talent
9. interview
10. violate
11. prior

3

resources   exhaust   campaign   industry

responded   national   specialize   official

productive   manufacturers   protesting

committee   coughed   considering

directly   government   slogan

4

A Hectic Time

The advertising budget for Car was just over one million dollars. 11
That budget was exhausted after a one-week advertising campaign. 20
During that week, the advertising agency received nearly a thousand 30
phone calls. The agency had to hire an answering service to handle 42
the calls. Joe Kappas spent most of his time on the phone, talking to 56
angry people. Some of them were dealers of Car. "We're out of Cars," 69
they complained. "We don't have enough brochures to hand out to 80
customers. We need big signs so that people know where our 91
dealerships are." ❶ 93

During the week, fifty-three new dealers were signed up to handle 104
Car. About one hundred others were considering becoming Car 113
dealers. Joe told each of the dealers interested in becoming a Car 125
dealer, "Remember, as a Car dealer, you are entitled to display a sign 138
in front of your showroom that says, 'The only real Car dealer in this 152
area.' " ❷ 153

Among the people who called the agency were reporters from the 164
television and radio networks and all the leading national magazines. 174
These calls went directly to the president of the advertising agency. He 186
had meetings with reporters almost every day, starting on the second 197
day of the campaign. Joe was present during the first interview. Three 209
reporters, two from local newspapers and one from a national 219
magazine, shot questions at the president of the agency. 228

One reporter asked, "Is this campaign legal?" 235

"Certainly," the president responded. "Do you think we would do it 246
if it weren't legal?" 250

"But," the same reporter continued, "isn't this campaign going to 260
hurt other manufacturers and car dealers? They won't be able to refer 272
to their cars as 'Car.' " 277

The president laughed. He then said, "Well, they can't call their 288
product cars because they're not Cars. There is only one Car <u>that</u> is 301
sold in this country today." ❸ 306

"Whose idea was this campaign?" the magazine reporter asked. 315

"It was a group effort," the president replied. "Our agency has vast 327
resources and has a reputation for doing a creative job for our clients. 340
We try to assess the needs of our clients and provide each client with 354
the most creative and productive approach we can develop." 363

"What does that mean?" the reporter from the national magazine 373
asked. "I mean, how did it really come about?" 382

The president coughed several times. Then he said to her, "Well, it's 394
difficult to describe how a total campaign is developed. As I said 406
earlier, it is a group effort, with all people putting their talent into the 420
talent pool." 422

"But didn't somebody actually come up with the idea? Whose idea 433
was it?" 435

The president glanced at Joe and cleared his throat. "I believe it 447
came out of our creative department, but I can't actually remember. I 459
don't believe that it was any one person's idea. As I recall, it was a 474
group effort." 476

Joe understood that the president was trying to make it look as if his 490
agency had created the Car campaign, and Joe didn't really care. After 502
all, Cars were selling, and Joe would receive one hundred dollars for 514
every car over three thousand sold during the year. Besides, Joe knew 526
who created the advertising campaign. ❹ 531

The interviews with reporters went on, and so did the campaign. By 543
the second week, Joe was beginning to tire of reading about Car in the 557
newspaper and of watching TV reports on it. A government 567
committee was investigating the situation. The labor union made a 577
strong statement protesting the slogan, "The only Car in this 587
country." The union said that Car wasn't even made in this country 599
and that it was undermining the nation's automobile industry. ❺ A 609
leading automobile manufacturer indicated that it was considering a 618
lawsuit against Car. Another auto company indicated that it did not 629
intend to drop the word *car* from any of its advertising and that it did 644
not feel that it was violating any rights by referring to its automobiles 657
as "cars." One company said that it had prior rights to the word *car* 671
because it had used the word in advertising that dated back more than 684
fifty years. A railroad car manufacturer was considering a lawsuit 694
against the makers of Car because the manufacturer had made 704
railroad cars before automobile cars were invented. 711

In all, the weeks that followed the launching of the Car campaign 723
were extremely hectic. ❻ 726

INFORMATION PASSAGE

feat	astronaut	propelled
galaxy	reposition	

The Hubble Space Telescope—Part 2

Putting the Hubble Space Telescope in space in 1990 was a remarkable feat. A rocket propelled it to 375 miles above Earth. The telescope circles Earth every hour and a half. That means the telescope travels about 400,000 miles every 24 hours. In a year, it travels almost 150 million miles. ❶

Putting the Hubble Space Telescope in space was very expensive, but repairing it is also expensive. The only way to repair it is to send astronauts into space. That's what scientists had to do before the Hubble Space Telescope worked properly.

When the first pictures from the Hubble Space Telescope were received, scientists recognized that there was a problem. The images were not clearly in focus. At the end of 1993, three years after the telescope had been in orbit, seven astronauts went into orbit to repair the problem. It took them ten days. The problem was that the mirror was not perfectly curved, so all the rays of light were not focused in a single spot. The astronauts corrected the problem by installing two smaller mirrors that gave the original mirror the right shape. ❷

The results were remarkable. The pictures on the next page show the image of a galaxy that contains billions of stars. On the left is the image before the repairs had taken place. The image on the right was taken after the repairs. ❸

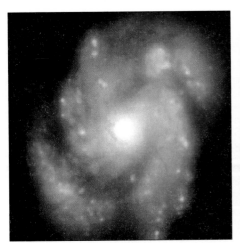
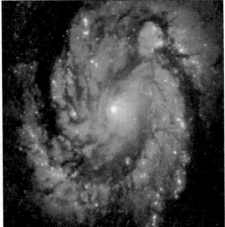

Although the Hubble Space Telescope is expensive to maintain, it has given astronomers a great deal of information about the universe. In its first ten years, it has observed 25,000 astronomical targets. It has captured images of distant stars that are not visible through telescopes on Earth, and it has also given more information about how distant they are. The telescope confirmed that the distances of far-off stars and galaxies change rapidly. All of them are moving farther and farther away from Earth and farther from each other. ❹

One of the incredible images the Hubble took occurred shortly after it was repaired. It caught the image of a comet striking Jupiter. This is something that happens only about every four hundred years.

The orbit of the Hubble Space Telescope is slowly changing, which means that it is getting closer and closer to Earth. If scientists do not reposition the telescope farther from Earth, it will move into the atmosphere and fall to Earth. This would happen sometime between the years 2010 and 2032. ❺

Lesson 109

1

un   less   sub

ness   pre   able   ly

2

furthermore   motionless

executives   disguised

3

survival   easily   exact   concerned

production   instead   convert

months   situation   convention

guarantee   Kamigo   estimate

heartily   schedule   broadcast

4

1. launch
2. translate
3. facilities
4. associates
5. profit
6. colleagues
7. thorough
8. devote

5   Just Too Much

Two months after the Car campaign had been launched, six   10
executives from the Niota factory in Japan came to the advertising   21
agency. Only one of them could speak English very well. Joe and four   34
people from the advertising agency met with the six Niota executives.   45
During the meeting, the one who could speak English talked to Joe   57
and the others. She then translated what was said to the other Niota   70
executives, who would shake their heads either up and down or from   82
side to side.   85

"We're concerned," the English-speaking executive said, "because   92
we do not have facilities to produce for export more than five hundred   105
thousand Cars each year. Already, we are at full production. And   116
already the orders from your country are greater than we can fill." ❶   128

"That's kind of a nice problem to have," the president of the agency   141
said and laughed heartily. Several other members of the agency   151
laughed, too.   153

Joe didn't laugh. He said, "I took one of the Niotas apart, and I   167
found out that it's almost an exact copy of a Miyada model that was   181
built in 1970."   184

"You say we copied Miyada!" the Japanese executive said.   193

She quickly translated Joe's comment to the other executives, after   203
which they shook their heads from side to side and said, "No, no, no!"   217

The president said, "Joe, what are you trying to do? We're not here   230
to insult Ms. Ogura and her associates."   237

"That's not the point. The point is that Niota could contract with   249
Miyada to build more Cars. ❷ I've looked into the situation, and I've   261
talked to the executives at Miyada. According to them, they can   272
convert part of the Kamigo plant into making Cars within only three   284

months. Furthermore, there are currently enough Niotas around to 293
fill all orders between now and <u>then</u>. There are nearly thirty thousand 305
of them in France, where they are not selling well. We could easily 318
pick up twenty thousand and have them shipped here within a month. 330
With the other shipments that are scheduled, we should have enough 341
Cars to last us until the Miyada plant starts producing." ❸ 351

Ms. Ogura was busy translating to the other Niota executives. Two 362
were nodding their heads up and down. Ms. Ogura then smiled 373
broadly and turned to Joe. "You are very thorough. However, we must 385
know what it will cost for us to have Niota produced by Miyada." 398

Joe said, "You will make a profit of about five percent, which is less 412
than you make on the cars you produce, but you will have no expense 426
in the production of these cars. Miyada will pay for setting up and 439
producing Cars if you give them a guarantee that you will take one 452
hundred thousand Cars." 455

Ms. Ogura's eyes became very large. "Oh," she said. "Oh, that's 466
many cars. Many cars." She translated for her colleagues. Four shook 477
their heads from side to side. 483

"Too many cars," Ms. Ogura said. "What happens if we can't sell 495
all Cars produced by Miyada?" 500

The head of the marketing department for the advertising agency 510
said, "Maybe I can help. I have done some figuring. Based on the sales 524
that we have made since the beginning of the campaign, I would 536
estimate that nearly half a million Cars will be sold in this country 549
during this year. That means that we will need more than one 561
hundred thousand Cars from Miyada this year alone." ❹ 569

A quick translation from Ms. Ogura to the other executives, and 580
their heads began to nod up and down. Ms. Ogura smiled. "Very 592
thorough, very thorough," she said. 597

Joe had known from the beginning that he was a super salesperson, ₆₀₉
but now he felt that the Niota situation was getting a little out of hand. ₆₂₄
It was becoming too crazy. Imagine Miyada producing Niotas that ₆₃₄
were to be sent here and called Cars. Imagine all the other major ₆₄₇
manufacturers in the country battling a second-rate import for ₆₅₆
survival. Imagine hundreds of pages of print in newspapers and hours ₆₆₇
and hours of broadcast time devoted to news on the Car situation. ₆₇₉
And imagine the amount of money Joe would make if half a million ₆₉₂
Cars were sold. He would make fifty million dollars! ₇₀₁

During the meeting, Joe found himself thinking, "This is just too ₇₁₀
much!" ❺ ₇₁₁

1

carbon   straight   Africa   zero   India

Montana   dioxide   atmospheric   Portugal

Rainier   Meghalaya   survive   Death Valley

2

1. extreme
2. endure
3. annual
4. climate

3

Climate

No matter how hot it is where you are, you're only a few miles from a place where it is bitterly cold. That place is high over your head. Jet planes fly there because the air is thin high above Earth. Therefore, there is less pull, or drag, against the plane. The temperature outside a high-flying jet, however, is typically -40°F.

Sometimes the temperature there is even lower. In 1963, the lowest atmospheric temperature ever measured was recorded high over Kronogard, Sweden: -225.4°F. At this temperature some gases, such as carbon dioxide, will freeze solid. ❶

Although temperatures on Earth's surface do not approach those high above Earth, some places on Earth do become amazingly cold. A record low of -128.6°F was recorded in 1960 at the South Pole. It seems astonishing that any creature could endure such cold, but there are animals at the South Pole who do just that.

At the other extreme, some places on Earth become extremely hot. In July 1913, the temperature in the shade at Death Valley, California, soared to a scorching 134°F. A temperature of 136.4°F was recorded in 1942 in northern Africa. However, the all-time high reading occurred in Portugal in September 1933. The temperature there suddenly jumped to 158°F. It remained there for two minutes and then dropped to less than 100°F. ❷

Here are some other interesting facts about temperatures:

A great temperature drop occurred in Montana in January 1916. During the day, the temperature was 44°F. That night the temperature fell to -56°F.

The world's hottest weather year after year occurs in Ethiopia, which has an average annual temperature of 94°F. ❸

The place with the greatest annual amount of snowfall is Mt. Rainier, Washington. From early 1971 to early 1972, 1,224.5 inches of snow fell there. That's more than one hundred feet of snow—enough to cover an eight-story building.

The record for the greatest rainfall during any period occurred in July 1861. More than 366 inches of rain fell in Meghalaya, India, in that one month. That's as much rain as will fall in New York or Chicago in eight years. The one-year record for rainfall in Meghalaya is more than 1,041 inches. ❹

1 specialize article countless

convinced pressure

2 reporter raises campaign honest

monster discussing unpopular serious

suddenly strategy overheard estimate

brochure filing creative broadcasting

accurate concluded patents

3
1. genius
2. domestic
3. intent
4. fraud
5. deceit

4 Sinner or Genius?

Joe felt that the Car campaign had turned into a monster, and he was   14
right. The head of the advertising agency's marketing department was   24
pretty close to her estimate about the number of Cars that would be sold   38
in this country during the year. Nearly a quarter of a million were sold   52
within six months. About the time the 250,000th Car had been sold, a   65
reporter from *Moment* magazine found out that Joe Kappas was really   76
the brains of the Car campaign. The reporter interviewed Joe, and two   88
weeks later, Joe's picture was on the cover of *Moment*. Beneath it, it said,   102
"Joe Kappas, Brains Behind Car." Inside the magazine was a four-page   113
story about Joe. The title was "Joe Kappas, Sinner or Genius?" The   125
article pointed out that the Car campaign had hurt sales of domestic   137
cars, that Joe had used a trick to turn an unpopular imported car into the   152
second-largest-selling import in the nation in 1975, and that he had done   164
this in one year. ❶ The article concluded, "The campaign created by Joe   176
Kappas certainly points out the power of advertising; however, it raises   187
serious questions about the rights of companies to use Joe Kappas's type   199
of advertising. There was no truth in Kappas's campaign, only tricks.   210
Yes, Joe Kappas could claim, 'We sell the Car that is Number One in the   225
Nation.' He can point out that his statement is true. In fact, the name of   240
the Car is 'Number One in the Nation.' But clearly the car has that name   255
so that Joe Kappas and the manufacturers of Car products can lie. ❷ As   268
a matter of record, the model that is named 'Number One in the Nation'   282
was not number one. It was the fourth-best-selling imported model and   293
the seventh-best-selling model of all cars <u>sold</u> in the country. The three   305
top-selling 1975 models were manufactured here. The Joe Kappas   314
campaign points out that truth in advertising involves more than words.   325
It involves intent. Joe Kappas's intent was clearly fraud." ❸   334

Joe read the article four times. It made him feel quite bad. Joe was 348
not a person with dishonest intent. He was a super salesperson, not a 361
fraud. He understood people and what made them tick. He had seen 373
the Niota as a challenge. It was an opportunity for him to take a 387
product that was not doing well and turn it into a success. To Joe, that 402
was a good thing because it didn't involve destroying; it involved 413
building something. At least that's how Joe had felt earlier. Now, 424
however, he had some doubts. Perhaps the *Moment* article was 434
accurate in suggesting that Joe had used tricks and deceit to sell Niota 447
cars. Although he had succeeded in turning the Niota into a huge 459
success, he had hurt other people along the way. ❹ 468

After reading the *Moment* article, Joe decided he needed time to 479
think. He didn't accept any phone calls during the next day. In fact, he 493
didn't spend much time at the agency. He spent a lot of time walking 507
around the city. Every time he passed one of the Car billboards, he 520
stopped and examined it. They didn't look too clever to him now. "See 533
the Biggest Selling Car at your Car dealer," he said to himself. "What 547
does that mean? It means see a little Niota at your Niota dealer. But 560
that's not what it says." ❺ 565

He listened to people talking to each other about Car. "My 576
daughter is an automobile dealer," Joe overheard one woman saying 586
to another. "And you would not believe the trouble that she has had 599
since that ugly Car came on the market. She gets phone calls from 612
people wanting to buy Cars. She's had to go to countless meetings. 624
Her company is filing a lawsuit against Car. It's a mess." 635

Joe overheard a couple of young men discussing Car. One of them 647
said, "I think it's great. I think this is just what we need to wake us up. 664
Maybe now we'll get some laws to make advertising honest." 674

The more Joe listened to people talk, the more he became convinced that he had to do something to fix the situation. But what could he do now? Nearly four hundred dealers were selling Cars. The campaign was legal––even if it was based on falsehoods. There was no way Joe could turn the clock back one year and change the events that had taken place. So what could he do? ❻

Joe now had a new challenge, and he loved challenges. Although he didn't know what his strategy would be, he knew that he would do something to correct the situation. However, he didn't want to hurt the people at the advertising agency or the dealers who were selling Car. That was going to be hard to do.

Joe had been walking, listening to people, and thinking for nearly a week when an idea hit him. He was walking through a park, past a small pond that was dotted with ducks, when suddenly, he stopped, snapped his fingers, and said, "I think I've got a plan that will work."

1   re   ness   dis   tri   ly   un   able

2   benefi<u>ci</u>al   <u>wh</u>ether   espe<u>ci</u>ally

<u>pr</u>evailing   p<u>a</u>rticularly

3   seriously   image   practically   accounts

curiously   remained   bellow   implement

waddled   interrupt   created   individual

canceled   concealed   demand

4
1. stroll
2. receptionist
3. conference
4. resignation

5 All in the Same Pond

Joe sat down on a park bench, took out his pocket notebook, and 13
began to make notes. He talked to himself as he wrote, and some of 27
the people strolling through the park paused to look curiously at him. 39
Joe remained on the park bench nearly all afternoon. At three thirty 51
he got up and ran the four blocks back to the agency. He ran up to the 68
receptionist and said, "Set up a meeting." He paused to take a deep 81
breath and continued, "I want to speak with the president and the 93
department heads." 95

"When do you wish to schedule this meeting, Mr. Kappas?" the 106
receptionist asked. 108

"Right now," Joe replied quickly. 113

"Oh, I don't believe that's possible." 119

"I don't care how possible it is," Joe said in a firm voice. "Do it." Joe 135
hadn't intended to be so rude, but he wanted to get his plan into 149
operation as soon as possible. ❶ 154

The receptionist made some calls and then informed Joe, "The 164
meeting is set up in the conference room in five minutes." 175

"Look," Joe said. "I'm sorry—I—" This was one of the few times 188
that Joe was at a loss for words. 196

The receptionist smiled at Joe and said, "It's OK." 205

Joe went up to the conference room and waited for the others to arrive. 219

When everybody was present and seated around the conference 228
table, Joe said, "We must deal with some facts. Fact: The Car 240
campaign has created a lot of ill will. Fact: The campaign has hurt a 254
lot of people. Fact: Articles like the one in *Moment* magazine give this 267
agency a bad image." 271

"What are you trying to get at with these facts?" the president 283
demanded. "I can give you a fact, too. The people at Niota feel that 297
our campaign <u>was</u> so beneficial that they have given us another two 309
million dollars for advertising. That's the fact that counts." ❷ 318

"Sure they do," Joe said. "But we have to consider other people, 330
too. Wouldn't it be a good idea to get some good will for Niota?" 344

"Sales are good will," the president said. "And we've made lots and 356
lots of sales." 359

"Look," Joe said. "I was sitting in the park looking at the ducks 372
swimming in a pond when I got this idea. Each duck is an individual, 386
but they're all in the same pond. Niota is a duck. It is in a pond with 403
all the other car manufacturers. But Niota has turned on the other 415
ducks. What I'm suggesting is that Niota should try to get along with 428
those other ducks." ❸ 431

"I don't know anything about ducks," the president said. "One of 442
our accounts is Mason's TV chicken dinner, but that's as close to 454
ducks as we get." 458

Everybody laughed except Joe. "Well, let me tell you my plan, and 470
please don't interrupt. We've got the dealers now, so we're sure of 482
selling Cars. That means we don't need our campaign anymore. And 493
we can get another ten million dollars' worth of news if we do 506
something to fix this situation with the lawsuits and the other 517
manufacturers." 518

"So what's the plan?" the president asked. 525

"Here it is," Joe said. "We keep on calling the Niotas 'Cars,' but we 539
do it a little differently. We call them 'Cars by Niota.' Then we sell 553
every other car manufacturer the right to call their automobiles 'Cars.' 564
We can sell them the right for practically nothing, because we're not 576
interested in the money; we're interested in the good will and the news 589
that we can create with this move." ❹ 596

"I like it," the head of the marketing department said. 606

"I don't," the president bellowed. "That's like admitting that we 616 were wrong in the first place. From the beginning, I said that we 629 should stand behind the Car idea." 635

The head of the marketing department said, "But it's a good idea. 647 As Joe says, we've got the dealers now. Why not do something 659 positive?" 660

The president stared at the marketing director and said, "It seems 671 that there are some people in this agency who don't think for 683 themselves. If Joe Kappas has an idea, they want to buy it, no matter 697 how sour it is." ❺ 701

The head of the marketing department stood up. Very quietly she 712 said, "Well, I'll tell you this. I don't feel good about the way the Car 727 campaign is going. I didn't know it would get so big or that it would 742 get so far out of hand. That's thinking for myself, and if you don't take 757 Joe's suggestions seriously, you'll have my resignation." 764

A deep silence fell over the conference room. 772

INFORMATION PASSAGE

expectancy   predictor   canine   per

Life Expectancy of Animals

Some species of animals live longer than others. As a rule, the smaller they are, the shorter their lives.

The worker honeybee has one of the shorter life expectancies. The worker never sleeps and dies about two weeks after it becomes a bee.

Mayflies often live as adults for less than a day. A long life for an adult mayfly is four days.

At the other extreme are large animals. An average elephant lives over 50 years, and some whales live over 200 years. ❶

The size of an animal is not a perfect predictor of how long the animal is expected to live. Different species age at different rates.

Worker Honey Bee

Mayfly

Turtles live a long time, some living 150 years. A crow lives longer than an average dog, but an eagle lives longer than a crow. Some birds live much longer than eagles. For example, a Canada goose lives over 30 years. Some parrots live 80 years. ❷

Dogs and other canines do not live as long as many birds. An average dog is expected to live about 12 years, but some types of dogs live much longer. Some small dogs may live as long as 18 years. Great Danes and other large dogs have a short life expectancy. Sometimes these dogs will die before they are 10 years old. ❸

The life expectancy of animals is usually related to how long it takes an animal to become an adult. Animals that have longer childhoods live longer. It takes a human 17 years to become adult, and humans are expected to live over 70 years. It takes a bunny a year to become a full-grown rabbit, and rabbits live only five years or less. Mice grow up faster than rabbits and have a shorter life expectancy. ❹

Mammals and birds that burn up fuel faster often have short life expectancies because they wear out faster, and their hearts beat faster. The heartbeat of a human is about 72 beats per minute. The heartbeat of a hummingbird or bat is about 600 beats per minute. That means birds and bats age faster than a human or a camel, whose heartbeat is about 30 beats per minute. ❺

Because smaller animals burn fuel at a faster rate than larger animals, smaller animals must eat more compared to how much they weigh. Every day, a weasel has to eat food that weighs as much as the weasel weighs. Larger animals don't eat amounts that are even close to their weight. An elephant may eat 200 pounds of food every day, but that elephant may weigh 4,000 pounds. So the elephant weighs 20 times more than it eats each day. Also, the heart rate of the elephant is much slower than that of a small animal or human. The elephant's heart beats about 20 times a minute. ❻

Lesson 113

1

especi<u>a</u>lly h<u>ea</u>dlines <u>au</u>dience f<u>u</u>rthermore

2

creative wandering dealership figure

announcement details several outfits

additional hurting basically general

remained official purchase

furthermore country suing

representative create waddling

3

1. withdraw
2. rowdies
3. term

4   Car by Niota

Joe stood up next to the marketing director and said to the   12
president, "I'll do more than quit if you don't take my plan seriously. 25
So far, you owe me more than six million dollars on our contract. If   39
you don't implement my plan, I'll take every cent of that money and   52
turn it over to one of the outfits that is suing Niota. Furthermore, I'll   66
get in touch with the major news reporters in the country and tell   79
them that I withdraw from the campaign, that I will take no money   92
from the campaign, and that the only reason the campaign is   103
continuing is because *you* want it that way." ❶   111

"What is this?" the president said, standing up. "There's no need for   123
shouting and acting like rowdies. I gather you must be speaking out of 136
great anger to talk about anything as crazy as giving away six million 149
dollars."   150

"I may be crazy," Joe said softly. "But I'm me. And I have to live   165
with me. And I don't think I would like myself with six million dollars 179
that I made by hurting other people. I think I would like me much   193
better if I knew that I was doing what I think is right. I'm a good   209
salesperson, and I'm going to sell you on my plan. Believe me, you'll   222
buy it before I'm done." ❷   227

The head of the creative department stood up. "I'm with Joe," he   239
said.   240

The art director stood up. "Me, too."   247

The president sat down. "Now, I don't recall saying that I was   259
against any plan to create good will. I don't know why everybody is   272
jumping to conclusions."   275

"Good," Joe said, sitting down. The others sat down, too. "Let's go   287
over the details of the plan. First, we have to talk Niota <u>into</u> changing 301

the name of Car to Car by Niota. That should be pretty easy to do   316

because they'll be happy to have their name advertised again."   326

"I see no problem on that count," the president said.   336

Joe continued, "Then, we'll have to fix up the signs at the Car   349

dealerships, so that they say 'Car by Niota.' I figure that should cost   362

no more than one hundred fifty thousand dollars. We must have those   374

signs within three weeks, so we'll have to move quickly."   384

The head of the marketing department said, "I think we can do that   397

without much trouble." ❸   400

Joe went through the rest of the details that would have to be   413

attended to. After the meeting, Joe remained at the agency and made   425

more than a dozen phone calls. He called several lawyers, two union   437

leaders, and several executives from other automobile companies.   445

During the next three days, Joe made more than a hundred phone   457

calls. He called reporters and executives from all the automobile   467

manufacturers that had distribution in the country, telling them of his   478

plan. He asked them to keep it a secret until the official   490

announcement, which was to take place on Friday. Joe asked for a   502

representative from each automobile company to be present at the   512

announcement. All the companies agreed to send one. ❹   520

Friday was extremely hectic at the agency, with people running   530

around carrying stacks of paper that would be handed out at the   542

meeting. Reporters were wandering around asking thousands of   550

questions. At last, representatives from twenty auto manufacturers,   558

thirty-five reporters, and a dozen lawyers went to the agency's meeting   569

room. The president of the advertising agency stood up and said,   580

"The Niota Motor Works has decided to sell rights to the word *car*.   593

These rights will be sold to all other car manufacturers so that they   606

can use the word *car*. Niota is charging each company that wishes to   619

purchase the rights one thousand dollars per year. This money will be   631

donated to the labor union. Finally, the name Niota will appear on all 644
cars manufactured by Niota. The name will be Car by Niota." ❺ 655

As the president talked, flashbulbs went off and cameras clicked. 665
Following the announcement, every reporter in the audience seemed 674
to ask a question at the same time. They asked which companies were 687
taking up Niota's offer. Joe told them that all had agreed to the terms. 701
Reporters asked whether any of the suits would be dropped against 712
Niota. They were told that most of the major suits had been dropped. 725

There were a lot of headlines in the newspaper during the days that 738
followed the announcement and a lot of articles. *Moment* magazine 748
ran an article that referred to Joe as "basically a good guy." Sales of 762
Car didn't drop off. If anything, they went up. And Joe felt a lot better 777
about the whole situation. 781

On the day after the meeting, Joe went for a walk through the park. 795
He stopped and looked at the ducks swimming in the pond, and he 808
said to himself, "That's the way it should be." ❻ 817

Lesson
114

1

less   ly   ness   re   able

2

ailment   surgery   knowledge   snout

sewer   cleanliness   penicillin

3

especially   medicine   referred   disease

patient   diphtheria   viewed   effective

bubonic   leather   plague   sweating

advanced   invisible   professional   dwellings

childhood   smallpox   wand   statues

4

1. treatment
2. organism
3. microscope
4. infected

5   Medicine Years Ago

The doctors of today are professionals with a great deal of   11
knowledge about the human body and what may go wrong with it.   23
Doctors understand what treatments are effective. They treat some   32
problems with surgery, which involves cutting into the patient's body.   42
To fight disease they may use some form of drug, such as penicillin.   55
They know that germs spread diseases, and that germs are tiny   66
organisms, so small they are invisible unless viewed under a   76
microscope. It is fair to say that today's doctors have a great   88
understanding of medicine—the science of curing ailments. ❶   96

The doctors of 1850 did not know many of the things that today's   109
doctors understand. They didn't understand that they should wash   118
their hands before touching a patient. If you had been living then and   131
had to go to a hospital, you probably would not have left that hospital   145
alive. Over half of the people who entered a hospital died there,   157
because hospital attendants and doctors didn't know as much as they   168
do today. ❷   170

Let's go back much further than 1850. Let's go back to the year   183
1350, and let's visit a large city in Europe. The scene is quite similar in   198
all large cities. The first thing you probably notice is the smell of the   212
city. Many cities did not have sewers, so the streets were used as sewers.   226
Another thing you notice is that the people are very dirty and that they   240
smell. They don't believe in taking baths. Even kings and very rich   252
people bathe only once or twice a year. The city, you observe, is   265
surrounded by a large wall, and the dwellings are packed together. The   277
great wall around the city was originally intended to protect it from   289
attack by neighboring kings or princes. But packing people together   299
<u>makes</u> for terrible filth. ❸   303

Lesson

114

You observe an interesting contrast between the filth of the city and 315
the beautiful paintings, statues, and hand-crafted objects made by the 325
talented artists and craftsmen of the city. Obviously, the people have a 337
great appreciation of beauty. And some of the music you hear is still 350
played today. What a contrast. On the one hand, the people's 361
understanding of medicine and cleanliness is far different from what 371
we know today. Yet on the other hand, the people are similar to 384
today's people in their understanding of the arts. ❹ 392

As you walk through the crowds of people in the streets of the city, 406
you notice a man dressed in a very strange outfit. He wears a large 420
leather coat and gloves. Over his face is a strange mask with a large 434
circle of glass in the middle and a long snout. He carries a long metal 449
wand, and as he walks down the street, the people run to get out of his 465
way. The man is a doctor. He treats people who are infected with the 479
most dreaded disease in the city—the bubonic plague. His costume is a 492
special one, worn only in times of plague. ❺ 500

The bubonic plague, called the Black Death at the time of our visit, 513
is the greatest single killer in the city. This dreaded disease spread 525
throughout Europe in the middle of the fourteenth century (the 1300s) 536
and killed probably at least one-third of the population. 545

Bubonic plague is not the only killer in the city. Smallpox and 557
measles and diphtheria are common. You probably notice that many 567
people's faces are covered with pitlike scars. These scars were caused 578
by smallpox. Almost everyone in the city suffered from smallpox when 589
they were children. Those who wear the scars lived. ❻ The graveyards 600
are filled with the thousands of children who didn't live. On the average, 613
a baby born in 1300 could have been expected to live less than twenty 627
years. (The baby's *life expectancy* was twenty years.) This was so 638
because many would not survive the diseases of childhood. Even those 649
who did might die from something as simple as an infected tooth. In 662

418 *Lesson 114*

contrast, the life expectancy of people in Europe and North America 673
in the twentieth century is about seventy years—because most children 684
survive childhood diseases. 687

As you stand in the street, watching people make way for the doctor 700
in the leather outfit, you decide to follow him and observe how he 713
cares for those who suffer from the bubonic plague. Perhaps you will 725
regret this decision. ❼ 728

Lesson
115

1

carried   Egyptians   official

combinations   syllables   English

Mandarin   billion   intelligent

hieroglyphic   language   represented

determine   inhabited   scenes

2

1. inscribed
2. tomb

3

Spoken Language and Written Language

Experts have not been able to determine exactly when people first began to use language. Experts agree that prehistoric people used language thousands of years ago. They expressed many ideas through pictures, one of the earliest forms of written language. Drawings in caves show scenes of animals and hunters. In the earliest type of pictures, each picture represented an object, an idea, or an action. Later the pictures stood for sounds, not things, but they were not symbols for words or syllables.

Burial tombs show that the Egyptians who lived four thousand years ago had a highly developed form of picture writing called hieroglyphics. Examples of elaborate hieroglyphic stories have been found inscribed on vases, boxes, and the walls of the tombs. ❶

Spoken language, however, came long before writing. While all groups of human beings have speech, the patterns and sounds of speech can differ greatly from one group to another. There are about three thousand languages spoken in the world today.

In the United States, English is the official language, but many other languages—for example, Spanish, Portuguese, and Japanese—are used. In some countries, there is no single official language. People from one part of the country cannot understand people from another part because each group speaks a different language. In India, about 140 languages and more than 700 regional variations are spoken. ❷

The language spoken by the greatest number of people is Mandarin Chinese. More than one billion people speak this language. The second most widely used language is English, which is spoken by about 400,000,000 people.

Of all languages, English has the greatest number of words: about 800,000. The average English-speaking adult doesn't use all these words, or even half of them. The average person probably uses only about 10,000 of all English words. ❸

There are some very long words in the English language. One has twenty-eight letters: antidisestablishmentarianism.

The longest word in the English language is the name of a lung disease that people who work in mines sometimes get. That word contains forty-five letters. Here it is:

pneumonoultramicroscopicsilicovolcanoconiosis.

Lesson 116

1 un   re   ly   able   ness

2 bre<u>a</u>thing   <u>fou</u>l   he<u>a</u>vens   offi<u>ci</u>al

3 perfumed   responded   wealthy

poison   curtains   wand   course

patients   plague   servant   victim

females   gloved   filthy   bubonic

conscious   hollow   bedding   indicates

4
1. unconscious
2. sprinkling
3. impure
4. purify

5 The Black Death

You are observing a doctor who is treating victims of the bubonic   12
plague in 1350. You follow the doctor down the narrow street where   24
houses are crowded side by side. The doctor pauses in front of a   37
house. A large black cloth hangs from the front door. This black cloth   50
indicates that there is a plague victim in the building and that nobody   63
can leave the building. Only a doctor can enter.   72

The doctor goes inside and enters the room of the victim, who is   85
unconscious in bed. The room is very dark and foul smelling. The   97
windows are closed. The bedding is filthy. The doctor walks over to   109
the bed and pokes at the victim with his wand. He uses the wand so   124
that he doesn't have to touch the victim with his hands or even his   138
gloves. The victim does not move. ❶   144

"What can we do, doctor?" the victim's brother asks.   153

"I will purify the air," the doctor responds, his voice sounding   164
hollow through the mask.   168

The doctor takes a bottle of perfumed water from under his coat.   180
He walks around the room, sprinkling the curtains, the floor, and the   192
patient's bed with the perfumed water. He then asks the patient's   203
brother for a cooking pot. After the doctor places some spices in the   216
pot and lights them, a powerful-smelling smoke fills the room.   226

"Should I bathe my brother?" the young man asks.   235

"Heavens no," the doctor replies through his mask. "The Black   245
Death is caused by impure vapors that enter the body through the   257
openings in the skin called pores. If you bathe the patient, the water   270
will open his pores further and more of the disease will enter his body.   284
The smoke of the spices will prevent any more impure vapors from   296
entering his pores." ❷   299

"Doctor," the brother asks, "will my brother live?" 307

It is difficult to see the doctor's expression through his mask. "I 319
don't know," he replies. 323

The doctor charges the healthy brother a fee for the services he 335
performed, and then, without washing his wand, he leaves the 345
building and continues down the street. 351

As you follow him, you notice a horse-drawn cart that is piled high 364
with the bodies of plague victims. 370

The doctor's next stop is a large house near the city wall. This is the 385
house of a wealthy family. The doctor is not allowed inside. A servant 398
meets him at the gate to the house. "My master is feeling ill," the 412
servant says. "It does not seem that he has the plague, but he wishes 426
your advice." 428

The doctor takes off his mask and shakes his head. He looks very 441
tired. "I will give you some pills that will clean out his system, but my 456
best advice is quick-far-late." 460

"What does that mean?" the servant inquires. 467

"It means be *quick* to leave the city. Go *far*. And come back *late*— 481
after the plague has run its course." ❸ 488

The doctor hands the pills to the servant. The servant says, "I shall 501
tell my master what you said." The master who owns the house has 514
ten servants and a great deal of money. He is lucky because he can 528
afford to leave the city during a time of great plague. Only the kings, 542
the princes, and the wealthy are able to follow the advice of 554
quick-far-late. Of those who can't leave, two-thirds become plague 563
victims, and as many as eight out of ten victims will die. 575

The doctor wipes his brow with the back of his gloved hand and 588
then puts his mask on again. He doesn't know that the stroke of the 602
glove across his forehead spread the germs of the bubonic plague to 614
him. He will be dead within a week. ❹ 622

1

surgeon   un<u>e</u>ducated   lect<u>u</u>re   challen<u>g</u>e   ignoran<u>c</u>e

2

Ambroise Paré   Leonardo da Vinci   intelligent

barber   conducted   spirits   popular

advice   ailment   penicillin   medicine

anesthetics   haircut   Latin   respect

schooling   dissected   anatomy   infected

unfortunately   warfare   physician   frequent

lanced   purify   muscles

3

1. wounds
2. sluggish
3. amputate
4. scalding
5. ignorant
6. suspicious

4   The Barber-Surgeon

Around the year 1500, there were three types of doctors. The three   12
types were called *surgeons of the long robe, physicians,* and   22
barber-surgeons.   23

The surgeons of the long robe, unlike the surgeons of today, never   35
operated. They dressed wounds, gave out pills or drugs, and "bled"   46
people. During the 1500s, people believed that some diseases were   56
caused by blood that was sluggish. The surgeons of the long robe   68
suggested that patients would recover from these diseases if some   78
blood were removed from their systems. ❶   84

Sometimes the surgeons of the long robe worked with physicians.   94
Physicians did not do any work on patients. They lectured at   105
universities and gave advice to people who could afford to hire them.   117
If a patient needed some kind of care, the physician would bring in a   131
surgeon of the long robe. The physician would give the advice, and the   144
surgeon of the long robe would take care of the patient's ailment. The   157
physician never touched the patient.   162

Both physicians and surgeons of the long robe went through a great   174
deal of schooling. They spoke Latin, and the books they read were   186
written in Latin. The great majority of the people of that time could   199
not speak or read Latin. In fact, most of them couldn't read at all.   213
Physicians and surgeons of the long robe were well-to-do and highly   224
respected, even though they knew very little about medicine, by   234
modern standards. ❷   236

The third type of doctor was the barber-surgeon. Most of the   247
barber-surgeons were uneducated, even unable to read. Many had   256
other jobs, such as tending pigs or cutting meat in a market. Most   269
people had little respect for the barber-surgeons, who had learned   279

their trade by working in a "barber shop." You could get a lot more 293
than a haircut in those barber <u>shops</u>. You could also get a wounded 306
leg amputated or have a boil lanced. You could have your teeth pulled 319
or a bullet removed. (Guns were just coming into use in warfare 331
around this time.) ❸ 334

Barber-surgeons usually had a number of charms hanging in 343
different parts of their shops. One of the most popular charms was a 356
stuffed animal that was hung from the ceiling. The animal was 367
supposed to keep the evil spirits away while the barber amputated a 379
leg or an arm. Amputations were frequent because the doctors didn't 390
know how to stop infections. They had no penicillin or other drugs of 403
that type, and they didn't realize that wounds should be kept clean. 415
When a wound became seriously infected, the patient would either 425
wait to die from the infection or have the infected part amputated. 437
The operation was conducted without any anesthetics because at that 447
time anesthetics were unknown. The barber-surgeon would tie the 456
patient to a chair and saw off the infected part. Then he would place 470
scalding hot oil on the wound to stop the bleeding and to "purify" the 484
wound. If the bleeding did not kill the patient, the scalding hot oil 497
sometimes did. ❹ 499

Although the barber-surgeons were not trained in the science of 509
medicine, their knowledge was not much less than that of the 520
physicians and the surgeons of the long robe. The surgeons of the long 533
robe never operated because they knew that the patient would 543
probably die from the operation. So they devoted their efforts to 554
impressing people by speaking in Latin, blaming diseases on evil 564
spirits, and attempting cures that did not work. ❺ 572

The religious ideas of the times made it very difficult for doctors to 585
find cures that did work. People believed that a person would not 597
reach heaven if the body were cut into pieces. It was, therefore, 609

considered a crime for doctors to study dead bodies. The doctors 620

knew very little about the parts of the body—the muscles, the bones, 633

the nerves. And they were prevented from finding out any facts by 645

studying dead bodies. In studying anatomy (the structure of the 655

body), they were allowed to operate only on animals such as dogs or 668

goats. Unfortunately, the human body is not the same as the body of a 682

dog or a goat. So the physicians and surgeons remained ignorant 693

about the human body, and they were suspicious of anyone who tried 705

to challenge their ignorance. ❻ 709

There were a few challenges around 1500. One came from a famous 721

artist, Leonardo da Vinci. Another came from a man named 731

Ambroise Paré, who became a surgeon of the long robe, even though 743

he did not go to a university. He began as a barber-surgeon and never 757

learned to speak or read Latin. Both da Vinci and Paré learned a 770

great deal because they sought the facts—not the beliefs that had been 783

passed along for hundreds of years. 789

1 **sub   able   dis   re   ly**

2 spe<u>ci</u>al   <u>sub</u>stance   <u>ex</u>tract   dese<u>r</u>ve   ac<u>c</u>epted

3
treatments   submarine   eventually

devices   conditions   filthy   corpses

dissected   sponge   anatomist

patients   completed   battlefield

muscles   amputate   contribution

arteries   achievements   publish

4
1. selection
2. sketches
3. masterpieces
4. anatomy
5. dressings
6. limbs

5   The Early Study of Anatomy and Surgery

After you read this selection, look up some of the paintings of   12
Leonardo da Vinci. When you examine these paintings, look at the way   24
Leonardo drew the human body. Leonardo understood the structure of   34
the human body probably as well as anybody who had ever lived. And he   48
reached this understanding of the body by studying its inner structure.   59
He worked with corpses (dead bodies), and he dissected them (cut parts   71
away so that he could study other parts). He recorded his findings by   84
making sketches of the body parts. He made detailed drawings of   95
muscles, bones, even nerves. He hoped to publish a great work on the   108
anatomy of the human body. Unfortunately, he died before he completed   119
the book. All that he left behind were hundreds of notes and sketches.   132
Many of these were lost after his death, but some were saved. These   145
notes and sketches found their way to different parts of Europe. ❶   156

Leonardo also left sketches of another kind. Among them were   166
details for building a submarine, an airplane, and other devices that   177
would not be "invented" for hundreds of years. Besides the devices   188
that remained on paper, he did invent machines that were actually   199
used to construct buildings, make statues, and create special effects   209
for plays. He created paintings that are considered masterpieces. He   219
helped open the door to the study of human anatomy. But he never   232
saw some of his greatest achievements accepted by the world. ❷   242

A very different kind of contribution to medicine in the 1500s was   254
made by a man named Ambroise Paré. Paré was not an anatomist or   267
an artist. He began as a helper to a barber-surgeon in a hospital of   281
more than one thousand beds. Conditions in that hospital were   291
terrible even by the standards of that time. <u>Rats</u> could be seen in every   305
part of the building. The bedding and the dressings of the wounds   317

were filthy. The odor was so bad that the attendants could not enter 330
the sickroom unless they held a sponge dipped in vinegar over their 342
nose and mouth. The patients were not fed regularly. ❸ 351

After three years of working in the hospital, Paré became an army 363
surgeon. Conditions for treating soldiers on the battlefield were as bad 374
as those in the hospital. The surgeons would amputate limbs or try to 387
extract bullets from gunshot wounds. Bullets were new in warfare, and 398
the surgeons did not know how to treat the wounds bullets caused. 410
Some cut out the bullet and then poured hot oil into the wound. These 424
surgeons used the slogan: "If the wound is not curable by using the 437
knife, use fire." (*Fire* meant "hot oil.") ❹ 444

Paré changed two things. First, he discovered how to tie off arteries 456
in amputations so that the patient did not bleed to death. Second, he 469
discovered that wounds healed better without boiling oil. Instead, he 479
used clean cloth and mild substances like egg whites to cover the 491
wounds. Paré's methods worked. Many of the soldiers that Paré 501
treated lived. Many didn't suffer as much as they would have if they 514
had received the usual treatments. They usually didn't develop fevers, 524
and the wounds healed more quickly. ❺ 530

People began to become aware of the work of Paré. He became 542
court surgeon to three kings. In his day, many other doctors thought 554
surgery was below their dignity. Paré helped raise the standing of 565
surgery. But many physicians and surgeons resented Paré. They didn't 575
believe in his methods. They thought he was an ignorant man because 587
he didn't even know Latin. 592

Paré did a lot of things to advance medicine. He developed new 604
methods for delivering babies and cut down the number of deaths among 616
mothers and newborn babies. The methods that Paré developed were 626
eventually adopted by others. In fact, when he died, his methods were 638
being used in the hospital where he had begun as a barber's assistant. ❻ 651

INFORMATION PASSAGE

occupation   electrician   frequent   repairer   electrocution

The Most Dangerous Occupations—Part 1

Some occupations are dangerous. People who work in an office or at home are far less likely to have an accident that is related to the job than somebody who works outside. The reason that outdoor jobs are more dangerous than indoor jobs is that some kinds of weather make an outdoor job dangerous. A worker who is trying to repair electrical power lines during a wind storm or thunderstorm is in far more danger of being injured or killed than the worker who does the same job during good weather.

Truck driving is a dangerous occupation. In fact, the trucking industry has the largest number of work-related deaths of any occupation. That doesn't mean that truck driving is the most dangerous job. There are a lot more truck drivers than there are workers in some of the other dangerous occupations. The most common cause of death for truck drivers is highway crashes, often in bad weather. ❶

If you look at 100,000 workers in each dangerous occupation and see how many deaths there are per 100,000, truck driving is the fifth most dangerous job. In the trucking industry, about 26 of every 100,000 workers are killed in work-related accidents. That's over five times the number of deaths compared to the average job.

For workers who install or repair electric power lines, 28 per 100,000 are killed. Almost all are the result of being electrocuted. Farming is also a dangerous job, almost as dangerous as trucking.

The reason is that the machinery is dangerous. Farmers use dangerous machinery to harvest crops, mow fields, or plant seed. ❷

For some jobs, the greatest cause of death is falling. These jobs include roofing and working on the construction of tall buildings or bridges. These jobs are more dangerous than either trucking or repairing electrical power lines.

The table below shows the top ten most dangerous occupations. The most dangerous are fishers and loggers, followed by airline pilots.

The third column of the table shows the most common causes of death. The most frequent cause of death for electricians is electrocution. The most frequent cause of death for airplane pilots is crashing. ❸

The top ten most dangerous occupations		
	Occupation	**Most frequent cause of work-related deaths**
1.	Fishers	Drowning
	Loggers	Struck by object
2.	Airline pilots	Airplane crash
3.	Taxicab drivers	Violence
	Construction workers and roofers	Falling
4.	Electric-power-line repairers	Electrocution
5.	Truck drivers	Highway crashes
6.	Farm occupations	Machinery
7.	Police	Violence, highway crashes
8.	Factory workers	Machinery
9.	Electricians	Electrocution
10.	Welders	Falling, fire

Lesson 119

1 **able   ly   re**

2 observations posture remarkable breast
mentioned courage concerned frequently

3 Vesalius Galen accepted explanation
scattered challenge managed conclusions
theories indicated dissect anatomy
conflict prominent suspicious

4
1. elaborate
2. proclaimed
3. common trait

5 Galen's Theories

Around 1500, some doctors began to question the medical theories 10
that had been accepted for hundreds of years. These doctors exhibited 21
a great deal of courage because most people were suspicious of 32
anybody who challenged established theories. 37

But a few doctors had the courage to record what they observed, 49
even though their observations were in conflict with long-standing 58
theories and with the accepted medical practice of the time. The basic 70
theory of medicine around 1500 had been accepted for over a 81
thousand years. It had been developed by a man named Galen, a 93
Greek who tried to explain how the body worked and how to cure its 107
ailments. ❶ 108

During Galen's time, doctors were not permitted to dissect (cut up) 119
dead bodies. Galen realized, however, that doctors could not work 129
with the human body unless they understood the anatomy of the 140
body. (The study of anatomy deals with the structure of the body— 152
the bones, muscles, nerves, and organs.) Galen wrote an elaborate 162
work on anatomy. He drew conclusions about human anatomy by 172
studying the anatomy of different animals. Since he couldn't work on 183
human bodies, he dissected animals, such as pigs and apes. ❷ 193

Galen proclaimed that human hipbones looked like those of an 203
ox—a conclusion based upon his dissection of oxen. Galen thought 214
that different human organs were identical to those found in the hog, 226
the dog, the ox, or the ape. He made these mistakes because his 239
conclusions about human anatomy were based upon animal anatomy 248
instead of human anatomy. 252

Galen's views of anatomy were accepted as law for well over a 264
thousand years. Few people questioned his findings; few surgeons 273
made observations of humans and said, "Galen is wrong." Instead, 283
physicians continued to teach Galen's theory and stood ready to fight 294
anybody who challenged it. ❸ 298

We <u>have</u> already mentioned one man who questioned Galen's 307
theory—Leonardo da Vinci. His works, however, remained scattered 316
around Europe for many years after his death. Another man who 327
challenged Galen's views was Vesalius. He was a doctor and a 338
professor at a leading university. Vesalius met Paré at one time. The 350
two men had a great deal in common. Both relied more on what they 364
saw than on what they were told. They were willing to question 376
long-standing theories and were willing to see what was there, not what 388
they wanted to see. ❹ 392

Another common trait of Vesalius and Paré was courage. 401
Remember, people were not encouraged to challenge accepted 409
theories. If they did, they could expect trouble. Both Paré and 420
Vesalius attacked practices of the day. Yet Vesalius was respected by 431
many people. Toward the end of his life he became physician to two 444
kings. His work helped lead the medical profession to a greater 455
understanding of the human body. ❺ 460

1

corpus callosum   greatest   basically

telephone   estimates   messages   electric

forehead   halves   dividing   current

hemispheres   tracing   lesion   tremor

melody   damaged   accurate   fibers   logical

2

1. composed
2. eliminate
3. function

3

The Brain

The human brain is one of the greatest wonders in the universe. Basically, the brain is composed of nerve cells that are packed together. A nerve cell is like a wire. It has a long shaft that works like the wires that carry telephone messages or electric current. The best estimates hold that there are hundreds of millions of nerve cells in the brain. Some of these are less than an inch long, but many are more than three feet long. ❶

If you were to draw a line from the tip of your nose, between your eyes, and up the middle of your forehead, you would be tracing the dividing line between the two halves of your brain. The fibers that join the two halves are called the corpus callosum, and the two halves are called hemispheres. ❷

Most theories state that each hemisphere has a different major function. A simple rule for describing what the two hemispheres do is this: The left hemisphere thinks, and the right hemisphere feels.

According to scientists' theories, this rule is not exactly accurate, but it does tell the major function of the hemispheres. Language is usually controlled by centers in the left hemisphere. If these are damaged, you could lose your ability to speak and even to understand what others are saying. When you try to reason logically, you are primarily using the left side of your brain. But when you experience feelings, you are using the right hemisphere of your brain. When you listen to the melody of a song, your right hemisphere is involved. When you see a face in the clouds, you're using the right hemisphere. When you feel strong emotion, your right hemisphere is involved. ❸

Although scientists understand a great deal about the brain, there is much they don't know. For example, there is the puzzle of the second lesion. A lesion is a cut. Let's say that you have a lesion on the left side of your brain, near the back. Your hands may shake so much that you can't hold a cup without spilling the contents. In some cases, this tremor can be eliminated by making another lesion on the opposite hemisphere. In this case, the lesion would be made on the right side, near the back. Why doesn't the second lesion make your condition twice as bad? Why doesn't the second lesion always work? These are very good questions; they haven't been answered yet. ❹

1

able   dis   re   ly   less   ness   sub

2

challenging   dis<u>ea</u>se   c<u>au</u>tious   dis<u>ci</u>pline

unbeliev<u>able</u>   starv<u>ation</u>   <u>c</u>ertain

3

Servetus   dangerous   shortly   convinced

structure   superstition   accept   publish

observation   Vesalius   dissected

professor   sketches   obvious

described   designed   shipwrecked

accused   centuries   revolution

4

1. gallows
2. criminal
3. liver
4. internal
5. cautious
6. predictable
7. position

5   Vesalius, Professor of Anatomy

Vesalius is called the father of anatomy. He lived from 1514 to 1564.   13
When he was a student at the university, he dissected a few animals   26
and observed work on dead human bodies. Once he stole a human   38
skeleton from the gallows. It was the remains of a criminal who had   51
been hanged. If Vesalius had been caught, he would have been hanged   63
himself. Vesalius studied the skeleton and made observations.   71

One of the first things he noticed was that the hipbones of the   84
skeleton were not like the hipbones that Galen described. ❶ Vesalius   94
wrote down all his observations, but he was not yet ready to publish   107
them.   108

When Vesalius was only twenty-three years old, he accepted a   118
position as professor of anatomy at a leading university. While   128
continuing his study of anatomy at the university, he discovered many   139
things that Galen had not noticed or described. Vesalius discovered   149
that the liver and other internal organs were different from those in   161
Galen's description. Vesalius carefully wrote down his findings and   170
made sketches of their details. For five years, he wrote and studied   182
and worked with artists who made detailed pictures based on human   193
anatomy. Then, at the age of twenty-eight, he published his work. ❷   204

The response of many of the doctors of the day was predictable.   216
Vesalius's former professor of anatomy accused Vesalius of being   225
mad. The doctors agreed that Vesalius was both crazy and very evil   237
for attacking the teachings of Galen. We can understand how these   248
men felt when we remember that they had spent a great deal of effort   262
learning to become doctors. They were convinced that they had   272
special knowledge about how to cure diseases. The work of Vesalius   283
said, in effect, "You don't know much about the human body." Many   295

doctors who read or <u>heard</u> about the work of Vesalius continued to 307

believe in Galen's work. After all, it had been accepted for centuries. ❸ 319

However, Vesalius was very cautious about challenging 326

long-standing beliefs. When he observed that human hips were 335

different from the hips that Galen had described, Vesalius didn't say 346

that Galen had been wrong. Instead, Vesalius suggested that people 356

had changed since the time Galen wrote his work. He suggested that 368

the shape of the hips had changed perhaps because people had been 380

wearing tight clothing for so long. ❹ 386

Vesalius probably did not believe this explanation, but he knew that 397

it was very dangerous to challenge long-standing beliefs. Shortly after 407

Vesalius's work on anatomy was published, another man, Servetus, 416

showed that the heart pumps blood to the lungs. Unfortunately, he 427

wrote a book that was not in line with some of the religious beliefs of 442

the day. All copies of that book were burned, and Servetus was tied to 456

a stake and burned to death. ❺ 462

Although Vesalius was not burned at the stake, he suffered many 473

insults. The insults were so intense and frequent that Vesalius became 484

depressed, quit his position at the university, and became the official 495

doctor at a royal court. In the course of his travels, he was 508

shipwrecked on a small island, where he died of starvation. At the 520

time of his death, he was still a fairly young man with a great deal to 536

offer the world. He had tried to help the people of his day by adding 551

to their knowledge about the human body. Doctors can't do much to 563

cure a disease of the liver unless they understand some facts about the 576

liver. Doctors can't do a good job of setting broken bones unless they 589

know something about the structure of bones. Vesalius was not 599

correct about everything he observed, but the doctors of his day could 611

not hide from the more obvious truths that Vesalius had pointed out. 623
After his death, anatomy became a scientific discipline. And medicine 633
became a profession. Vesalius helped to start a scientific revolution. **6** 643

Vesalius had opened the door to modern medicine, but the practice 654
of medicine still had a long, long way to go. Vesalius got rid of some 669
medical superstitions, but there were many more superstitions left to 679
be fought. The pattern of these fights was often the same— 690
long-standing beliefs had to give way to new knowledge. **7** 699

1

introduction specializes fright centuries

2

Semmelweis Pasteur Jenner fever

division infection garbage childhood

convinced pasteurization smallpox

improvements typhoid affects

diphtheria organisms poisoning purify

3

1. bacteria
2. vaccination
3. substance
4. explanation
5. life expectancy
6. resist

4 | Contributions of Jenner, Pasteur, and Semmelweis

Let's skip ahead in time to about 1850. During the 350 years since   13
1500, a number of improvements had come about in medicine;   23
however, conditions were still very different from what we know   33
today. The average life expectancy of people born in the cities was   45
now about thirty-seven years. If people survived childhood, they   54
could expect to live far beyond their thirty-seventh birthday; however,   64
chances of living through childhood were not too good.   73

Diseases like smallpox, typhoid fever, and diphtheria still took the   83
lives of thousands of children every year. Another killer was blood   94
poisoning. Blood poisoning is a serious infection that affects a   104
person's whole system. A fever starts, and if the infection continues to   116
develop, the person dies. The doctors of 1850 did not understand that   128
blood poisoning is caused by tiny organisms called bacteria. ❶   137

An Englishman named Edward Jenner had introduced a method   146
for preventing smallpox about fifty years earlier. The method was   156
called vaccination. Even by 1850 some people were not convinced that   167
vaccination worked. They feared being stuck with a needle and having   178
some strange substance injected into their body. Even some doctors   188
were slow to accept vaccination. ❷   193

During the twenty-five-year period following Jenner's introduction   200
of vaccination, about six million people in Europe died of smallpox.   211
The toll was especially great in the United States, particularly among   222
the Native Americans, who had no resistance to the disease. Entire   233
villages of Native Americans died from smallpox. In fact, one hundred   244
years after Jenner introduced vaccination, there was a severe outbreak   254
of smallpox in the town where Jenner had lived and worked. ❸   265

One of the greatest of all medical scientists was Louis Pasteur. He 277
discovered that diseases were spread by bacteria. He demonstrated 286
that bacteria were living things and were born, like all other 297
life-forms. Until <u>his</u> theories were accepted, many doctors believed that 307
flies and other small life-forms simply grew out of garbage or dirt. 319
They didn't believe that these animals were born from a parent, like 331
larger life-forms. Most of these doctors did not even believe that 342
bacteria existed, because they were invisible to the naked eye. **4** 352

Pasteur showed how to control the spread of disease. He 362
demonstrated that harmful bacteria in milk could be killed by 372
applying heat. This method, called pasteurization, assured a safe milk 382
supply. His other great life-saving contribution resulted from his work 392
in the area of vaccination. He discovered that harmful bacteria 402
(germs) cause some diseases by multiplying in the human body. He 413
discovered how to stop this process by vaccinating a person with a 425
weakened form of the germs. It is impossible to estimate the number 437
of lives saved by Pasteur's work. **5** 443

A doctor named Semmelweis lived in Europe around 1850. He wasn't 454
familiar with the work of Pasteur. But he showed that some problems 466
of controlling bacteria could be solved by using common sense. 476

Semmelweis was in charge of a large hospital that specialized in 487
caring for women who were having babies. The women went into the 499
hospital to have their babies, and a few days after the baby was born 513
the mother and the baby went home—if the mother was still alive. 526

There were two divisions in the hospital. Semmelweis noticed a 536
striking difference between them. In one division, one of every ten 547
women died after giving birth. In the other, fewer than one of every 560
thirty died. **6** 562

Semmelweis studied the figures and asked himself, "Why do more   572
women die in Division One than in Division Two?" Division One was   584
staffed by doctors and medical students. Division Two was staffed by   595
nurses. What was the difference between the doctors and the nurses?   606

An explanation had been offered by some medical officials. It might   617
be that some women in Division One died of fright because Division   629
One had a bad reputation. Some women might have died of heart   641
attacks caused by fear. ❼   645

The Most Dangerous Occupations—Part 2

The table on page 433 shows that fishing and logging are the most dangerous occupations. Both occupations are outdoors, and both become more dangerous in bad weather. Logging on a flat surface is far less dangerous than logging on a steep mountainside. Fishing in calm waters is far less dangerous than fishing during a storm.

Both of these occupations are about 25 times as dangerous as the average job. That means the risk of dying for workers who have these jobs is 25 times greater than the risk for somebody who has an office job. For both logging and fishing, there are 125 deaths for every 100,000 workers. ❶

The most dangerous kind of logging occurs on steep mountainsides or hillsides, where it is much harder for workers to get out of the way of a falling tree or machinery that slips. Some logging operations use cables to move the logs down the slope. When workers attach cables to logs, they may be in danger if they are on the downhill side of the log and the log slips. Some trees are rotten on the inside but look healthy on the outside. Sometimes, when these trees are cut down, they split or fall in a direction the loggers do not expect. ❷

The table on page 433 indicates that the most frequent cause of death for loggers is being struck by objects. In 65 percent of the cases, the objects are trees or logs. Some logs may weigh more than ten thousand pounds.

A job as a fisher is about as dangerous as logging, but the most dangerous occupation is crab fishing in Alaska. The risk of death for crab fishers is 200 deaths per 100,000 workers. That's nearly twice the risk taken by the average fisher. Most deaths are caused by drowning. ❸

The work is dangerous because of the machinery and the weather. Workers drop steel cages that weigh 800 pounds to the bottom of the ocean; then later the workers pull up the cages they hope will be filled with Alaskan king crabs.

Crab fishing is permitted for only a few days in the winter. The workers often sleep less than 4 hours a day during this period. The waves may be more than 15 feet high. There are ropes and water and sometimes ice on the deck. A king crab may weigh more than three pounds; therefore, a cage filled with crabs may weigh 1,600 pounds. The workers have to haul the cage up from the ocean floor, position it on the deck, empty the cage quickly, put in fresh bait, and drop the cage to the ocean floor again. If one detail of this operation goes wrong, a worker may be seriously injured or killed. ❹

1 ly   dis   re   able   less   un   ness

2 occurred   procedure   solution   arrange

resistance   rejected   laundry   replaced

examine   weather   consider

3 bacteria   harmful   explanation   series

Semmelweis   solve   clue   insisted   concluded

dissecting   childbirth   contact   ridiculous

patients   indicated   serious   diet   infectious

4
1. stale
2. punctured
3. frequently
4. hostility

5   Semmelweis Solves the Problem

Semmelweis tried to figure out what caused the higher death rate in   12
Division One of his hospital. He rejected the explanation that fear caused   24
the higher death rate. He considered other explanations. One was that   35
changes in the weather caused the higher death rate. Semmelweis pointed   46
out that the weather was the same for Division One and Division Two.   59

Another explanation was that patients were crowded together in   68
Division One. Semmelweis pointed out that deaths occurred in   77
Division One even in areas where patients were not crowded. He also   89
showed that high death rates did not occur in the parts of Division   102
Two where patients were crowded together. ❶   108

Semmelweis considered a number of other possible explanations   116
and rejected each of them. The bed sheets were equally dirty in   128
Division One and Division Two. Semmelweis concluded that the   137
condition of the bed sheets could not cause the difference in the death   150
rates. Poor diet and stale air were also rejected as causes because both   163
were present in both divisions.   168

Then something happened that gave Semmelweis a clue to the cause   179
of the high death rate in Division One. A doctor who worked in   192
Division One was dissecting a dead body when his knife slipped and   204
punctured his finger. Within a few days, he came down with a fever. It   218
was the same kind that killed so many women in the hospital. It was   232
called childbed fever. People had thought that the fever occurred only   243
after childbirth, but the doctor's illness and death proved them wrong.   254

Semmelweis did not know that the doctor had been infected by   265
bacteria that cause childbed fever (blood poisoning). But he assumed   275
that something must have entered the doctor's body when he dissected   286
the infected body. ❷   289

Since childbed fever was more serious in Division One, where   299
<u>doctors</u> and students attended patients, Semmelweis concluded that   307
the disease must be carried by the doctors and students, but not by the 321
nurses in Division Two. So he began to examine what the doctors and   334
students did. He found that they frequently dissected the bodies of   345
women who had died of the fever. The nurses did not do this. The   359
doctors and students frequently went directly from an operating room   369
to deliver a baby without bothering to wash their hands. When they   381
did wash, they used only soap and water. ❸   389

Semmelweis took steps to cure this problem, but they were met with   401
a great deal of resistance. First, he insisted that all doctors must wash   414
their hands in a solution that would kill the infectious material on   426
their hands. Next, Semmelweis removed all dirty materials from the   436
patients' rooms. Each room was cleaned frequently, and bed sheets   446
were replaced when they got dirty. ❹   452

The changes that Semmelweis introduced caused a great drop in the   463
death rate in Division One. During the first year the new procedures   475
were put into operation, the death rate dropped from one out of every 488
ten women to one out of every hundred women—a drop of ninety   501
percent. During two months of that year, not one woman died in   513
Division One.   515

Semmelweis should have been treated as a hero. Instead, he was   526
greeted with hostility. Many respected doctors said that his procedures 536
were ridiculous. They felt that he had no right to tell doctors how to   550
wash their hands. ❺ Semmelweis couldn't stand the constant battles, so   560
he left the hospital. Shortly afterward he became ill and went to a   573
hospital for an examination. He found out that he had infected his   585
finger during one of his last operations. The infection was blood   596
poisoning (childbed fever). Semmelweis died of the very disease he had 607
learned to control.   610

Semmelweis was a great man because he used common sense, facts, 621
and figures. He didn't work out a cure for blood poisoning. He didn't 634
work out ways to kill bacteria that had entered a wound. But he did a 649
great deal for the field of medicine because he showed how cleanliness 661
can prevent the spread of harmful bacteria. The techniques he 671
introduced have been improved over the years, but they follow the 682
same basic principle: Whatever comes in contact with a wound must 693
be clean. ❻ 695

1

identifi<u>a</u>ble occ<u>u</u>rred incredib<u>ly</u>

m<u>ea</u>nt spe<u>ci</u>alize

2

excellent increased rejected surgeon

frequently taunted function infection

available infantile crippled anesthetics

transplant paralysis assist vaccine

doubled thorough punished antiseptic

3

1. penicillin
2. attitude
3. symptoms

Lesson
124

4   Medicine Now

A doctor's office of today is very different from the office of the   13
barber-surgeon of 1500. It is also quite different from a doctor's office   25
of 1900 because a great deal has happened since then. Knowledge   36
about medicine has grown like a snowball rolling downhill.   45

At first, the knowledge of medicine developed very slowly. Before   55
the 1500s, few advances were made. Then the pace of change began to   68
increase. By the beginning of the 1900s, doctors had far more   79
knowledge than those of the 1500s. Doctors practicing in 1900 knew   90
about germs, about antiseptic procedures, and even something about   99
anesthetics, which are drugs that kill pain. ❶ But there was no cure for   112
the terrible disease that crippled young children—infantile paralysis   121
(polio). There was little knowledge about heart disease, its symptoms,   131
and how to prevent or treat it. Many diseases of the kidneys, heart,   144
and liver meant certain death. Doctors didn't know how to transplant   155
kidneys or how to replace valves that didn't function properly. ❷   165

In the last 100 years, knowledge of medicine has snowballed faster   176
and faster. New instruments, new operations, and new drugs have come   187
to the medical scene almost yearly. A vaccine was developed to prevent   199
polio. The discovery of wonder drugs such as penicillin made it possible   211
for doctors to control infections that had formerly killed patients. ❸   221

Another change that has occurred in medicine has to do with   232
women. A little over one hundred years ago, all doctors were men.   244
Women were allowed to assist doctors as nurses, and many women were   256
midwives. (A midwife specializes in caring for a woman in childbirth.)   267
Women, however, were barred from attending medical schools.   275

454   *Lesson 124*

In 1849, Elizabeth Blackwell received her medical degree from a   285
school in Geneva, Switzerland. She was the first woman to graduate   296
from a medical <u>school</u>. She was resented by the male doctors, taunted   308
by other women, and rejected by her teachers, even though she was an   321
excellent student. Although her problems did not end when she   331
graduated from medical school, she set the stage for other women to   343
become doctors. At first there were only a few, but the number of women   357
doctors slowly increased. The attitude has changed—today, at some   367
medical schools, there are nearly as many women students as men. ❹   378

The snowballing of knowledge in medicine has made it difficult for   389
the average doctor to keep pace. When there were only a few diseases   402
known and a few types of treatments, it was not difficult for doctors   415
to keep pace with the available knowledge of medicine. As the amount   427
of information about treatments and the number of identifiable   436
ailments increased, doctors were required to learn much more in   446
order to keep pace with the available knowledge. Some experts have   457
estimated that the amount of medical knowledge doubled between the   467
years 1900 and 1940, doubled again between 1940 and 1960, and yet   479
again between 1960 and 1970. This trend continues today. Medical   489
knowledge doubles at a faster rate, making it very difficult for a   501
doctor to have a thorough understanding of medicine. Doctors are   511
humans, and humans can learn only so much during the time that is   524
available to them. ❺   527

To solve the problem of snowballing information, many doctors no   537
longer attempt to deal with all medical problems. They specialize.   547
Some specialize in ailments of the nose and throat; others specialize   558
in a particular type of surgery, such as brain surgery. There are eye   571
specialists and bone specialists, foot specialists and of course dentists.   581
These specialists are able to keep pace with the medical knowledge of   593
their particular field. There are still doctors who deal with all   604

ailments; however, after reviewing symptoms, these doctors often refer ~613~ patients to specialists. ❻ ~616~

  The medical profession has grown through the work of many brave ~627~ people who said what they thought to be true, even though they knew ~640~ their ideas would not be popular. We've looked at a few of these ~653~ people—Paré, Vesalius, da Vinci, Pasteur, Jenner, Semmelweis, and ~662~ Blackwell. There are many others. You can read about them in books ~674~ on the history of medicine. ❼ ~679~

1

Rochetain   funambulist   frightened

gorge   endurance   daring   Blondin

swayed   Niagara   bowed   impressed

Canadian   feat   balance   fad   crews

stroll   incredible   agent

2

1. casually
2. secured

3

Famous Funambulists

Nearly everybody who lived in the year 1885 knew what a funambulist was. Although the word is not used much today, it stood for feats of great daring to the people of the late 1800s. A funambulist is a tightrope walker. Tightrope walking became quite a fad after Charles Blondin performed his incredible walk 160 feet above Niagara Falls. The rope was three inches in diameter and was 1,100 feet in length. ❶ The crews experienced great difficulty in securing the rope, and Blondin's agent wasn't satisfied that the rope was adequately secured for his scheduled walk on July 30, 1885. Blondin, a famous French funambulist, was apparently not worried. He tested the rope, which swayed more than 29 feet from side to side in the middle of the span, and indicated that the crowd of people that gathered for the event would not be disappointed.

With the wind blowing and the silent crowds on both sides of the river, Blondin walked across as casually as one would stroll on a sidewalk. He stopped in the middle, put down the long pole that he carried for balance, and bowed to the crowd. Then he continued. What impressed people more than anything else was how easy Blondin made the walk look. Others attempted the same feat. According to one story, a man who had never walked a tightrope before in his life made a bet that he could walk across Blondin's rope, and he did. According to the report, he walked from the United States side to the Canadian side of the river at night.

Blondin, however, was not to be outdone. Five years later, he crossed above Niagara Falls with his agent on his back. His agent had never been on a tightrope in his life and was so frightened that he became quite sick after the walk had been completed. ❷

The longest tightrope walk was recorded in France in 1969. To cross from one side of a gorge to the other, the funambulist Rochetain walked 3,790 yards (more than two miles). The walk took almost four hours.

The endurance record for being on a tightrope is 205 days, set by Jorge Ojeda-Guzman of Orlando, Florida. The previous endurance record for being on a tightrope was 185 days and was set by Rochetain. Doctors were puzzled by his ability to sleep while balanced on the wire. During the 185 days, he walked to stay in condition. In all, he walked about 310 miles. Food was brought to him regularly, but he never left the wire. ❸

One of the strangest tightrope exhibitions occurred in New York City in 1974. A French funambulist walked a wire between the twin towers of the World Trade Center. When he crossed between the towers, he set the record for the highest crossing—1,350 feet above the street (about 100 stories). He was charged with trespassing.

Glossary

A

abnormal	not normal
abruptly	suddenly
accurate	correct
achieved	attained
acoustics	the quality of sound in a place
acquainted with	know
adapt	do something to get along in a new situation
adequate	sufficient, enough
adjust	make a small change
adjustment	a slight change
advantage	favored to win
adventurous	likes to take risks and do new things
advice	a statement of what you think a person should do
agency	a business that represents clients
aggressive	quick to fight
ail (you)	make you feel bad
air pressure	how hard the air pushes against things
alert	paying close attention
amazement	(with amazement) how you act when you are very surprised
amputate	cut off
amusing	funny

anatomy	the study of the body
anchor	an object used to hold a boat in one place
ancient	very old
anesthetic	medicine that deadens pain
announce	tell something new
annual	every year
antics	clowning behavior
anxiety	worry
apparatus	equipment
apparent	obvious
approach	get close to a thing
approval	an OK
area	a region or place
argument	a disagreement
aroused	awakened, stirred up
arranged	made plans
assess	evaluate
associated	related
associates	people who work together
assuming	supposing
assured	guaranteed
attained	reached
attentive	paying attention
attitude	how you respond to things
auction	a sale where things are sold to the highest bidders

average	something that is in the middle, ordinary
avoid	don't deal with something, stay away from something

B

bacteria	germs that produce disease
bargain	try to buy something at a reduced price
barge	a long, flat-bottomed boat used for carrying things
beaker	a container used in chemistry labs
bellow	shout loudly
beneficial	good
bid	make an offer to buy
bill of lading	a list of everything in a truckload or carload of things
bombardment	a shower of particles
bonds	forces that hold things together
bored	don't have anything to do
bothersome	bothers you
bounding	jumping and leaping
breadfruit	a large, tropical fruit
breaker	a big wave
brilliance	(has brilliance) sparkles and shines
brittle	breaks, doesn't bend
brochure	a folder

buckles	folds, collapses
budget	a breakdown of how money is to be spent
bulge	stick out in places
buoy	a float that marks something in the water
business	buy and sell things to make money

C

calculate	figure out
calculator	a small device that is used for mathematical calculations
campaign	an organized effort
canopy	a roof
capable	qualified, able to perform
capacity	the amount that can be held; the ability to hold an amount
carnivorous	eating mainly meat
cascading	falling or tumbling
casually	without paying much attention; calmly
cautious	careful
century	one hundred years
challenge	something that presents a question or a contest
champion	a person who is the best at something
charred	burned and blackened

chimney	a tube to carry smoke from a fireplace or furnace	complicated	involved, difficult to understand, having many parts
chisel	a tool with a sharp point used to chip rock or wood	composed	made of
chores	daily jobs	computer program	set of directions that tells the computer what it is supposed to do
chowder	a thick soup	concealed	hidden
churned	stirred up very hard	concerned	interested
claim	pick up something you own	conclude	reach a decision, figure out a reason for something
clients	people who pay a company for work	conclusion	(draw a conclusion) use facts to figure something out
climate	weather conditions	conference	a meeting
coastal	along the edge or coast of an ocean	confidential	secret
coiling	winding around	confirm	show that something is right
coincidence	something that happens by chance	confused	mixed up, jumbled
collapse	fall apart	conscious	very aware
colleagues	associates	considering	thinking about
collide	crash into each other	continue	keep doing
combine	put together	contract	a pledge
comment	say something	convert	change
commercial	an advertisement	convey	get across
commission	money paid for selling something	convince	make someone believe
common trait	a way in which living things are the same	coordinated	working together smoothly
comparison	a statement of how two things are the same and how they are different	copyright	the right to make copies of something that is printed
		craft	a boat

crease	a mark that's left after something has been folded
created	made for the first time
crest	top
criminal	somebody who commits a crime

D

daggerlike	pointed like a dagger
data	facts
deadlocked	when neither side can win
deafening	very loud
dealership	a business that is licensed to sell a particular product
deceit	lying
deceive	trick, fool
deceptive	misleading
decide	make up your mind about something
decision	a choice about what to do
delicately	gently and carefully
demand	a need; insist on
descended	came down
deserve	earn
detect	find
determination	(have determination) keep trying to do something
determined	firm in your decision
device	an object made to do something special

devote	give a lot of attention
diet	all the things you eat
disadvantage	opposite of advantage
disapprove	not approve
disassembled	taken apart
disguise	makes something look different
dismantled	taken apart
distinguish	tell how things are different
disturbed	worried or upset
doctoral degree	the highest degree you can get
domestic	not foreign
downed	knocked out
dressings	bandages that cover a wound
drizzly	like a light, quiet rain
ducts	tubes
duplicated	made a copy
dwellings	places in which people live

E

echo	sound bouncing back from something
effective	working well
efficient	without wasted movements
elaborate	complicated
electromagnetic waves	very small waves that travel through space very fast
eliminate	get rid of

emerge	come out of	**extracted**	pulled out
encounter	come up against	**extreme**	far from normal
endure	put up with something unpleasant	**F**	
enforce	make someone follow the rules	**facilities**	things built to be used for a special purpose
enlarged	made bigger	**failure**	something that does not reach its goal
enormous	large, immense	**faint**	very weak
erupted	suddenly burst	**faked**	pretended
estimate	a smart guess	**familiar**	something that is known
evaporate	when water is heated and goes into the air	**fascinated**	really interested
evolution	a slow change	**fault**	something wrong
exaggerated	stretched the truth	**favor**	something you do for someone
examine	carefully look over	**feast**	eat a lot
exceed	go beyond	**feat**	a great achievement
exceptionally	unusually	**fidget**	twist and turn
exclaim	cry out	**fierce**	very violent
executive	a person who runs a company	**figurehead**	a carved figure on the front of a ship
exhaust	use up	**filtering**	straining things out of something
expectations	thoughts that something will happen	**flail**	swing around like crazy
expert	someone who knows a great deal about something	**flask**	a container with a narrow top and wide bottom
explanation	a statement that makes something clear or tells why something happened	**flexible**	bends easily
		flinch	jump as if you're startled
expression	the look on your face	**flounder**	flop around; the name of a fish
extension	something that is added		
extinct	no longer living		

fluttered	moved back and forth rapidly
focused	concentrated
foliage	leaves on a bush or tree
formal	stiff and polite
formulas	sets of rules
fossilized	what happens to the remains of a living thing from a past geological age
foul-tasting	bad-tasting
franchise	the right to sell something
frantic	very excited and upset
fraud	a trick to cheat somebody
freeway	a wide highway that costs no money to travel on and has limited access
frequently	often
fret	worry
function	a purpose
futile	cannot succeed
future	time that is to come

G

gale	a strong wind
gallows	a device for hanging people
gash	a deep cut
gasp	take short, fast breaths
gear	equipment
genetic	a living thing's inherited pattern of growth
genius	a person who is very talented or smart
gimmick	a trick used to do something
glance	look at something quickly; bounce off
glands	parts of the body that produce important chemicals
glimpse	a quick look
glistening	sparkling
grade	slope
graduate student	someone who has an undergraduate degree and is working on a higher degree
grant	money that researchers receive for doing a particular job
grazing	eating grass
greedy (person)	a person who wants a whole lot of something
grumble	talk in an unhappy or a pouty way
guaranteed	assured
gymnastics	tumbling, stunts on parallel bars, etc.

H

hailed	called to
hammock	a swinging bed made of net or cloth
harmless	something that will not hurt you
hassle	something that causes trouble
hazy	not clear
hectic	frantic
helicopter	an aircraft that can go straight up and down
herd	a group of animals that live together
hesitate	pause for a moment
Himalayas	the largest mountain chain in the world
hoist	lift
hostility	unfriendliness
hulk	a person who is clumsy and overweight
hull	body of a ship
humiliating	very embarrassing
hurl	throw
hurtle	fling or hurl violently
husks	the dry outer coverings of some fruits

I

identify	know, recognize
ignorant	unaware, uninformed
ignore	not pay attention
illegal	against the law
ill-tempered	mean, grumpy
image	a picture or reflection of something
immediately	something happens right away
impatient	tired of waiting
impish	full of mischief
import	bring into the country
impression	an image or a feeling
impressive	very good
impure	not pure
incredible	very hard to believe
incurable	can't be cured
incurred	caused
indeed	for sure
indicate	point out; signal
indifferently	without interest, without caring
inexpensive	doesn't cost a lot of money
infected	diseased
inhabitants	people who live in a place
initial	first
innocent	not guilty
in range	close enough
in relation to	how things are compared
inscribed	written
insist	demand
inspect	look over carefully
instant	very fast
instantly	quickly

insurance	a guarantee that you won't have to pay for some things that might happen
intent	an aim, a purpose
internal	inside
interpretation	an explanation
interruption	a break
interview	a talk with someone about a particular topic
intriguing	interesting
intruder	someone who goes where they aren't wanted
invent	develop
investigation	a close examination of something
invoice	a list of prices for things that are being sold
irritated	a little angry

J

jokester	a person who plays a lot of jokes on people
jostled	tossed around

K

keen	sharp
knee-deep	up to your knees in something

L

label	a piece of paper attached to an object that gives information about that object
laboratory	a place where experiments are done
launch	start
lava	hot melted rock that comes out of a volcano
ledge	a narrow shelf
legal	actions done according to the law
leisurely	at a slow and easy pace
leveled	flattened to the ground
life expectancy	the number of years the average person is expected to live
limbs	arms and legs
lingered	hung around for a long time
litter	debris
liver	an organ in the body
location	a place
logical	makes sense

M

magnificent	very great, wonderful
maintenance department	made up of people who maintain things
mammal	a warm-blooded creature that has hair

manner	way
manufacturer	someone who makes a product
marine	living in the sea
marvelous	very good, wonderful
masterpieces	fine works of art
matted	pushed and flattened
mature	full-grown
mechanic	a person who fixes cars
media	newspapers, magazines, radio, TV
microscope	an instrument used to look at things that are very small
minerals	materials (like stone, coal, salt, and gold) found in the ground
minnows	small fish frequently used for bait
mission	a serious duty
modeled	demonstrated
moderator	a person who runs a meeting, discussion, or debate
modified	changed
mole	a small animal that spends most of its life underground
momentary	lasts for only a moment
motive	reason
mounting	the base you put something on

N

nagged	constantly scolded, annoyed
nervous	edgy or jumpy
nitrogen	a gas that has no smell or color
nonsense	something that makes no sense
nudge	a gentle push
nutrition	the food needs of the body

O

observe	watch
occasional	once in a while
occupied	used
official	backed by an authority
offspring	descendants, children
organism	something that is living
original	first
outfit	a set of clothes
outskirts	the areas on the edge of a town

P

paleontologist	a scientist who studies fossils and ancient forms of life
panic	sudden fear
particularly	especially
patent	a license that protects the person who invents an object

peak	the highest point of a mountain	**prevented**	kept something from happening
peeved	irritated	**prickly**	sharp and stinging
penetrate	go through	**prior**	before
penicillin	a medicine used to kill bacteria	**probably**	likely that something will happen
perch	a small fish; to stand on something unsteady or high	**procedure**	a series of steps for doing something
personality	character	**proceed**	go ahead
physicist	a person who works in the field of physics	**process**	a series of steps
		proclaimed	announced
physics	the science of how nonliving things behave	**productive**	achieves a great deal
		profit	money left after all expenses have been paid
pleaded	begged		
plentiful	when there is a lot of something	**programmed**	always follows the same steps
plumes	fancy feathers	**prominent**	well known and important
plunge	dive		
podium	a high desk used by speakers	**prop**	short name for **propeller**
polite	considerate, courteous	**property**	a feature
position	a job	**proposition**	a plan
pounced	jumped on	**protection**	something that guards
prance	step high and move in a frisky way	**provides**	gives
		punctured	poked a hole in
precious	very special, rare	**puny**	small and weak
predator	an animal that kills other animals	**purchase**	buy
		purify	kill germs
predictable	when we know what will happen	**R**	
		reaction	a response
presentation	a speech	**receipt**	a paper that proves that something was paid for
preserved	lasted a long time		

receptionist	a person who greets people in an office	**resignation**	a statement that one quits a job
recommend	suggest	**resist**	do not give in
recreational vehicle	a camper, a jeep, a four-wheel-drive pickup, etc.	**respected**	treated as a special person
		respond	answer
rectangle	a four-sided figure	**responsible**	when it's your job to do something
reduced	made smaller		
referred	directed attention to	**resume**	begin again
refused	turned down	**retreat**	go backward
rehearse	practice	**retrieve**	recover
reinforced	strengthened	**ribs**	bones located in your chest
rejected	turned down		
related to	has to do with	**rig**	a device
reliable	can be counted on	**rigged**	fixed up
remarkable	surprising or amazing	**rigid**	will not bend
remarked	commented	**risk**	a gamble
remodel	change the way something looks	**roamed**	wandered
		routine	something that is presented in the same way over and over
reply	answer		
represent	stand for		
reptiles	animals like snakes and lizards	**rowdies**	disorderly people

S

reputation	what people think of you	**salary**	the money a person makes by working on a job
request	ask for		
required	(to do something) must do	**salvage**	valuable objects saved from someplace
rescue	save	**sarcastic**	saying the opposite of what you mean, often to poke fun
researcher	a person who tries to discover new facts		
resident	a person who lives somewhere	**scalding**	burning
		scan	look over very quickly
		scarcely	only just

scavengers	animals that eat what other animals leave behind
scent	an odor
schedule	set up a time
scold	talk to someone about something done wrong
scramble	move quickly
scrawl	write poorly or quickly
screens	keeps out
scurried	moved fast
sea level	the height of the ocean at the edge of land
secluded	well hidden
secured	put firmly in place
selection	a portion of something
sensed	felt
serious	important and not funny
set a record	do something better than anyone else
several	more than one and less than many
severe	very fierce
shad	a type of fish
shade	screen from light
sheer	very steep
shimmering	seems to be covered with shiny, moving lights
shorings	things that are used to hold something up
shortage	not enough

shrill	high-pitched
silt	very fine mud
site	a place
situation	what goes on
sketches	rough, quick drawings
skid	slide
skirt around	go around
skyscraper	a very tall building
slanting	not flat or level
slime	slippery coating
slither	to slide along
sluggish	slow
smoldering	burning and smoking without a flame
snaked	twisted
snout	the nose of an animal
solution	the answer to a problem
sound	in good condition
speck	a tiny piece of something
sprawl	stretch out
sprinkling	a spray or light drip
sprout	shoot out new growth
sprouts	new shoots or buds
stale	not fresh
stampede	run together in panic
starvation	dying from lack of food
statue	a likeness made of stone, wood, or metal
stern	the back end of a boat

stout	strong and heavy	**symbol**	something that represents something else
strain	put forth too much effort		
stranded	cannot move	**symptoms**	signs
strategy	a procedure		

T

strides	long steps	**talent**	a special ability to do something
stroll	walk at a slow pace		
stunt	a hard trick done to get attention	**tantrums**	fits of anger
		taut	stretched tight
stunted	not grown as large as it is supposed to	**technical**	not understood by everyone, only by people in a special field
subsided	died down		
substance	material		
suddenly	something happens all at once	**term**	a part of a contract
		termites	bugs that eat wood
suggest	hint	**theory**	an explanation
suitable	just right	**thorough**	careful and accurate
summary	a short version of a speech or writing	**thrash**	move about violently
		tick	an insect that sucks blood
superb	very, very good		
surface	the top	**tides**	daily variations in sea level
surfer	a person who rides a surfboard		
		tiller	handle that steers a boat
surge	a sudden movement		
surpass	outdo	**tingly**	a slightly stinging feeling
survive	live through		
suspended	hanging	**tomb**	a building for the dead
suspicious of	when you don't trust	**toppled**	fell over
swayed	moved slowly back and forth	**torch**	a big fire on a sticklike object
		trace	track down
swell	get larger	**trample**	stamp into the ground
swirl	twist around	**trance**	a daze

transform	change	**valves**	movable parts that let air or liquid in and out
translate	change something from one language to another	**vast**	very big
		vegetation	plant life
transmit	send, convey	**vein**	a thin line in a rock where gold is found
treatment	a cure		
tremendous	very large, great	**venom**	the poison that poisonous snakes spit
trough	a container with its bottom shaped like a long V		
		venture	do something daring
tug	pull strongly	**verses**	the parts of a song that are not sung over and over
tunnel	a passage through water or mountains		
		viciously	fiercely
typical	predictable	**violate**	break
		visible	can be seen
U		**volcano**	a mountain that hot, burning liquid rock comes out of
unbelievable	not believable		
unconscious	asleep; knocked out		
unconvincing	weak	**volume**	a book
undergraduate	a student who is studying for a regular college degree	**W**	
		waddle	walk in a clumsy manner
unfortunate	unlucky		
unison	at the same time	**wail**	cry out in pain
unsteady	shaky, not steady	**waist**	around the middle of the body
unusual	uncommon, rare, not usual		
		whir	a soft humming noise
urge	a desire to do something	**wick**	the string part of a candle or a lamp
V		**wispy**	very light and dainty
vaccination	a shot that prevents a person from getting a disease	**withdraw**	take back
		wounds	cuts, injuries